International Political Economy Series

Series Editor: **Timothy M. Shaw**, Visiting Professor, University of Massachusetts Boston, USA and Emeritus Professor, University of London, UK

The global political economy is in flux as a series of cumulative crises impacts its organization and governance. The IPE series has tracked its development in both analysis and structure over the last three decades. It has always had a concentration on the global South. Now the South increasingly challenges the North as the centre of development, also reflected in a growing number of submissions and publications on indebted Eurozone economies in Southern Europe.

An indispensable resource for scholars and researchers, the series examines a variety of capitalisms and connections by focusing on emerging economies, companies and sectors, debates and policies. It informs diverse policy communities as the established trans-Atlantic North declines and 'the rest', especially the BRICS, rise.

Md Mizanur Rahman, Tan Tai Yong, Ahsan Ullah (*editors*)
MIGRANT REMITTANCES IN SOUTH ASIA
Social, Economic and Political Implications

Bartholomew Paudyn
CREDIT RATINGS AND SOVEREIGN DEBT
The Political Economy of Creditworthiness through Risk and Uncertainty

Lourdes Casanova and Julian Kassum
THE POLITICAL ECONOMY OF AN EMERGING GLOBAL POWER
In Search of the Brazil Dream

Toni Haastrup, and Yong-Soo Eun (*editors*)
REGIONALISING GLOBAL CRISES
The Financial Crisis and New Frontiers in Regional Governance

Kobena T. Hanson, Cristina D'Alessandro and Francis Owusu (*editors*)
MANAGING AFRICA'S NATURAL RESOURCES
Capacities for Development

Daniel Daianu, Carlo D'Adda, Giorgio Basevi and Rajeesh Kumar (*editors*)
THE EUROZONE CRISIS AND THE FUTURE OF EUROPE
The Political Economy of Further Integration and Governance

Karen E. Young
THE POLITICAL ECONOMY OF ENERGY, FINANCE AND SECURITY IN THE
UNITED ARAB EMIRATES
Between the Majilis and the Market

Monique Taylor
THE CHINESE STATE, OIL AND ENERGY SECURITY

Benedicte Bull, Fulvio Castellacci and Yuri Kasahara
BUSINESS GROUPS AND TRANSNATIONAL CAPITALISM IN CENTRAL AMERICA
Economic and Political Strategies

Leila Simona Talani
THE ARAB SPRING IN THE GLOBAL POLITICAL ECONOMY

Towards a Political Economy of the Underground in Global Cities
International Political Economy Series
Series Standing Order ISBN 978–0–333–71708–0 hardcover
978–0–333–71110–1 paperback

You can receive future titles in this series as they are published by placing a standing order. Please contact your bookseller or, in case of difficulty, write to us at the address below with your name and address, the title of the series and one of the ISBNs quoted above.

Customer Services Department, Macmillan Distribution Ltd, Houndmills, Basingstoke, Hampshire RG21 6XS, England

Global Governance and Regulatory Failure

The Political Economy of Banking

Roman Goldbach
Deutsche Bundesbank, Germany

First published 2015 by
PALGRAVE MACMILLAN

Palgrave Macmillan in the UK is an imprint of Macmillan Publishers Limited, registered in England, company number 785998, of Houndmills, Basingstoke, Hampshire RG21 6XS.

Palgrave Macmillan in the US is a division of St Martin's Press LLC, 175 Fifth Avenue, New York, NY 10010.

Palgrave Macmillan is a global academic imprint of the above companies and has companies and representatives throughout the world.

Palgrave® and Macmillan® are registered trademarks in the United States, the United Kingdom, Europe and other countries.

ISBN: 978–1–137–50002–1

This book is printed on paper suitable for recycling and made from fully managed and sustained forest sources. Logging, pulping and manufacturing processes are expected to conform to the environmental regulations of the country of origin.

A catalogue record for this book is available from the British Library.

A catalog record for this book is available from the Library of Congress.

For my parents and for Lisa, with gratitude

Contents

List of Figures

List of Tables

Acknowledgements

Like with any other book, writing this one was only possible with the help of many colleagues and friends along the way. I wish to acknowledge the many persons, who have helped me in developing this book. The cooperation with Andreas Busch at the University of Göttingen provided an invaluable, fruitful framework for this project. During many discussions, his invaluable feedback challenged my ideas and pushed the project in the right directions when necessary. Like Andreas, Martin Höpner, Till Martin Kaesbach, and Michael Breen read earlier versions of the manuscript and commented extensively. Many of the theoretical claims were refined due to their invaluable feedback. Till's extremely detailed and painfully critical comments on the first draft improved the following ones substantially. At Palgrave Macmillan, Christina Brian and Timothy Shaw provided excellent feedback and support in finishing this book.

I was also blessed with many extraordinary colleagues at the Department of Political Science at the University of Göttingen. Among them, Tobias Jakobi commented on several chapters and was willing to discuss the issues at so many times, that it is really difficult to measure his contributions to this manuscript. I, furthermore, received very helpful feedback on different aspects of this book from Christoph Hönnige, Bernd Schlipphak, and Julia Schwanholz. During research stays at the Max Planck Institute for the Study of Societies and the Political Economy and Transnational Governance Research Group at the University of Amsterdam Brian Burgoon, Renate Mayntz, Annettee Freyberg, Paul van Hooft, and Geoffrey Underhill challenged my project and provided very helpful guidance. In particular, I want to thank Geoffrey Underhill, who took a lot of time out of his busy schedule and supported me in framing the problem stemming from the simultaneity of regulatory delegation and transgovernmental network cooperation in financial regulation. Yet, it goes without saying, that all remaining errors are mine alone. Furthermore, the views expressed in this book are those of the author and should not be reported as or attributed to the Deutsche Bundesbank.

Finally, I am grateful for Lisa and Naomi. Without their unique patience and passion I would not have finished the manuscript with the same excitement and distance.

List of Abbreviations

A-IRB	advanced internal ratings based approach
ABA	American Bankers Association
ACB	America's Community Bankers
AIG	Accord Implementation Group
AMA	Advanced Measurement Approach
BaFin	Bundesanstalt für Finanzdienstleistungsaufsicht (Federal Financial Supervisory Authority)
BaKred	Bundesaufsichtsamt für das Kreditwesen (Federal Banking Supervisory Office)
BCBS	Basel Committee on Banking Supervision
BdB	Bundesverband deutscher Banken (Federal Association of German Banks)
BIA	Basic Indicator Approach
BIS	Bank for International Settlements
BVR	Bundesverband der Deutschen Volksbanken und Raiffeisenbanken (Federal Association of German Co-operative Banks)
CET1	Common Equity Tier 1
CGFS	Committee on the Global Financial System
CP-1	consultative paper 1
CP-2	consultative paper 2
CP-3	consultative paper 3
CP-4	consultative paper 4
CPSS	Committee on Payment and Settlements Systems
CRA	Credit Rating Agency
CRMPG	Counterparty Risk Management Policy Group
CSBS	Conference of State Bank Supervisors
DK	Die Deutsche Kreditwirtschaft (Umbrella Organisation of five German Banking Associations, formerly ZKA)
DSGV	Deutscher Sparkassen- und Giroverband (German Association of Savings Banks)
EAD	exposure at default
ECA(I)	External Credit Assessment (Institution)
EIA	Export Insurance Agency
EL	expected losses
EU	European Union

EU-FSAP	EU Financial Services Action Plan
F-IRB	foundational internal ratings based approach
Fed	Federal Reserve System
FDIC	Federal Deposit Insurance Corporation
FINRA	Financial Industry Regulatory Authority
FGG	Financial Guardian Group
FSB/F	Financial Stability Board/ Forum
FSR	Financial Services Roundtable
G7	Group of Seven (industrialised countries), in particular Heads of State/Government and Finance Ministers
G8	Group of Eight (G7 plus Russia)
G10	Group of Ten (industrialised nations with globally relevant financial markets); Original Group of Countries participating in the general arrangements to borrow to the IMF
G20	Group of Twenty (industrialised and emerging market countries), in particular heads of state/government and finance ministers
GE	Germany
GHOS	Group of Governors and Heads of Supervision (oversight body of the Basel Committee)
IAIS	International Association of Insurance Supervisors
IASB	International Accounting Standards Board
ICAAP	internal capital adequacy assessment process
ICBA	Independent Community Bankers of America
IFI	International Financial Institutions (IMF and World Bank)
IIF	International Institute of Finance
IMF	International Monetary Fund
IMF-FSAP	IMF Financial Sector Assessment Program
IOSCO	International Organisation of Securities Commissions
IRB	internal ratings based approach
ISDA	International Swaps and Derivatives Association
LCFI	Large Complex Financial Institution
LGD	loss given default
LTCM	Long Term Capital Management
MRA	Market Risk Amendment
NASD	National Association of Securities Dealers
NPR	note for proposed rule-making
OCC	Office of the Comptroller of the Currency

OTS	Office of Thrift Supervision
PD	probability of default
ROSC	Reports on the Observance of Standards and Codes
RCAP	Regulatory Consistency Assessment Programme
SIA	Securities Industry Association
SIFMA	Securities Industry and Financial Market Association
SME	small- and medium-sized enterprise
SREP	supervisory review and evaluation process
TNC	transnational corporation
TRR	transnational regulatory regime
UL	unexpected losses
US/USA	United States of America
VaR	Value-at-Risk
VDP	Verband deutscher Pfandbriefbanken (Association of German Pfandbrief Banks)
VÖB	Verband öffentlicher Banken (Association of German Public Banks)
ZKA	Zentraler Kreditausschuss (Umbrella Organisation of Five German Banking Associations, now DK)

1
The Great Recession, Regulatory Failure and Global Governance

Succumbing to one form of interdependence may be the price one pays for avoiding another.

(Keohane & Nye 1974, 61)

1.1 Global governance and financial crisis

Did *global governance* through transgovernmental networks lead to regulatory failure that caused the Great Recession? And, if yes, should we enhance global cooperation to prevent future crises or focus on the national level? In 2005, bank supervisors from industrialised nations – within the transgovernmental network of the Basel Committee on Banking Supervision – agreed to harmonise their regulatory standards with the purpose of controlling excessive risk-taking of globally active banks and pre-empting global financial turmoil. In 2009 these standards were considered a cause of the Great Recession as they had facilitated the spread of imprudent practices globally, rather than enhancing regulation. Their origin, the transgovernmental network of the Basel Committee, is frequently considered problematic with a view to regulatory failure. Nevertheless, in 2010, the BCBS presented its new framework, Basel III, as the centrepiece of global regulatory reform, which the G20 happily endorsed. Can we expect that these standards, this time, increase rather than undermine financial stability even though they originate in the same governance networks and through the same policy processes?

More generally, should we enhance the global approach to prevent future financial crises? Or should we rather focus our efforts to regulate banks on the national, or maybe the regional, level? In the public's attempt to regain control over the financial sector without choking its growth engine, the seeking of the optimal, or at least best possible, locus for policy and regulatory action is crucial. Pundit and scholarly opinion is divided. Some tend to favour global or transnational governance approaches to the standard-setting problem (Slaughter 2004), some see the nation state as the locus of authority to be better suited to providing the necessary confluence of polity and market (Germain 2010). Probably, most authors (including those mentioned above) would argue that the spectrum of *realistic* options involves some mix of both national and global/transnational authoritative structures and agents. This leaves us with a complex global governance (dis)order (Cerny 2010b, Lake 2010), in which nation state bound and nation state-transcending governance layers interact in setting the rules to reduce risks of future global financial turmoil.

In this book, I argue that a *persistent* key problem of global financial regulation as well as other transnationally governed areas of the global political economy is that policymakers pursue both, national and transnational governance, but do not reconcile these approaches. The unchecked simultaneity of national and transnational influence in (transnational) standard-setting is a major, unresolved problem at the core of global governance, since it leads to durable disorder and, in consequence, to global policy failure. With a view to the financial governance reforms in response to the Great Recession, I argue that the unreconciled competition of national and transnational governance continues to condition global policymaking, which implies the undiminished probability of future regulatory failure and turmoil – the reforms actually foster this aspect of the pre-crisis constellation.

1.2   Transgovernmental governance and regulatory failure

This book is about the transgovernmental harmonisation of standards to regulate globally active banks – in short global banking regulation – and in particular about the structures and dynamics of its global political economy. More specifically, the study is about the effects that the Basel Committee on Banking Supervision (BCBS, Basel Committee) and its most recent agreements, the Basel II and III frameworks, have on the stability of the global financial system. Thus, my aim is to explain the role that global governance plays in regulatory failure, a main cause of the Great Recession.

It is by now accepted wisdom that this latest crisis, the most severe financial turmoil in six decades, was in part caused by regulatory failure to prevent imprudent banking strategies, which, in turn, resulted in global financial instability. It is, furthermore, a widespread conviction that the transnational harmonisation of regulatory standards between developed nations in the Basel Committee was a crucial element of this regulatory failure – by diffusing faulty standards, the infamous Basel II rules, transnationally. This is particularly concerning, since it was the Basel Committee that was commissioned to strengthen financial stability after the crisis – the same transgovernmental network of the G20 nations' regulatory agencies with its problematic transnational governance structure (Verdier 2013). Accordingly, as first evidence suggests, the resulting Basel III reforms remain largely insufficient to enhance the provision of (global) financial stability (Admati & Hellwig 2013, European Systemic Risk Board 2014). Moreover, with the reconstitution of the Financial Stability Board (FSB), the centrepiece of the governance reforms is the addition of another transgovernmental network – with potentially comparable structural effects. These BCBS and FSB reforms are arguably the most important changes to the global regulation of banking and financial stability. Therefore, with the aim to explain global regulatory politics and failure, and given that largely the same transgovernmental regulatory networks that have harmonised the faulty rules of banking regulation prior to the crisis are also the central hubs of post-crisis reforms, I will investigate how this governance structure conditions influence in regulatory processes and outcomes. At the same time, I will assess the question of whether the post-crisis reforms, Basel III and the FSB in particular, actually constitute significant change.

In sum, then, the *question* that guides my analysis is how the transnationalisation in the governance structure of regulating banks and financial stability conditions the influence of actors in the political process of standard-setting, and, thereby, the content of regulatory standards.

There are several excellent studies on the Basel Committee and its standards. Ethan Kapstein (1989, 1992, 1994) has revealed how supervisors assembled informally in the early 1970s within the Basel Committee to overcome control problems in their jurisdictions. Following his example, other studies have emphasised that standards are set through a two-level game of national and international politics, with a particular focus on the influence of US-based market power in setting these global rules and domestic US interests – Congress, banks, regulators – driving this cooperation (see e.g. Simmons 2001, Wood 2005, Singer 2007, Drezner 2007, Tarullo 2008). A second group of studies rather puts emphasis on the transnational mechanisms driving Basel standards, be it the transgovernmental epistemic community of supervisors within the BCBS or the transnational banks and their associations (see e.g. Underhill 1995, Slaughter 2004, Porter 2005, Goodhart 2011, Young 2012). The present investigation, however, is motivated by the promise of what the integration of these state-bound and transnational approaches can yield in explaining global politics and regulatory failure.

My aim is to combine previous insights to construct an encompassing, systemic understanding of how the different actors and institutions that affect global banking regulation interact in bringing about the global standards, and how this relates to regulatory output and, potentially, failure. I will introduce a theoretical framework that synthesises these diverse mechanisms and will provide new empirical data on the politics and policies of the Basel Committee and its Basel II/III frameworks, which adds up to a detailed account of the global political economy of banking regulation during the time period from 1998 to 2014. While I am interested in regulatory failure, I designed the empirical analysis rather neutrally, with a view to explaining who was influential, through which channels, and which policies resulted from that. This, however, allows me to draw substantiated conclusions about the link between governance structure and regulatory failure. Furthermore, I assess whether the post-crisis reforms have changed the governance structure's conditioning of influence and outcomes.

A new aspect in the area of transgovernmental banking regulation, which however builds on Goodhart's (2011) historical study on the Basel Committee's early years from 1974 to 1997, is my emphasis on the evolution of the Basel Committee and its surrounding governance and opportunity structure. Thus, the Committee constitutes a prime example of the incremental evolution of global politics. As such, the continuous development mirrors the incremental transnationalisation of the political process and the deepening global institutionalisation of the governance structure. In order to explain how global harmonisation works in this setting, I delineate how standards are diffused transnationally through, and how the rule development takes place within, the *transnational regulatory regime* that connects national, interstate, and transnational actors and institutions. This constellation, however, is prone to asymmetric influence and policy failure.

1.3   Interdependence and the collision of competition state and global governance

Beyond these policy and governance challenges of global banking regulation, this study is also rooted in the fascination of the broader phenomenon underlying these issues. That phenomenon is the transnationalisation (or globalisation) of politics and political economies, and the resulting tensions of the simultaneity of nation state-bound and state-transcending mechanisms.[1] In accepting that there is neither a neat international system of state units nor a global polity, my interest is rooted in two sets of closely intertwined questions concerning the state of the global political economy. First, how does the (partially) global political economy structure the policy process and the influence of different actors? And, second, how do the multiple factors of this complex constellation dynamically interact in affecting (global) policy outcomes, i.e. regulatory standards?

Underneath these questions lies the continuous transformation of structures and processes in the international political economy since the 1950s and 1960s – and in particular the transformation of the nation state. This trend and its effects can be stated succinctly to encompass three broader developments: (1) the incremental break up of the (never complete) unity of national polity and economy and the corresponding reduction of national independence in setting rules for the economy; (2) the state's adaptation as 'competition state' that pursues the competitiveness of its economic actors in the global market place in order to enhance its citizens' wealth; (3) the growth of complex governance regimes that do not make the state vanish, but rather integrate its partially disaggregated components as well as interstate and transnational mechanisms in the societal attempt to govern partially globalising political economies.

This spans (at least) from the post World War II order of 'embedded liberalism' (Ruggie 1982), during which the free trade regime deepened the economic interdependence of nations, i.e. the activities of national economies increasingly unfolded reciprocal, transnational effects (Keohane & Nye 1977). Notwithstanding its wealth-enhancing effects, however, this also widened the gap between national governments' aspiration for control and the capability to achieve it, i.e. this transnationalisation created a new quality of a 'control gap' (Nye & Keohane 1971b, 343). Attempts to narrow this horizontal control gap of economic interdependence through transgovernmental cooperation resulted in 'policy interdependence' (ibid) due to the emerging transnational governance layers. Yet, the incomplete compatibility between national and transnational rules and processes resulted in vertical governance gaps. Thus, in effect, global governance efforts change the nature of the gap rather than narrowing it. 'Succumbing to one form of interdependence may be the price one pays for' moderating the consequences of another (Keohane & Nye 1974, 61). As I will demonstrate in later chapters, it is this governance gap, first identified in the 1970s, that is constitutive of regulatory failure.

The challenges of this governance gap were augmented through the onset of free-floating currencies and the removal of capital controls. Furthermore, the third industrial revolution since the late twentieth century accelerated the globalisation of societal interaction and introduced new dynamics. Philip Cerny (1995) has delineated the core challenge to the spatial unity of state and market: in a world of increasingly open economic exchange, private market activity can relatively easily widen its transnational scale of production, while, however, the much more difficult endeavour of creating a spatially coherent public authority that can embed this market activity cannot catch up with the private interaction. Now, this is important to remember with a view on current global banking regulation, since the consequence of deepening interdependence was the incremental loss of national policymakers' capacities to curb their own banks' activities as well as transnational spillovers of financial turmoil from other countries (Kapstein 1994).

In other words, the global reach of financial intermediation – facilitated through the technological advancements that enabled electronic trading discerned from geographical space – was considered to make the state obsolete in governing economic relationships. With regard to the globalisation of finance, however, studies from the 1980s and 1990s revealed how states were active supporters of this development as it suited their governments' and bureaucracies' agendas (Helleiner 1994, Pauly 1997), even though many implications were rather unintended (Goodman & Pauly 1993). Moreover, several scholars have qualified the 'retreat of the state' (Strange 1996) by demonstrating that the state, rather than vanishing, is adapting to the circumstances created by globalisation. This adaptation has many faces (Berger 2000), however in this study's context it is the new role as 'competition state' (or 'regulatory state', see Majone 1997) that is crucial (Cerny 1997, 2010a). Domestically, the development into the competition state was rooted in the diversion from the public goal of the positive or welfare state that widely engaged in producing goods itself and protecting many aspects of individual and social life from free market uncertainties. Under pressure of public fiscal constraints and neoliberal policy agendas the competition state reinterpreted the main aim of the state as one of enabling free markets to flourish. For that purpose, competition needed to be facilitated to the goal of which the state would focus its public interventions. This meant arm's length regulation, rather than production and welfare spending (Cerny 2010b). Globally, the competition state logic implies that all actors of disaggregated states aim to maximise the competitiveness of the nation's economic actors in the global market place in order to spur economic growth and enhance its citizens' wealth. This logic is very important in the context of the global political economy, since it is the reasoning that underlies strategic decisions and the idea that underlies ideological actions of politicians, regulators and economic actors (Cerny 2010b). Whenever the competitiveness of a sector is supposedly threatened, ideational automatism and/or strategic calculation move parliamentarians in their support of crucial constituents. Likewise, governments are easily convinced of the need to negotiate for a specific exception or addition to international agreements, while public or sectoral concern is easily aroused and organised through appeals to national competitiveness in a globalised world.

As a result, national actors become international competitors for market share and industry location. In this context, regulatory policies become increasingly important as transaction costs for globally active firms, and may provide a competitive disadvantage, if other jurisdictions attract companies with less costly stipulations (Mattli & Büthe 2003). Regulatory/competition states, therefore, engage in 'interjurisdictional competition', which means that regulators have not only to ensure the societally beneficial functioning of markets, but also to ensure the attractiveness of their jurisdiction to global firms and the competitiveness of their jurisdiction's main companies (Murphy 2005). Financial regulators, thus, 'must walk a fine line between stability and competitiveness' (Singer 2007, 23). The implications for the global quality of regulatory standards are far more complex than a race to the bottom of lowest possible standards (Vogel 1996). For the purpose, of this study, nevertheless, it is important to note that there are multiple factors that might incentivise regulators to adopt and enforce lenient supervisory approaches – and that these incentives are driven in considerable part by the logic of the competition state.

At the same time, however, deepening economic interdependence led policymakers to coordinate transnationally as well as internationally. In contrast to the state-unit bound approach of International Relations, the approach of global governance states that authority relationships do not neatly function in a hierarchical context of national and international organisation, but through the messy, often uncoordinated, interaction of national, transnational and interstate mechanisms (Rosenau 1995). 'These centralizing and decentralizing dynamics have undermined constitutions and treaties in the sense that they have contributed to the shifts in the loci of authority' (Rosenau 1992, 3). The reduced costs of transportation and communication have facilitated the immense increase in cooperation across the globe (Keohane & Nye 1998). As a result, global governance of state and non-state actors, in its numerous forms, deepened continuously. In sum, the increase in global governance efforts have created complex, dynamic governance regimes that do not make the state vanish, but rather integrate its partially disaggregated components as well as interstate and transnational mechanisms in the societal attempt to govern partially globalising polities and political economies.

A pivotal role in global governance is played by transgovernmental actors – sub-units of several nations' governments and executive agencies that build transgovernmental networks – which, with increasing frequency of contact, have moved from early information sharing, to policy coordination, cooperation and even transgovernmental, informal agreements (Slaughter 2004). The deepening transgovernmental cooperation in banking and financial regulation, as in several other policy areas, has implied the incremental transnationalisation of governance structure and policy process (Cerny 2001, 2010b). While central banks have been building such a web at least since the 1930s in the context of the Bank for International Settlements, banking regulators have been deepening close transgovernmental coordination ties since the early 1970s (as will be discussed in Chapter 2).

Thus, at its current stage, the global political economy is simultaneously characterised by interjurisdictional competition among competition states and by the transgovernmental cooperation among the same actors from these disaggregated states.

1.4 Transnational layering and the New Interdependence Approach

This overlap of state-bound and state transcending authority leads to the layering of national and transnational rules and policy processes, which can create considerable loopholes in regulating economic activity, i.e.

a global governance/regulatory gap. This global layering (national + transnational [+ international] layers = global layering) and the corresponding governance gaps have two aspects, one institutional, i.e. rule-layering, and one procedural, i.e. process-layering. Whereas the latter refers to the interaction of influence, or influential actors and coalitions, in the setting of global standards, the first refers to the interaction of national and global rules in enforcing regulation. Both aspects are crucial in global banking regulation and are covered in this book. My argument in this contribution, however, puts particular emphasis on the *simultaneous, unreconciled influence that national and transnational coalitions wield in the process of setting harmonised regulatory standards*.

But lets briefly outline the institutional aspect of global layering and governance gaps first. Thiemann (2014) has recently demonstrated how globally harmonised regulatory standards and their loopholes incentivise national regulators to turn their back on regulatory arbitrage strategies of banks in their jurisdictions. The underlying cause, Thiemann argues, were regulators' fears that global market reach would pull financial activity into other jurisdictions, if the regulator would push legislation or regulation that went beyond the perforated global Basel standards. In other words, the global reach of markets and the ensuing global competition undermines the capacity of regulators to implement and enforce higher standards in their jurisdictions. Globally harmonised rules fail to remedy this problem, since they do not cover – and thereby replace – all relevant aspects of national rule-making. Rather, transnational standards complement national laws, which causes the movement of regulatory arbitrage strategies into other shadowy areas, what Thiemann calls the 'fringes' of national regulation.

More generally, legal scholars like Tim Bartley (2011) have revealed that the layering of domestic and transnational rules results in complex rule constellations of a complementary, rival and hybrid character. Harmonised rule-setting, thus, might work in highly successful ways as intended or might actually inhibit national enforcement. The simultaneity of global governance and competition states, therefore, can create problematic governance gaps. This setting, furthermore, might even be considered as competing authoritative claims over setting standards for global banking (or any other socio-economic) activity. In other words, the transnationalisation of governance structure and policy process leads to the cross-cutting of state-bound with state-transcending authority. Put succinctly, the transnationalisation in the governance structure produces authoritative overlap without a procedure to reconcile these competing claims.

But loopholes do not only emerge out of the incompatibility of national and transnational rules. Gaps can also emerge within transgovernmental agreements themselves. With the aim of contributing to the understanding of the interaction between national and transnational governance layers, I approach this phenomenon at an earlier stage, namely during the stage of transnational standard development. I will demonstrate that the conflict of domestic and transnational mechanisms begins already during the development and negotiation of global standards. Accordingly, I show how negotiating global rules becomes subject to the simultaneous pressures of transnational pro-harmonisation networks and national competition state interests – without a procedure to counterbalance these special interests. This creates additional loopholes, and contributes to some of those that Thiemann, Bartley and others have revealed, and that play a crucial role in explaining patterns of national regulatory failure with potential global repercussions.

In the field of political science the increasing importance of interacting layers of national and global rules is mirrored in the merging of the sub-disciplines of international and comparative politics/political economy. Combining the layering perspective on institutions and processes, Farrell & Newman (2014, 2015) have provided an extremely valuable framework for the dynamic assessment of national and cross-national mechanisms – the 'New Interdependence Approach'. Postulating a new research agenda, their core argument is that the global political economy is characterised by cross-national layering of rules and sequencing of politics that take place within and between nation states, which, in turn, alters political opportunity structures in a way that leads to a partially transnational political economy. This dynamic complex, in turn, is a crucial mechanism in explaining institutional change in the global and national political economies.

Farrell & Newman (2015, 501–508) delineate how opportunity structures incrementally have come to transcend the established notions of national (comparative) preference formation and interstate bargaining. First, globalisation augments interdependence as a result of increased interjurisdictional activity of firms. Being exposed to distinct rules in different jurisdictions, transnational firms are confronted with rule overlap, which leads them to push for global harmonisation with their regulators.[2] The result is transgovernmental cooperation among regulators, which, in turn, alters the political economies' opportunity structures that now become partially transnational. Such transnationalisation, then, constitutes a source of change within jurisdictions, which unsettles the pre-existing domestic competition structure. Finally, nationally oriented actors, that were until then opposed to global rules, face the facts of transgovernmental cooperation and the resulting unlevelling of the national playing field, which leads them to engage politically to alter transnational rules (or achieve the favourable adaptation in the national context). I would add that these firms with a rather intra-jurisdictional business model are likely to pursue indirect strategies that go through established national channels to get to the regulators, rather than directly approaching transnational fora. The outcome of this process is a transnationalisation of the political economy, which is characterised by the simultaneous influence of pro-harmonisation coalitions and national coalitions that pursue the balance of the intra-jurisdictional level playing field.

The point is, then, that in explaining global regulatory policy and the influence in developing transnational standards one has to take national, transnational as well as interstate, where applicable, opportunity structures into account – and how these elements build a partially global political economy structure. More specifically, returning to Thiemann's (2014) intriguing insight of the structural constraints that global Basel standards pose for prudent national supervision, it is important to scrutinise the pivotal role of regulatory agencies in this constellation. From their perspective, the political economy of global banking regulation is characterised by distinct opportunity structures in their different national and transnational roles. These incentivise them to coordinate transgovernmentally, but at the same time also to enforce leniently at home. For example, German banking regulators felt they had to agree on developing the new Basel II standards, even though they were rather opposed to such a comprehensive approach, since they feared loss of reputation and influence in the Basel Committee. This, nevertheless, did not stop them knowingly accepting capitalisation levels that were not in line with these standards. Likewise, US supervisors pushed the Basel fellows to agree with the Basel II endeavour, yet failed to even adopt many of the resulting rules due to Congressional opposition. These contradictory actions are rooted in the differing structural constraints that the supervisors face in their domestic regulatory regimes and the transnational cooperation fora. As a result, the political economy of global banking regulation is characterised by the global layering of rules and processes, and this does not necessarily result in enhanced policy outcomes or narrowing governance gaps.

1.5   Eclecticism in the study of world politics

This New Interdependence Approach and the concept of global layering bring us a long way towards understanding global politics. But they do not explain how this constellation is related to (1) the (a)symmetry of influence in the political process, and (2) policy outcomes of global standards. Therefore, with this study I want to contribute to the New Interdependence/global layering agenda of explaining partially globalised politico-economic processes and outcomes, by assessing how the dynamic interaction of national, interstate and transnational mechanisms condition influence in the political process and, thereby, the outcomes of global banking regulation. For that purpose, I delineate a theoretical framework of these opportunity structures and assess their conditioning effects on influence and policy outcome empirically. To derive this framework (see Chapter 3), however, I have to draw on several insightful approaches to the study of world politics and political economy – I have to theorise synthetically, or eclectically.

Accordingly, in this project I apply a theoretical approach that integrates state-structure bound – national and international – actors and institutions as well as state-transcending, transnational activities and structures. Several scholars postulate the necessity of such an approach. Avant et al. (2010) have called upon scholars of world politics to analyse all actors that affect a global policy area. Cerny (2010b) has put forward the theoretical paradigm, 'Transnational Neopluralism', according to which nation states are not the only relevant global actors, which have to be complemented by non-state, transnational actors – together these all produce new transnational policy processes. Helleiner & Pagliari (2011) have argued that a meaningful analysis of global financial governance that is capable of grasping the complex interaction effects necessitates the careful consideration of national, interstate and transnational factors. Finally, from a pragmatist, problem-analytic stance, a complex phenomenon such as transnational regulatory failure cannot be investigated by separate analyses of one or two groups of actors/institutions, but necessitates an 'eclectic inquiry [that] takes on ... the messiness and complexity of concrete dilemmas facing "real world" actors' (Sil & Katzenstein 2010a, 411; see also Sil & Katzenstein 2010b).

1.6   The argument: the transnational regulatory regime and regulatory failure

The theme that guides this book is the relationship between global governance and regulatory failure to provide the public good of financial stability. But how can we connect the messy real-world problem of financial turmoil due to regulatory failure to the conditioning governance structure? This has to be considered against the background of the current state of the global political economy, which is characterised by a deepening institutionalisation of a global governance structure on the one hand as well as a nation state order organised around the concept of the competition state on the other hand. This overlap of state-bound and state-transcending authority leads to the layering of national and transnational rules and policy processes, which – if not reconciled – create considerable loopholes in regulating economic activity, i.e. global governance/regulatory gaps. This is, as discussed, particularly concerning, since these standards can in addition even undermine national authorities' capacity and incentives to enforce strict national rules. Hence, the result could be more, rather than less, gaps.

My main contribution concerns the analysis of how these loopholes are created at the stage of developing transgovernmental standards. I reveal how the simultaneous, unreconciled influence that national and transnational coalitions wield in the process of setting harmonised regulatory standards undermines their prudence. My argument is that in global banking regulation this unreconciled influence is entrenched in the global governance structure. More specifically, I claim that global banking regulation is characterised by a complex governance and opportunity structure – the transnational regulatory regime (TRR) – that is conducive to policy failure (and resulting financial instability). With the synthetic theoretical framework of the TRR, I provide an approach that interlinks transnational, national and interstate mechanisms to explain the influence on the partially globalised policy processes and the effect on the content of transnational regulatory standards. In order to understand the basic opportunity and governance structures, let us briefly take a preview at the Basel II deliberations (the subject of Chapter 4).

Once the development of the framework was under way in 1998, the most influential actors were the regulators themselves, with some influence exercised by transnational banking associations, although the Committee was keen to keep its distance from them. This exclusive influence of transgovernmental and dominant national regulators (especially the US Fed) was soon over, when two dissatisfied coalitions entered the deliberations with force. On the one hand, national banks, who saw their domestic competitiveness negatively affected, put pressure on members of the national parliaments. This, in turn, alerted Congress and the Bundestag to the effect of the politicisation of the Basel II process. However, unfortunately, these politicians enforced leadership selectively on behalf of the powerful voice coalitions in their constituencies. These, not surprisingly, pursued private interests of integrating specific options into the global framework, so that their competitiveness at least remained unchanged. This put substantial pressure on the transgovernmental network of the Basel Committee to integrate these specific options, thereby making it substantially more difficult to find a solution satisfying everyone yet also safeguarding financial stability. On the other hand, however, transnational banks were dissatisfied with the Basel Committee's proposals and increased their input into the Committee's working groups, in order to find their specific technical advancements integrated into the global standards.

The mounting pressure regarding the competitiveness of local banks in the US, national banks in Germany, international banks, etc. forced the Basel Committee to water down the Basel II framework. For example, almost the entire set of standards for the treatment of securitised assets as well as the beneficial treatment of residential mortgages and credit card commitments were integrated into Basel II after substantial US Congressional pressure. At the same time, German politicians ensured that small loans to small and medium-sized enterprises and certain forms of equity were treated beneficially. No such persistent pressure, however, insisted on standards to regulate systemic stability or asked whether banks would take on too much leverage.

The crux with all this is that the simultaneous pressure by national voice and transnational harmonisation coalitions – both reinforced through selective political intervention on behalf of concerns of competitiveness – did not only result in the neglect, but in the end even undermined the regard, of the public good of financial stability. The resulting standards were, then, diffused transnationally into the regulatory rules applied in jurisdictions. The public agencies, mandated to regulate banks in order to minimise the risks of negative externalities of imprudent banking on financial stability, were captured and hindered in providing this public good due to the unreconciled influence that national and transnational coalitions wielded in the process of setting harmonised regulatory standards. Thus, the complex governance constellation of the TRR conditioned the policy process in a manner that was conducive to asymmetric influence of private interest coalitions and the disregard of negative externalities and systemic financial stability.

In sum, in terms of how the governance structure is related to regulatory outcomes, the institutional structure systematically conditions the asymmetric influence of private vis-à-vis public interests. Interestingly, regulators at first were quite keen to protect financial stability. However, intervention by national politicians on behalf of particular, well organised interests altered and weakened the regulatory framework selectively. While these interventions were numerous, and complemented by selective pressure from transnational banks, advocacy on behalf of the public good of financial stability was disregarded. This systematic institutional condition, which is to the detriment of the provision and protection of the public good of financial stability, remains a crucial characteristic of the current institutional framework after the financial crisis. Any rules that originate within this institutional arrangement are likely to reproduce regulatory standards that benefit private interests, rather than providing the public good of financial stability.

In abstract terms, we can delineate the following politico-economic process: (1) an endogenous or exogenous initiation of harmonised rule-setting; (2) the transgovernmental network sets standards that change the domestic market equilibrium; (3) national coalitions raise their voice and achieve a selective intervention by politicians to integrate their interests into the global framework; (4) transnational coalitions raise their voice with the transgovernmental network and achieve integration of their interests; (5) the combined influence weakens the regulators' capacities and incentives to provide regulation that protects public goods.

What aggravates this problem is that the Basel rules are regarded as global benchmark standards, which leads to domestic regulators facing substantial pressure, if they aim to go beyond them domestically. This results in loopholes between national and transnational standards, which enable imprudent banking strategies. Put bluntly, rather than closing regulatory gaps, transnational regulatory standards diffuse perforated rules, while undermining domestic regulators' capacities to close them.

In sum, the core argument is that the TRR conditions the policy process of setting globally harmonised standards in a manner that entrenches asymmetric influence of national voice coalitions and transnational harmonisation coalitions, which, in turn, reduces the protection of financial stability. The latter is due to the preferential influence by the private interest coalitions as well as the missing counterbalancing for public good provisioning. In effect, the transnational regulatory regime raises the possibilities for organised special interests to integrate their preferences into policy outcomes, while at the same time decreasing the incentives for, and capacities of, public officials to regulate externalities and protect the public good of systemic stability.

As Admati & Hellwig (2013) argue, there are clear recipes for better, yet not perfect or best, societally beneficial banking regulation. However, the crucial road block for meaningful reform is the governance and opportunity structure of the political economy (Admati & Hellwig 2013, 190–227). The important question to be answered is how the governance/opportunity structure affects the quality of (global) banking regulation. This book provides a theoretical framework and new empirical evidence as a starting point for this analysis.

1.7   Plan of the book

The following chapter introduces briefly the logic for regulating banks. Crucially, it is outlined that financial stability constitutes an essential public good of modern economies, to which banks are important contributors. Since they provide a major part of the payments system, on which a diversified market economy relies, a systemic failure of this sector can have detrimental repercussions beyond its private activities. This is the reason why, that the public intervenes in banks' businesses by setting standards that constrain imprudent behaviour. I, furthermore, delineate to what extent this public good has global dimensions, and how transnational spillovers of turmoil undermine national capacities to regulate banks. Against this background, I provide a detailed introduction into the politics of the global harmonisation in banking regulation and in particular the Basel Committee. The theme that guides this chapter is that in banking regulation a transnational regulatory regime has evolved (and continues to evolve) around the Basel Committee. I argue that here we are witnessing the incremental transnationalisation of the governance structure and policy process.

In Chapter 3, then, I construct the eclectic theoretical framework of the TRR that builds the basis for assessing the simultaneous and interacting mechanisms of influence driving global standard setting. I synthesise the relevant explanatory mechanisms into an encompassing framework that delineates these interactions and how they result in regulatory loopholes being created at the stage of developing trans-governmental standards. Essentially, what differentiates my approach from previous studies is the framework's simultaneous delineation of national, transnational and interstate mechanisms of influence and their interaction within the global political economy of banking regulation. In essence, it encompasses the state unit-bound mechanisms of a refined two-level game of international politics – i.e. national intra-level regulatory regime dynamics and interstate G7/20 deliberations – plus transgovernmental and transnational mechanisms as well as dynamic feedback processes between these three arenas. The chapter provides a theoretical blueprint for the empirical analysis by outlining institutionalised governance and opportunity structures as well as involved actors' interests, strategies and potential coalitions. The framework reveals how the simultaneous, unreconciled influence that national and transnational coalitions wield in the process of setting harmonised regulatory standards originates in the transnationalisation of the regulatory governance structure, and how it can undermine the provision of financial stability.

On that basis, Chapter 4 presents a differentiated measurement of influence in the global politics of regulatory standard-setting, and, furthermore, how this influence translates into the content of regulatory policies. For that purpose, I carry out a systematic empirical assessment of the policies and politics of the Basel II agreement during the period 1998–2008. Departing from the two previous studies on the politics of Basel II (Wood 2005, Tarullo 2008), I simultaneously investigate the degree of influence exercised by international, transnational and various domestic actors and the global political dynamics underlying the regulatory outcome. Accordingly, the study combines a correlational content analysis of actor positions and their integration into the Basel II framework to measure influence in transnational standard setting with a process tracing analysis to identify which political channels were underlying these outcomes. This enables us to assess how the Basel II policy details reflect the success of distinct, national, transnational and interstate actors. Furthermore, I trace the underlying political processes within the G7, the Basel Committee, transnational banking associations, parliamentary committees of both US Congress chambers, and the financial committee of the German federal Parliament. In contrast to previous studies, I pay particular attention to the dynamics in national regulatory regimes through an in-depth analysis of parliamentary involvement. Of particular interest are the exact hearing documents from the finance committee of the German Bundestag, which were made available for this study: the non-public discussions, due to the detailed reports by regulators and industry on the Basel II negotiations, provide highly valuable historical source material to understand the politics of global banking regulation. In sum, the content analysis systematically evaluates the success and failure of certain actors in pursuing their interests, which allows clear interpretations of influence in the transnational political process. The process tracing devoted to highlighting which political structures were supportive for these outcomes provides clear insights into global political dynamics that drive global banking regulation.

This empirical approach bridges the gap of Basel II research between technical studies and political evaluations, by systematically evaluating the success and failure of actors in pursuing their policy-preferences. It reveals that the framework ensured the protection of competitiveness of the entire sector, sub-sectors and nation-specific sub-sectors, while losing sight of the negative external effects on systemic stability. It has promoted policies that met the short-term interests of the economic and political actors (politicians as well as regulators) in the TRR by introducing standards that were supportive of the many sectoral competitiveness-related concerns. Yet, the analysis reveals how Basel II neglected the protection of systemic financial stability and operated as a diffusion device of regulatory practices that were at the root of the Great Recession.

The Great Recession has caused politicians and regulators to respond by adapting the rules governing global banking (and finance more generally). The fifth chapter takes on the question of whether these reforms constitute significant change with regard to the problems that originate in the transnational governance structure. In light of my question, how the governance structure of global banking regulation affects influence in and the outcomes of regulatory standard setting, I review how the post-crisis changes may or may not affect the problematic TRR-conditioned dynamics of transnational regulatory cooperation. I discuss the main reforms outside the realm of nation state authority: the development of the Basel III framework to enhance harmonised banking regulation and the additional stipulations for systemically important banks, the reconstitution of the Financial Stability Forum as Financial Stability Board (FSB), and the strengthening of the G20 as the locus of interstate coordination for financial regulation. My analysis reveals that regulatory change in response to the Great Recession was substantial. Yet, with regard to this study's main argument of the conditioning effects that the TRR has on influence and outcomes of regulatory standard setting, the change, to date, is modest – and was *not* paradigmatic or significant. Reforms have not addressed the structure and dynamics of the TRR, since transgovernmental networks of national bureaucrats remain the pivotal actors in designing the global governance answers to politically embed global financial activities. Global layering of national and transnational rules continues to produce governance gaps, as the layering of national and transnational processes continues to facilitate the simultaneous, unreconciled influence of national and transnational coalitions that creates regulatory loopholes in global standards. In other words, the TRR-structure and transnational networks continue to drive the process, subject to comparable limitations. The reforms might even exacerbate the problem identified in this study.

Finally, the concluding chapter discusses how these results relate to the financial crisis that started in 2007 and what the insights, when combined with the current reform and clawback developments, mean for the future of global financial governance. This discussion is inspired by the quest for the right political control mechanisms in an incrementally globalising political economy. I outline how the persistent TRR structure around the Basel Committee is prone to asymmetric regard of well-organised sectoral interests vis-à-vis the neglected public good of systemic stability. Moreover, I will discuss how global layering gaps and the opportunity structures of TRRs provide theoretical frames to explain why post-crisis reforms in financial regulation are 'feeble' (Rixen 2013) and not paradigmatic. Finally, I discuss whether there are similar gaps in other areas of the global political economy, and how political control mechanisms can narrow or widen these gaps.

2
Global Financial Instability and the Evolution of Global Banking Regulation

In this chapter, I outline the evolution of the global politics around the Basel Committee since the collapse of the Bretton Woods agreement in the early 1970s, with a focus on the period 1998–2014. Next, however, I briefly introduce the essentials of financial stability as a public good, whilst highlighting its increasingly global character, and banks as businesses subject to regulation. In Section 2.2, I explain how a transnational regulatory regime has evolved (and continues to evolve) around the Basel Committee. I argue that we are witnessing incremental transnationalisation of the policy process, deepening global politicisation, and growing transnational institutionalisation in the governance structure. Finally, I discuss which actors wield influence through which institutional channels in this constellation.

2.1 Financial stability and banking regulation

The banking sector is not just another economic sector, it also has systemic relevance. While it is one of the most important and influential sectors, contributing to overall economic growth through the resulting tax revenues, regulatory fees, labour incomes and capital return, banking receives its distinguished role in the economy, as well as in politics from its twofold systemic relevance (Santos 2001). Its credit intermediation and creation can be a potential impulse of economic growth. If banks reduce their activity in lending this can slow down investment, therefore reducing growth dynamics. During recessions it might even come to a credit crunch, in which banks reject even those credit demands that promise highly profitable and secure prospects (which banks would normally be happy to accept) as a result of their increased caution. This tendency can take hold of large multi-million euro investment projects at national and international levels, as well as at the local level, where small businesses and private households cannot receive credit, or at least not under acceptable conditions. As a result, banks' lending activity affects a wide variety of actors, including many not directly concerned with banking (Rosenbluth & Schaap 2003, Keefer 2007).

Banks are an essential institution in a money-based economy due to their role as liquidity/deposit providers, which is the main difference compared to most other financial intermediaries (Goodhart et al. 1998, 10–12). Modern economies, which are not based upon the exchange of goods of comparable value but on monetary exchange, need a payments system with a provider of legal tender, the central bank, and institutions that provide deposits to market participants. The latter is an essential function of efficient exchange in a market economy, which establishes banks as institutions with systemic relevance. However, if one bank in a competitive market fails, it merely constitutes an individual problem to its depositors, not a systemic problem. An insolvent bank transforms from a private to a public bad if resulting *bank runs* create a threat to financial stability. A bank run, i.e. customers withdrawing all their deposits from a bank, occurs if customers are concerned about the safety of their deposits. The fear of bank insolvency becomes a self-fulfilling prophecy as the withdrawals weaken a bank's capital base to a point where it cannot serve its liabilities.

The underlying logic is rooted in the illiquidity of banks' assets relative to their short-term callable deposits and their widely interconnected nature through inter-bank lending (Diamond & Dybvig 1983). The resulting interdependence on the mutual servicing of liabilities makes banks' stability, in part, dependent upon competitors' ability to serve the liabilities. One institute's failure might have systemic repercussions due to the defaulting on liabilities to trading partners and creditors. An individual bank's solvency is particularly vulnerable to systemic instability due to the specific contract form of bank credit intermediation: banks typically lend over long time horizons (e.g. a real estate mortgage over 20 years), the return on which is naturally subject to time-dependent insecurities; at the same time, the refinancing or borrowing is structured over short time horizons, since depositors can typically withdraw their funds immediately without prior notice. The tension of liquid liabilities with illiquid assets demands sophisticated risk management, which is not very problematic in everyday banking since the probability of simultaneous withdrawals up to an endangering amount is very low – unless a bank run occurs. Since customers are aware of the possibility of a bank's insolvency, an event which has very negative consequences for a depositor, but are not capable of identifying the health of the relevant institute appropriately, it is individually rational to withdraw money as a precaution. Consequently, latent instability and diffusion of information about potential bank failures can turn into a full-blown banking crisis (Diamond & Dybvig 1983).

The consequence of banks' systemic relevance is that private credit transactions have a public dimension, an externality beyond the producer–consumer relation. Their lending activity and the criteria of credit supply have often become political issues in the past (Rosenbluth & Schaap 2003, 307). Furthermore, their role in the payments and depository system transforms them into a contributor to the public good of financial stability. Financial stability can be regarded as a public good (Santos 2001, 44–50) as it has substantial utility to all members of a society and, from the viewpoint of overall societal wealth, is pareto optimal, i.e. its provision increases overall welfare without disadvantaging any member of society (of course this disregards several special interest groups, which profit from the overall losses). As such, it is non-excludable and non-diminishing in usage (Kaul et al. 1999, Ostrom 2010).

It is apparent that the public or democratic polity has a considerable interest in regulating banks. Securing deposits, reducing the probability of bank insolvencies, and preventing systemic collapses from inter-bank contagion are at the core of the public interest, which is why supervision[1] of banks in industrialised countries is typically built upon three fundamental provisions (Llewellyn 1999, Santos 2001).[2] The first element is deposit insurance, i.e. reducing the threats of a bank run by ensuring banking accounts up to a certain degree. Most developed countries have adopted a variant of this approach, although via very different institutional designs (Davies & Green 2008, 155–186). The second main mechanism of stabilising the system of payments and credit intermediation is the lender of last resort function. In order to prevent the negative spillovers from a bank insolvency destabilising the entire banking system, a lender of last resort would provide sufficient funds to keep the bank's business running so that it can meet its credit and payment obligations. By doing this, the likelihood of another destabilised institute due to failed credits owed by the insolvent bank is reduced, as is the probability of a bank run. While this can be provided through different organisational channels, e.g. a consortium of all other banks, it is typically provided by a nation's central bank (Goodhart & Illing 2002).

The third major fundamental of current banking regulation are stipulations for prudential borrowing and lending. The main approach since the 1980s is risk-weighted capital adequacy stipulations. This instrument is intended to reduce banks' excessive risk-taking and leveraging of debt.[3] These stipulations aim at reducing the probability of a bank's insolvency from misjudged risk in lending and borrowing activities (Santos 2001, Tarullo 2008, 15–44).

The basic regulatory approach of capital adequacy regulation forces banks to collect a certain amount of equity, which provides a buffer against unexpected losses (for a review of the literature on capital adequacy regulation, see Santos 2001). Thereby, the probability of the institution's failure is considered to be reduced.[4] The adequate amount of capital to be held against a certain mix of credits is calculated by risk-weighting each credit with a factor that is considered to reflect the riskiness of this asset class. Put succinctly, it works as follows: regulators assign risk weights to different asset qualities (typically between 0 and 150 per cent, e.g. a developed country's government bonds receive 0 per cent, corporations of medium creditworthiness receive 50 per cent). The banks then have to multiply the respective assets in their books with the respective weight, with the sum of all risk-weighted assets depicting the consolidated risk position of a bank. Considering this monetary amount as the denominator of a fraction, the bank has to collect an amount of equity in the numerator so that the fraction is equivalent to the minimum percentage of regulatory capital stipulated. The magic Basel I and Basel II threshold was 8 per cent, which the bank had to meet at all times.

As we will see below, the Basel committee has focused on risk-weighted capital regulation in the context of the harmonisation of its members' regulatory standards since the 1980s. It continues this focus in the context of regulatory reforms of the financial crisis that started in 2007 (Goldbach & Kerwer 2012). Without going into detail it is worth mentioning that this approach has become heavily criticised by a considerable number of leading scholars of banking regulation (Admati & Hellwig 2013). These scholars argue that the highly complex risk weighted calculations combined with accounting loopholes – both elements in part due to Basel regulation – enabled the excessive risk-taking of banks in the run-up to the crisis. Banks were allowed, actually even incentivised, to invest in assets with low risk weights or those assets that had not to be accounted as risk bearing assets – i.e. all these assets had nominally 0 per cent of risk and resulted in zero capital requirements. The present study demonstrates how these detrimental standards came into being and became globally diffused.

With regard to the question 'in whose benefit?' one has to bear in mind that the interest in banking and its regulation is characterised by two dimensions, the promotion of which can be contradictory to a substantial degree. On the one hand, the concerns of private sector profitability and public economic growth tend to demand the high risk taking of banks and limited regulatory intervention in credit transactions. Due to the safety net provided by the state, private actors tend to underemphasise financial stability with regard to business and regulatory decisions. On the other hand, the mainly public concern about the stability of depository institutions promotes decreased incentives for high risk taking, as well as increased incentives to internalise the transaction externalities of credit intermediation.

Since the 1990s, international finance has become an economic activity of global character (Strange 1994, Helleiner 1994, Kapstein 1994, Cerny 1994, Cohen 1996, Deeg & O'Sullivan 2009). In effect, this means that financial intermediation is carried out internationally on (almost) truly global markets, i.e. supply, demand, and prices are determined in a global arena. Derivatives markets provide a fitting example of truly global markets, with almost unrestricted cross-border trading. In fact, foreign trading shares are higher at almost all big exchanges and all over-the-counter derivatives markets around the globe. This is demonstrated by descriptive data of trading volumes provided by Duffie & Hu (2008): highly specialised market segments are located within different national jurisdictions and electronic trading is undertaken independently of the market's location. Moreover, banks have become transnational conglomerates with interlinked operations in many jurisdictions. Through a series of takeovers and the banks' diversification of their business activities, especially into highly profitable security trading activities, national and transnational financial conglomerates emerged. This resulted in steadily growing conglomerates, and an increasing opacity of risk profiles and supervisory responsibilities (Group of Ten 2001).

As a consequence of this transnational interconnectedness, supervisors lost their ability to control bank activities. Whether foreign branches or subsidiaries act prudently within its jurisdiction is hard to control or even assess for the regulator acting unilaterally. At the same time, it is difficult for the regulatory agency of the country of incorporation to assess and control operations of the foreign branches or subsidiaries. As a result, which the recent crisis has demonstrated convincingly, the defaulting of a bank and a systemic turmoil in one country can easily spill over transnationally into other jurisdictions and develop into a global crisis (Singer 2007). Accordingly, the provision of financial stability has to a considerable degree become a global public good (Wyplosz 1999).

Once economic activity and the provision of private goods becomes increasingly transnational the provision of public goods and political rules is not geographically congruent anymore (Cerny 1995). In other words, once economic actors interact increasingly beyond national borders, existent political and regulatory institutions do not provide an appropriate framework of rules any more. If one aims for global financial markets while at the same time preventing global financial instability some form of regulatory coordination is necessary.

2.2   Evolution of the Basel Committee

While the national level continues to be the most influential political framework for banking regulation (Busch 2009), world politics have gained increasing relevance due to transnational harmonisation of regulatory standards since the 1970s (Wood 2005). Accordingly, while standards remain ingrained in the national context, the transnational harmonisation of regulations also has a considerable effect on the supervision of global and national banks.

In the absence of an intergovernmental authority to regulate international financial activities, this transnationalisation has been mostly driven by the responsible national regulatory agencies and/or central banks. Against the background of deepening global financial integration, domestic supervisors considered the international coordination of foreign banking supervision a necessary measure. Since 1974, under pressure from international financial crises during which national turmoil spilled over to other jurisdictions, the regulatory agencies have coordinated the exchange of information on transnational banking activity and have informally harmonised their regulatory standards through the transgovernmental network of the Basel Committee (Kapstein 1994, Wood 2005, Singer 2007, Goodhart 2011).[5]

In this book, I argue that the BCBS and its governance structure constitute a mechanism of transnational diffusion, and that it is a prime example of the transnationalisation of governance structures and policy processes (Cerny 2010b). Moreover, I argue that it becomes increasingly institutionalised, a trend that reached a new depth between 1998 and 2014, the period of investigation. In this section, I will, first, outline how this evolution has taken place so far and, second, how the BCBS works and exercises its influence.[6]

Evolution and functions

The Basel Committee has come a long way since its inception, evolving from a gentlemen's club of mostly informal information sharing into a transnationally institutionalised regulatory authority with a written and publicly available Charter (though still not of a legally binding nature). The scope and scale of these functions and consequently the Committee's role have continuously widened so substantially since 1974 that it nowadays fulfils all of the three main functions that Slaughter (2004, 53–61) ascribes to transgovernmental networks: first, sharing information, through which best practices are exchanged and codified, and reputation is exchanged; second, harmonising the standard setting and content of national laws; third, enforcement, i.e. enhancing cooperation among national regulators to enforce existing national laws and rules, sharing intelligence and capacity building to strengthen the weakest link in the chain of national regulatory agencies.

The following paragraphs provide a brief overview of the three functions, and how seven historical touchstones resemble the development from gentlemen's club to transnationally institutionalised regulatory authority: inception, Basel Concordat, Basel I Accord, Markets Risk Amendment, Core Principles of Banking Supervision, Basel II framework, and Basel III reforms. However, one should bear in mind that the Committee and its cooperation evolved continuously and incrementally, rather than through seven big negotiations (Goodhart 2011). Rather, their changing foci resemble the incremental adaptation of the BCBS's work from information exchange and coordination to cooperation and harmonisation, to transgovernmental rule-setting and institutionalisation.

The Committee's origin lies in the collapse of the Bretton Woods agreement and the concurrent macroeconomic shocks and bank failures. The combination of increased internationalisation of bank activities – through the so-called Euro-markets[7] – and newly floating exchange rates increased international financial volatility and resulted in bank collapses (particularly worrisome were the collapses of the German Herstatt and the US Franklin National Bank in 1974) and ultimately brought the insight that the new financial order created international externalities of bank failures (Goodhart 2011, 10–54). Against this background, the Bank for International Settlements (BIS) provided an established, suitable institutional setting for the discussion of supervisory concerns (Goodhart 2011, chs 2 and 3). Since the 1930s, central bank governors of the Group of Ten (G10) have met frequently to exchange information on and coordinate their monetary policies at the BIS headquarters in Basel (Toniolo 2005). The central banks are, however, very often, and in the 1970s were predominantly, also responsible for the prudential supervision of banks, and the rising global financial instability was a major concern for them.

In 1974, therefore, the governors established the Basel Committee as a committee of banking supervision authorities.[8] The original goal of the creation was information exchange to improve the transparency of international banking activities, while harmonisation was explicitly refused as being a goal of the BCBS – nevertheless, from the 1980s onwards it would move increasingly in this direction.

The initial function of the Committee's efforts was the exchange of information on transnational banking activity as well as on banks' conditions in situations of crisis. In light of globalised, opaque banking the enhancement of a supervisor's knowledge about foreign banks' business in his jurisdiction was deemed highly desirable. This early information exchange also led to increased trust and reputation building among supervisors (Kapstein 1994). Accordingly, the supervisors themselves considered the Basel Committee an informal club for the purpose of confidential information exchange and the building of common ideas and trust (Goodhart 2011). Furthermore, from this the exchange of best practices and the definition and diffusion of common codification in principles emerged. By creating a common language of risk and how to monitor and control these challenges, best practices are created that impact on banks in their business behaviour and regulators in supervising these activities (Tarullo 2008, Buchmüller 2008).

This information exchange deepened quickly into coordination of supervising internationally active banks. The Committee's first written agreement, the Basel Concordat of 1975, was a reaction to the international spillovers from the bank failures of the German Herstatt and the US Franklin National Bank in 1974.[9] To ensure that no foreign banking establishment in one of the member states' jurisdictions would be unsupervised, the Concordat clearly laid out principles that divide responsibilities for supervising foreign establishments and established the principle of home country control, which made this regulator the key supervisor of foreign bank establishments. Buchmüller (2008, 59) describes the division of supervisory responsibilities between home and host country supervisors precisely: the regulatory agency of the home jurisdiction of a bank is responsible for the consolidated banking group's supervision, while the supervisor of the host country, i.e. where branches and subsidiaries reside, takes responsibility for the partially consolidated foreign parts of the bank. While the host country supervisor can require additional capital requirements from legally independent subsidiaries, it cannot do so with respect to legally dependent branches. Furthermore, the Concordat outlined guidelines for the consolidated supervision of bank holdings, which was a particular aspect of the modifications in response to the devastating fraud events of Banco Ambrosiano and Bank of Credit and Commerce International. The Concordat was exclusively applied to supervisors (not to banks directly) and is seen as an effective coordination mechanism, with the basic principle of home country control remaining a key cornerstone of all Basel agreements until today (Kapstein 1994, 48–52).

What is important to note is that the Concordat was not a one-shot agreement, negotiated over some time and then accepted. It started as a working paper in the BCBS, introduced by one member, repeatedly revised and then accepted by the BCBS, and later endorsed by the G10 governors as a set of guidelines for G10 supervisors. It was altered repeatedly between 1975 and 1992. Its latter amendments mirror the incremental move from guidelines to more binding rules, which were expected to be met by BCBS members (Goodhart 2011, 96–126). This aspect of continuous, incrementally deepening supervisory cooperation characterises the Committee's work until today.

Evolving from mere coordination, starting in the mid-1980s, the BCBS began to focus on its new second function, namely the harmonisation of regulatory standards across jurisdictions. Probably the best known agreement, the Basel I Accord agreed in 1988, mirrors this move from coordination and cooperation in supervision towards harmonisation of regulatory standards (Goodhart 2011, 146–223). It was a cooperative reaction to the very low capitalisation levels and the international banking problems revealed during the Latin American Debt Crisis. Supervisors wanted to close regulatory loopholes and prevent regulatory arbitrage by international banks that chose the jurisdiction with the most lenient regulation. Accordingly, in order to improve regulation without tilting the global level playing field, the harmonised approach seemed most promising (Singer 2007). The BCBS answer was the introduction of minimum capital adequacy and risk weights regulation (see description above). Moreover, it introduced several important elements of transnational regulatory standards which are still important today, in particular the core of capital adequacy regulation. It was a highly influential agreement, with fast, comprehensive implementation into national law that has even extended to non-negotiating countries – in sum more than 100 countries implemented the Accord. It is said to have raised capital ratios substantially (Jackson et al. 1999). Moreover, bank stability was high in the 15 following years. While this cannot be convincingly attributed to the Basel mechanism directly, it is perceived to have worked indirectly as a focal point in investor and regulator evaluation of banks (Tarullo 2008). Basel I and its perceived success made the BCBS a globally respected authority.

On the basis of the Basel I success and the Committee's widely accepted authority, the BCBS increasingly engaged in developing new rules within the transgovernmental network, which would then be diffused into its participating domestic regulatory regimes. While Basel I had already constituted the turn to developing *new* elements within the BCBS (in contrast to mere harmonisation), this trend was fostered during the development of the Market Risk Amendment, which complemented the Capital Accord (Basel Committee on Banking Supervision 1996). The Amendment was a response to the increasing trading activities of international banks (in contrast to strategies of holding assets until maturity) that undermined the Basel Accord. The Market Risk Amendment's importance lies in two innovative aspects: first, the introduction of a regulatory approach that relies on complex risk calculation based on banks' internal risk management capacities.[10] The internal models approach, widely known as Value-at-Risk (VaR) models approach, mirrored the Basel Committee's beginning reliance on statistical risk calculation, as well as the inception of building risk regulation upon internal bank resources – since the main information for the VaR calculations were generated within the banks themselves (Claessens & Underhill 2010). Second, transnational banks' considerable advancement in risk-calculation via statistical modelling led the BCBS to raise the involvement of banks in the development of the regulatory standards (Goodhart 2011, 224–264). More specifically, the Committee's entrusted working groups that developed the Amendment chose to gain the international, technically advanced banks' input on innovative risk modelling techniques. For that purpose, the working group setting provided a suitable forum for informal, yet intense interaction with international banks. Another relevant innovation of the Amendment, which we will discuss in detail below, was the introduction of a public consultation process.

Due to its growing role as standard-setter since the Market Risk Amendment, the BCBS has become increasingly subject to politicisation. There is, however, a second reason for this politicisation that we should turn to briefly, namely the global perception of the Committee as global regulator with authority for non-G10 countries, in particular emerging markets. The Committee's role as global regulator with authority reaching well beyond its G10 world was tremendously strengthened through the Core Principles for Effective Banking Supervision (Basel Committee on Banking Supervision 1997), the only rapidly developed agreement of the BCBS (Goodhart 2011, 286–316).[11] It constitutes a set of guidelines to be adopted by emerging market economies, with less developed regulatory regimes.[12] In 1996, the G7 and IMF began to be worried about international financial stability in light of questionable prudence in the emerging markets. They pushed the BCBS to develop standards in this area, which resulted in the quick development of the Core Principles during a few months in 1997. These guidelines became highly successful in diffusing Basel standards to non-BCBS states, since the IMF and World Bank strengthened the Core Principles through the monitoring of countries' adherence to them (see discussion in Chapter 4) – market pressure, then, worked as the sanctioning mechanism (Goodhart 2011, 299–300). The Core Principles' political relevance lies in the acceptance of the BCBS by the G7, the IMF, the World Bank, and most global policy-makers as the international institution responsible for standards in the area of banking regulation – within and beyond the G10 (Goodhart 2011, 299). Since then, the BCBS has been considered as the international regulator, and the IMF as international supervisor (Goodhart 2011, 554).

The development of new rules in the transnational realm – and the according politicisation – intensified especially during the Basel II and III processes. These two agreements and their deliberation processes were characterised by the politicisation as well as the formalisation they introduced in to the BCBS. Basel II deliberations were initiated to overcome the antiquated and insufficient nature of the Basel Accord – to close regulatory loopholes on the one hand, and update to new market standards on the other hand. It fostered two aspects of the Committee's development, namely reliance on market-based regulation and transnational politicisation. In terms of content, it established the regulatory approach that is still fundamental to its recent Basel III reforms: a strong focus on the market-based regulatory approach that relies on a combination of (1) complex risk calculation based on (2) banks' internal risk management capacities, and (3) information disclosure and market scrutiny (Wood 2005, 123–151). The Basel II framework was an encompassing, innovative global policy product. Furthermore, the Basel II negotiations from 1998 to 2005 were the first (documented) time that politics got involved in the transnational policy process (Goodhart 2011, 554).

More specifically, the Basel II deliberations introduced the element of *multi-level negotiations* and complex interaction between international, transnational and domestic politics (Wood 2005). It also revealed early signs of deepening institutionalisation, namely in the form of a public consultative process, and the inception of an implementation monitoring mechanism (all these issues will be discussed in detail in Chapter 4). In sum, the Basel II framework harmonised the rules that guide the investment decisions of globally active as well as nationally oriented banks. It was the crucial element of global financial regulation preceding the sub-prime crisis. Most of its results continue to be relevant in the post-crisis architecture, since Basel III, the new agreement, does not replace but complements Basel II (Goldbach & Kerwer 2012, Lall 2012). As we will see below, this immense project to set rules that govern the entire banking sector was doomed to failure. Nevertheless, in the context of reforms responding to the Great Recession, the Committee became the central locus for global reforms (Verdier 2013).

Basel III and the corresponding agreements, ironically, built on the governance structure and processes that generated Basel II, and fostered their institutionalisation. Just after Basel II had failed, the BCBS decided to enhance its framework, and the G20 relied on the Committee's expertise to develop the new regulatory framework to stabilise global banking. As a result, less than one year after the Lehman Bros collapse, in July 2009 the regulators agreed on the Basel II.5 rules to close the worst loopholes, and only slightly more than one year later, in December 2010, the Basel III rules to reform global banking regulation, supposedly, fundamentally. These standards are one of the cornerstones of the global reforms in response to the Great Recession, and will have substantial impact on the future of global banking and its regulation (Goldbach & Kerwer 2012, Verdier 2013). I will reveal in detail in Chapter 5 that these reforms, while substantial in terms of altered policy-content and of governance structure, were insignificant in so far, as they further the transnationalisation of banking regulation without reconciling the TRR-problems of global layers and gaps. What stands out is the global political mandate for the BCBS, the repetition and deepening of politicisation of the Basel process, and the fostered institutionalisation in the governance structure. While I will discuss these aspects in detail in the following section and in particular in Chapter 5, three main aspects need to be mentioned here due to their role in the evolution of the transnationalisation of governance structures and policy processes. First, the BCBS, in January 2013, gave itself a written, publicly available Charter, which constitutes a major step in the hardening of its soft law approach. There, with explicit denial of legal effect, the Committee outlines such crucial aspects like the members' responsibilities to uphold financial stability and the public consultation process. A second, important aspect that was strengthened through further formalisation of principles is the coordinated supervision of internationally active banks by supervisors from multiple jurisdictions.

Finally, the reforms aim to enhance enforcement – the third transgovernmental network function, i.e. enhancing cooperation among national regulators to enforce existing national laws and rules – which so far has been the least developed function. Until 2009, it relied exclusively on the logic of appropriateness and peer pressure, but scrutiny and peer pressure for adequate national adoption and implementation has been weak. To strengthen implementation, the Accord Implementation Group (AIG) was created midway through the Basel II negotiations in December 2001. It was, however, initially *not* designed as an implementation monitoring body, but as one that merely exists to discuss implementation challenges. As part of the reform efforts since 2009, Committee members agreed to replace the AIG by a strengthened peer review mechanism. Under the Regulatory Consistency Assessment Programme (RCAP), which I discuss in detail in Chapter 5, member jurisdictions' implementation of Basel II, II.5 and III (Basel Committee on Banking Supervision 2013a) is becoming increasingly subject to institutionalised peer review, although without hard law sanctioning mechanisms.

There is, however, a potentially counter-balancing trend to this institutionalisation. Due to already outlined competition state strategies (Cerny 1997), states may continue to coordinate and share information to their benefit transnationally, while simultaneously engaging in cosmetic or 'mock compliance' in their jurisdictions (Walter 2008). Thus, regulations are adopted merely formally, but in practice not applied faithfully in the supervision of banks. This strategy was, for example, the choice of East Asian emerging market regulators in implementing the Basel I Accord (Walter 2008, Chey 2013). Likewise, Thiemann's (2014) already cited study on the interaction between national accounting rules and banking laws on the one hand and transnational regulatory standards of the Basel I Accord on the other hand, has revealed how eight out of ten analysed OECD countries knowingly oversaw regulatory arbitrage strategies by banks in their jurisdictions. As we discussed before, Thiemann argues that regulators feared that global market reach would pull financial activity into other jurisdictions if the regulator were to push legislation or regulation beyond the perforated global Basel standards.

In sum, then, we have a deepening institutionalisation of a transnational regulatory regime on the one hand as well as a nation state order organised as competition state on the other hand. These contrary trends of competition state strategies put the nature and actual effects of the TRR into question. As I said before, this problem of global rule layering is a persistent and deepening challenge of global cooperation, which is, furthermore, worsened through the fact that asymmetric influence during the negotiation process increases the number and size of these perforations. The size of this problem has increased over the past 20 or so years. I will reveal and discuss the deepening of this problem during the period 1998–2014 in the following chapters.

Between 1974 and 2014, the transgovernmental network structure has become a crucial forum to approach regulatory problems that regulators perceive to overwhelm their separate national capacities. Supervisory agencies are driven to it as the suitable collective action forum with established informal decision-making rules for a like-minded community. The Basel Committee's augmented importance in the global political economy is mirrored in the cornerstone character of its recent Basel II and III initiatives. Broadly speaking, three trends characterise the Committee's development: incremental transnationalisation of the policy process, growing global politicisation, and deepening transnational institutionalisation in the governance structure. Accordingly, the once secluded club has become subject to incrementally growing publicity and inclusiveness of the process and governance structure – from only regulators at first, to the integration of international banks, national politics (i.e. banks and politicians), and now increasingly public interest groups.

Organisation, decision-making and transnational diffusion

The evolving role of the BCBS makes it all the more important to understand how decisions are taken in the Committee and how the processes of standard-setting unfold. However, even though the studies by Wood (2005), Tarullo (2008) and Goodhart (2011) have provided invaluable insights into these processes, we still need a more encompassing understanding of the politicisation of global banking regulation within and through the Basel Committee since 1997. In an attempt to synthesise the above authors' insights with the new information from the present study, I briefly outline below how the BCBS is organised, how its policy process unfolds, how it takes decisions, and how its decisions affect regulatory standards. I present the current state of September 2014, while I point to the main prior stages during the investigative period of this study from 1998 to 2014.

Organisation

The Basel Committee is a transgovernmental network, the governance structure of which has been subject to increasing institutionalisation since its inception. It encompasses the national regulatory agencies from industrialised nations with globally relevant financial markets.[13] Countries are represented by upper/middle-ranking officials from their central bank and – in case where there is an institutional division of labour – also from their authority that is formally charged with the responsibility for prudential supervision of banking businesses (the exception is Luxembourg, which is represented by its supervisory agency only). The Committee is a continuous forum of regulatory coordination and cooperation, as supervisors meet regularly (at least four times a year) in Basel to discuss issues of bank regulation and supervision (additional meetings take place when necessary, as e.g. during the negotiations of the Basel II and III agreements).

The Basel Committee is subordinate to the Governors and Heads of Supervision (GHOS), which assembles the central bank governors and heads of banking supervision. The Committee's agreements have to be approved by the GHOS.[14] However, the Basel Committee's decisions are always approved. Since the country membership is identical in Committee and GHOS, all conflicts are resolved within the Basel Committee as the crucial forum of decision making (Buchmüller 2008, 19–20). This is no doubt the result of the very careful deliberation in the Committee, which hands proposals for adoption over to the governors only after prolonged discussion and compromise within the BCBS, as well as the traditional very close, regardful interaction between the BCBS Chairman and the governors (Goodhart 2011).

The BCBS is a transgovernmental network without formal legal international standing. Its organisation and decisions have the legal character of soft law. It has from its beginning been hosted by the BIS and has neither a high number of personnel nor a substantial budget, which are both provided by the BIS. Of the approximately 15 to 20 staff members, less than five are permanent secretariat staff, while those remaining are domestic central bank or regulatory agency employees on secondment to the Committee – they remain employees of the respective national institution, to which they are primarily responsible.[15] Rather than being an intergovernmental organisation, instead the Basel Committee enfolds its influence through its network structure among merely informally interconnected national regulators.[16] Figure 2.1 reveals that, while the Basel Committee reports upwards to the GHOS, it is a group that steers and coordinates the work of several working groups, task forces and ad hoc committees which feed the BCBS with the necessary policy-making groundwork.

The BCBS working group structure is a crucial feature of the transgovernmental network. These working groups and task forces, as depicted by the many boxes surrounding the BCBS circle in Figure 2.1, carry out the bulk of the work in the Committee and provide detailed analyses to the BCBS. They are composed of upper/middle-ranking officials from domestic supervisory agencies, who communicate extensively and intensively with the (international) banking community. The first such group was established in 1976 (the working group on bank confirmation enquiries), 'but the number of such groups ramified in the mid-1980s with, and following, the work on [capital adequacy requirements]' (Goodhart 2011, 85). During the Basel II process, the number of groups increased as did their influence due to the sheer amount of technical decisions to be made.[17] The Capital Task Force, a particularly relevant example, prepared and selected the topics for the Committee's Basel II negotiation meetings. These groups' importance in affecting the BCBS agenda and outputs is mirrored in the restructuring of them by every new Chairman as well as the fact that 'each working group had its own dynamic (and chairman and secretary)' (Goodhart 2011, 85). As a consequence, these groups of regulatory staffers determine to a substantial degree the content of several regulatory standards, which are then put on the Basel Committee's agenda for agreement.[18] Its problem-oriented spirit and tremendous technical expertise in a semi-institutionalised environment provides the Basel Committee with considerable problem-solving capacities in the absence of political or public interference. Furthermore, it provides an opportunity to integrate the expertise and interests of internationally active banks.

The club-like atmosphere and working group spirit of the Committee's first 25 years, however, has become, since the onset of the Basel II exercise, increasingly subject to incrementally deepening formalisation and institutionalisation. Two formalised aspects reformed in 2013 stand out. First, the BCBS has recently begun to present its official governance

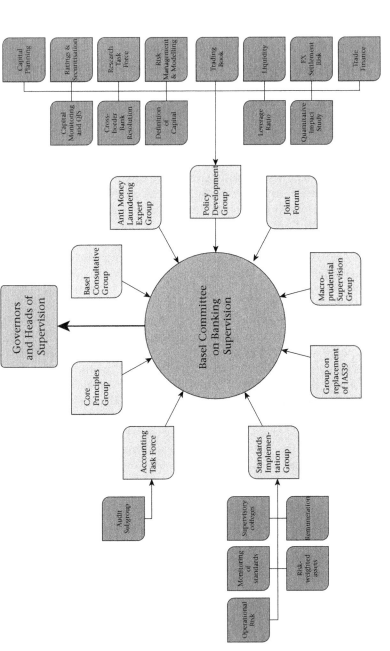

Figure 2.1 The Basel Committee on Banking Supervision, organisational chart (official version until 2012)

Source: Bank for International Settlements (www.bis.org/bcbs; accessed on 27 July 2012).

structure in the hierarchical manner of Figure 2.2.[19] Note that this depiction differs from the earlier presentation of Figure 2.1 (which the Committee promoted until mid-2012) in that the new one suggests a clear-cut hierarchical structure and streamlining of working groups. Yet, as outlined in the preceding paragraph, the BCBS is still mostly organised in the same groups depicted in the earlier organigram. In effect, the BCBS has differentiated its governance structure. It has streamlined the inner circle of formerly nine working groups (of a more continuous kind) to six that are now called 'Groups',[20] and has given them a permanent status in its Charter. According to section 9 of the Charter, these groups 'report directly to the Committee ... and are composed of senior staff from BCBS members that guide or undertake themselves major areas of Committee work. [They] form part of the permanent internal structure'. Hierarchically subordinated now are the 'working groups', which 'consist of experts from BCBS members that support the technical work of BCBS groups'. Finally, again situated one hierarchical level deeper, are the 'task forces', which 'are created to undertake specific tasks for a limited time [and which] are generally composed of technical experts from BCBS member institutions'. In sum, this mirrors a deepening of formalisation and institutionalisation. Nevertheless, the regulatory work remains to be carried out through a continuing complex network structure of groups, working groups, and task forces (the Committee website lists 23 such groups in September 2014), which is arguably still better reflected by Figure 2.1.

Second, the Committee has given itself a written, publicly available Charter, which formalises the hitherto informal rules that governed the Basel Committee between (roughly) 1999 and 2012. There it positions itself as 'primary global standard-setter for the prudential regulation of banks and [as] forum for cooperation on banking supervisory matters'. The Charter outlines the BCBS activities and responsibilities of informational exchange, supervisory coordination, regulatory harmonisation, development of new standards, and implementation monitoring. It, moreover, stipulates member states' responsibilities, where these range from the cooperation to promote financial stability to the faithful implementation and application of the Basel rules. The Charter goes as far, as to stipulate the mandatory participation in regular BCBS reviews as well as the responsibility to 'promote the interests of global financial stability and not solely national interests'.

While the new Charter explicitly states that the 'BCBS does not possess any formal supranational authority [and that] its decisions do not have legal force', it emphasises that it 'expects full implementation of

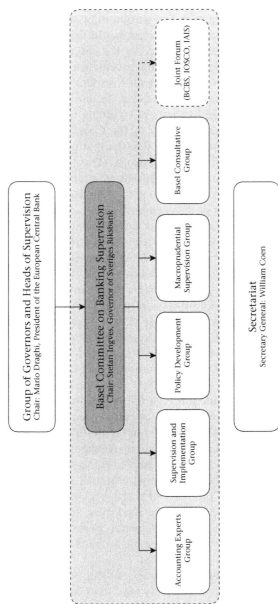

Figure 2.2 The Basel Committee on Banking Supervision, organisational chart (official version since 2013)
Source: Bank for International Settlements (www.bis.org/bcbs/organigram.pdf; accessed on 3 May 2015).

its standards by BCBS members and their internationally active banks', which translates into the incorporation 'into local legal frameworks through each jurisdiction's rule-making process'. The Charter continues to differentiate between three sets of rules, namely standards, guidelines, and sound practices, which constitute a differing degree of bindingness. Another, crucial feature is the now 'compulsory public consultation process', under which the Committee solicits comments from interested parties within 90 days, where the consultative papers as well as the comments are made publicly available on the BIS website. The Charter, furthermore, delineates a periodical review of membership and potential integration of new members as well as the BCBS relations to other international organisations. In sum, thus, the Charter positions the Basel Committee as a central authority in world politics, and how it relates to other elements of this order – another clear element of formalisation and institutionalisation.

Effect of BCBS decisions

So, in the absence of supra- or international legal force and given the fact that agreements have merely soft law character that do not force countries into adoption,[21] how do the BCBS decisions affect national regulations and supervisory practices? This is difficult to answer, since the degree and mechanisms of domestic implementation and application remain poorly researched (with the exception of Asian emerging markets, as will be discussed below). What can be said is that BCBS rules work through two analytically distinct yet inextricably intertwined mechanisms, namely faithful implementation and transnational diffusion of principles.

Notwithstanding the soft law character of the Basel agreements, BCBS supervisors have typically adopted and implemented them faithfully and thoroughly. Regulators subject themselves to these restrictive contracts for three reasons, namely market enforcement, jurisdictional competitiveness, and reputational risks. First, due to the third-party enforcement power exercised by the global financial market (Wood 2005), the diffusion of regulatory standards provides simple benchmarks through which investors calibrate their investment decisions. Market pressure on banks and supervisors rises as they aim to attain the 'seal of approval' (Singer 2007, Gray 2009). Second, domestic regulatory agencies pursue implementation to prevent competitive disadvantages for their banks' international activities in other jurisdictions (Chey 2007) as well as the need of attracting international investors, who favour globally harmonised rules. Third, the network character of the

Basel Committee results in the importance of mutual trust relationships, which makes – due to a logic of appropriateness – defection from agreements or the lack of cooperation in the BCBS an activity with considerable negative consequences, where a regulator's international reputation would suffer. Supervisors need to coordinate with foreign counterparts in light of transnationally active banks and fear losing this possibility (March & Olsen 1998, Singer 2007).

There is, however, variance over time in the faithfulness of adoption and implementation: with increasing precision of stipulations, evasive strategies have also risen (Walter 2008, Chey 2013). In contrast to the Concordat, the faithfulness and thoroughness of implementation has decreased in the context of Basel I and the Market Risk Amendment, has worsened under Basel II; a reversal of this trend is not occurring in the context of Basel III. Accordingly, implementation is increasingly subject to two limitations. First, many of the elements of the agreements are designed as optional choice sets, which consider national specificities substantially. This policy has become a major strategy of the BCBS to uphold compromise and guarantee international agreement – as we will see in Chapters 4 and 5. Second, implementation is adapted to the national context, and might be subject to evasive strategies.[22] As already noted, this results in cosmetic or mock compliance, where regulations are adopted formally, but in practice not applied faithfully in the supervision of banks (Walter 2008, Chey 2013).[23]

Against this background, the second form of influence gains in relative importance, namely transnational diffusion of regulatory and supervisory principles. The BCBS has always functioned as a forum for information exchange and deliberation directed at the goal of developing best practices. It was and is considered appropriate, if not mandatory, for a reputable regulator to adopt these best practices. The Basel interactions also transnationalised the regulators' perspective on problems and approaches. This is exemplified by the application of the rules to domestically active banks. Accordingly, while the rules are primarily directed at the activity of transnationally active banks, the rules are frequently considered as some kind of best practice, which leads regulators to apply them also to banks that are only active within the limits of a jurisdiction. In other words, even nationally/locally oriented banks become somewhat the target of the transnationally harmonised regulations. These regulatory standards resulted in widespread harmonisation in many countries, even though no formal, legally binding agreement was ever adopted. The following analyses of Basel II and III will reveal that Basel standards are, in addition to being implemented into national regulations, also transnationally diffused through the integration of the regulatory approaches and principles that supervisors learned in Basel.

A highly important, and under-researched, area concerns the layering of domestic and transnational rules into complex rule constellations (what legal scholars refer to as complementarity, rivalry and hybridity), which implies that a straightforward assumption of transgovernmental agreements impacting on national rules is not possible (Bartley 2011). A particularly interesting aspect in this regard is that there probably are a variety of domestic – transnational rule-layering combinations, and that these patterns affect how Basel standards function in reality. In this context, we should turn to a potentially problematic pattern, according to which countries implement those aspects faithfully that are less controversial and are reconcilable with national regulatory systems and standards, while they, however, fail to comply faithfully – i.e. they implement half-heartedly or strategically to their domestic banks' advantage – with those rules that they conceive to be disadvantaging for their national economies and banks' competitiveness. For example, they adopt complex risk calculation approaches, but forfeit the compliance with capital definitions that are unfavourable to traditional domestic approaches. This problematic pattern is facilitated through the TRR's governance structure, since the unreconciled cross-cutting of state-bound with state-transcending authority, i.e. the layering of national and transnational rules and processes, leads to the serving of well organised specific interests and the simultaneous neglect of public goods.

In sum, therefore, the BCBS is highly influential due to its facilitation of the transnational diffusion of major regulatory principles through its network, while cosmetic compliance is increasingly becoming a major problem.

Policy process and hybrid interaction mode

One of the reasons why regulators feel bound to the Committee is its club-like atmosphere and the overarching principle of consensual decision making. This is mirrored in the unanimous decision making approach, which, in turn, is characterised by an absence of voting.[24] Since its inception, a vote has never been taken – yet unanimity in the Committee was somehow always achieved (Bundestag Finance Committee 2001d, Goodhart 2011, 546–547). Before Germany latently threatened to veto negotiations during the Basel II deliberations, no country in the Committee had exercised its right to veto in the

25 years prior (Bundesaufsichtsamt für das Kreditwesen & Deutsche Bundesbank 1999, 14–15).

Against this background, the policy process from initiation to endorsement by the GHOS can be roughly sketched through a standard series of stages, though this has changed somewhat over the years. Until 1996/1997, the agenda setting was mostly driven endogenously by the supervisors' current problems, which one or several of the agencies would table for discussion over the two-day meetings in Basel (Goodhart 2011). In case of a commonly perceived problem, this would usually result in a paper that would be discussed and revised over a series of BCBS meetings until every member could agree to the substance and wording.[25] Such an agreed paper, if important enough, would then be transferred to the G10 governors who, then, would support and recommend it for adoption in the G10 jurisdictions (which, in turn, would be undertaken by the BCBS supervisors). Since 1997, however, the rising politicisation and exogenous influence on the policy process as well as the public consultation process, have complicated the procedures considerably. While the basic internal process remains unaltered, three aspects constitute major amendments: now, agendas can be affected from the outside, the process becomes subject to industry and political influence in the course of the consultation process, and there is follow-up debate regarding (and in the future even monitoring of) implementation. As I will demonstrate throughout this book, the policy process surrounding the rule-setting in the BCBS has become a global policy process with national, transnational and interstate interactions throughout the extensive deliberation and commenting periods.

As a result of these changes to the policy process, the modus of interaction has changed over time. Accordingly, the Basel Committee's interaction mode has been characterised differently, where these different modes, in reality, are partially overlapping.[26] It is my aim to synthesise the relevant aspects of these explanations to come to an accurate description of the BCBS and its interaction mode(s). This theoretical approach is presented in the subsequent chapter. Here, I briefly discuss the four major perspectives on the Committee, namely the transgovernmental network, the epistemic community, the club of powerful regulators, and the international negotiation forum.

As outlined before, according to the transgovernmental network perspective (Slaughter 2004, Barr & Miller 2006), bureaucrats with comparable challenges that cannot be solved individually within their own jurisdictions, meet informally to exchange information, harmonise their approaches, and make sure that all transnational externalities are dealt with under this roof of transnational cooperation. This approach draws on a rational/functional bureaucratic perspective of problem detection and solution. Accordingly, bureaucrats share problems, therefore interests, come to an optimal solution, and commit to it.

Going beyond this rational/functional approach, the constructivist/ideational perspective considers the BCBS as an epistemic community, i.e. a 'network of professionals with recognised expertise and competence in a particular domain and an authoritative claim to policy-relevant knowledge within that domain or issue-area'. (Haas 1992, 3). Following this logic, financial regulators – in collaboration with the epistemically coherent financial industry – perceive their policy area through a common lens, based on the same presumptions. In the area of finance, the common denominator is education in a Western university economics programme that transferred mainly neoliberal ideas of perfectly functioning free markets (Porter 2005, Tsingou 2010, Porter 2011). On this ideational common ground, regulators (in collaboration with the industry) can find a common solution to similarly conceived problems.

For the purpose of this study's inquiry we can leave aside the question of rational or ideational motivation/action. Arguably, it can be assumed that all involved actors are motivated by and decide/act on the basis of a mix of rational, ideational and further factors (Kahneman 2012). Both, transgovernmental network and epistemic community perspectives leads to the conceptualisation of the BCBS as an at least partially cohesive collective actor that can be seen as distinct from the national regulatory agencies. As such, the Committee develops agency in itself, as the supervisors merge on a common evaluation and preference. In such instances it constitutes a collective actor, that is (at least partially) distinct from domestic regulatory agencies.

However, while Basel banking supervisors reveal several characteristics of an epistemic/functional community, they fail to offer a clear case as the interests and activities of national regulators are substantially constrained and influenced by their respective domestic circumstances (Kapstein 1992, 266–267, Singer 2007). Therefore, while trust and logic of appropriateness as well as rational choice and logic of consequence are constitutive elements of the BCBS and affect the domestic adoption and regulation of the soft law standards, national deviation in adoption and implementation as well as domestically oriented negotiation *ex ante* countervail these trends. Accordingly, the Committee rather resembles an international negotiation forum – one with a flexible, informal setting – where powerful regulators from developed nations' with important financial markets meet to negotiate the terms of mutual adjustment for the purpose of borderless financial intermediation. In a similar sense, the Committee is depicted as a club of like-minded developed countries that choose the forum consciously due to the similar interests of its members – in contrast to a more encompassing international organisation with diverse interests, which makes agreement much more difficult (Drezner 2007, 119–148).

To summarise, we can synthesise these different perspectives in outlining the Basel Committee's hybrid interaction mode. On the one hand, it is a transgovernmental network that operates according to rather informal (though increasingly formalising) rules and can even constitute (in part) a collective actor with common interests. On the other hand, it resembles an exclusive negotiation forum of the most powerful countries, where international adjustment is negotiated within a flexible setting. Both aspects characterise the Committee's activity in reality, which is why the theoretical approach of the subsequent chapter will integrate them.

Global banking regulation is an area of growing political globalisation. The BCBS has become a pivot of global policymaking, in particular since the Basel II and III agreements, which are two fundamental building blocks of the global political economy's (dis)order. Over the course of the last 40 years, the BCBS has proven a prime example of the incremental, partial globalisation of political processes and political economies. Moreover, during the years since 1998 this trend has intensified. Yet so have countervailing dynamics of international negotiation and cosmetic compliance. This leaves us with a complex global political economy that is simultaneously driven by national, transnational and international politics.

Against this background, I argue that the governance constellation of the TRR conditions the policy process of setting globally harmonised standards in a manner that entrenches asymmetric influence, which has detrimental effects on the regulatory content (reducing financial stability provisioning). Thus, in order to explain how global governance is related to regulatory failure, it is necessary to consider all factors that might affect the transgovernmental setting of harmonised regulatory standards. More specifically, in order to explain, how the global governance of banking regulation is related to the content of standards, it is important to account for who is influential within the governance structure and how this influence translates into interests being integrated into transgovernmentally developed standards.

3
Theory: Influence in Global Banking Regulation and the Transnational Regulatory Regime

This book's aim is to reveal how the transnational regulatory regime conditions influence, and how this translates into regulatory failure. Therefore, in this chapter, I outline a synthetic theoretical framework that delineates the TRR and how it conditions the interaction of influential actors and institutions, and, thereby, results in regulatory loopholes being created at the stage of developing transgovernmental standards. The framework's approach is to delineate mechanisms of politico-economic influence of national, transnational and interstate actors within the global political economy of banking regulation. I reveal how the simultaneous, unreconciled influence that national and transnational coalitions wield in the process of setting harmonised regulatory standards is entrenched in the governance and opportunity structure of the TRR, which is conducive to regulatory failure (and which can undermine the provision of financial stability).

More specifically, I construct the eclectic theoretical framework of the TRR that builds the basis for assessing the simultaneous and interacting mechanisms driving global standard setting. In order to understand how politico-economic opportunity structures affect policy outcomes in the partially globalised political economy of banking, a theoretical approach needs to encompass national, transnational and international elements. In particular, such a framework has to conceptualise domestic regulatory regimes, the transgovernmental network and how these interact with each other. This is best facilitated by the transnational regulatory regime concept. Eberlein & Grande (2005, 91–96) characterise transnational regulatory regimes as established national regulatory states which are interlinked via mostly informal transnational networks: they define (domestic) regulatory regimes as the 'full set of actors, institutions, norms and rules that are of importance for the process and the outcome of public regulation in a given sector'. Between such regimes, transnational regulatory gaps exist in areas where regulatory coordination would be desirable, but nation states block formal delegation upwards, as in banking activity across borders; the transgovernmental network of regulatory agencies fills this gap by establishing informal coordination.

On this conceptual basis, I propose to consider the setting of transgovernmental regulatory standards as a two-level game of international politics, which is further characterised by feedback processes from the transnational arena into domestic preference formation. Essentially, what differentiates my approach from previous studies is the refinement of the two-level heuristic by integrating additional intra-level but in particular dynamic inter-level mechanisms. In such a setting, domestic regulators are pivotal actors who balance the demands in their national jurisdictions and the transnational challenges of global banks within a transgovernmental network. In addition to the traditional two-level game, the complex national preference formation among domestic regime actors is integrated into the framework. Further to this, I regard dynamic transnational feedback processes between the domestic and the transnational realms as a crucial addendum. Finally, one has to consider the potential influence of international negotiations between G7/20 heads of state or ministries of finance as affecting the actions of regulators.

The key argument of this chapter's framework is that opportunity structures incentivise public officials – regulators and politicians – to advance domestically and transnationally active banks' competitiveness, while neglecting the provision of financial stability. Two aspects of political delegation contribute to this constellation: first, in national regulatory regimes authority is divided, delegated and opaquely dispersed among public officials. This separated responsibility weakens political control mechanisms on behalf of the public good of financial stability. Furthermore, in the context of globalising politics, the dispersion of authority and the inherent weakening of political control mechanisms is amplified by the transnationalisation of the regulatory regime through cooperation in the Basel Committee, i.e. the layering of national and transnational processes and institutions. Thus, the chapter will delineate the problems connected to this twofold authority dispersion in the TRR, in particular the simultaneous influence of national and transnational coalitions, by delineating, first, the opportunity structures of the competition state and domestic regulatory regimes, and, second, the opportunity structures of global governance and the transnational regulatory regime. Before I outline how influence is conditioned in these governance structures, however, I briefly present the established explanations of who is influential in global banking regulation.

3.1 Influence in global banking regulation

Since the seminal studies of Kapstein (1989, 1992, 1994), several explanations have been developed regarding who is influential through which channels in global banking regulation.[1] Previous studies have focused on specific elements of the governance architecture and provided us with several competing explanations.[2] But in order to explain how the governance constellation conditions influence and, thereby, policy outcomes, one has to integrate the insights from these explanations and consider their dynamic interactions. Accordingly, I develop the TRR framework that synthesises state-structure bound – national and international – actors and institutions as well as state-transcending, transnational activities and structures. This framework can build on six established, typological[3] explanations of agency-based influence within the conditioning institutional environment of the TRR.[4]

The BCBS as transgovernmental network organisation

The first explanation relates to the predominance of the transgovernmental network (Kapstein 1994, Slaughter 2004, Porter 2005, Barr & Miller 2006). The Basel Committee's influence was discussed at length in the last chapter. Accordingly, since it is the BCBS that sets the standards in quite a secluded atmosphere, it is reasonable to expect it to be particularly successful in integrating its interests into the standards. As discussed, according to this view, the Basel Committee is an at least partially cohesive, collective actor that can be seen as distinct from the national regulatory agencies. In other words, the interests of the involved staffers from national agencies – that cooperate closely during the Basel weekends and within the BCBS working groups – are distinct from individual interests within, and the aggregated interest of, their specific jurisdictions.

Transgovernmental network – BCBS – explanation: Thus, the common position of the regulators' community in the Basel Committee should set many of the aspects of their global regulations according to their common preferences. Therefore, the BCBS can be viewed as one collective supervisory organization if the regulators perceive a common challenge that they prefer to pursue via the transgovernmental network, share a common opinion (i.e. more aspects are agreed upon than not), and approach the solution through the web of Basel Committee working groups. In such instances it constitutes a collective actor that is (at least partially) distinct from domestic regulatory agencies.

Capture: transnational banks' influence in regulatory standard-setting

The second well established explanation is transnational capture, i.e. that transnationally active banks with substantial resources capture the regulatory process and dominate the rule-setting by advancing standards according to their preferences (Underhill & Zhang 2008, Young 2012). The potentially extensive influence is due to two factors. On the one hand, supervisors need the informational support from transnationally oriented banks, since they neither have the detailed knowledge and data about organisational and credit business details, nor do they command comparable resources. On the other hand, transnationally active banks (and their associations) actively demand specifically designed, and globally harmonised, regulatory standards from the supervisory network. This is likely to succeed, since the international banking industry has better access to the transgovernmental network than locally/nationally oriented counterparts, and shares a cross-national perspective as opposed to the rather limited domestic view. Transnational banks and their international associations, the Institute of International Finance (IIF) and the International Swaps and Derivatives Association (ISDA), have in the past directly attempted to capture the Basel Committee (Claessens & Underhill 2010). At the same time, they have national options to go directly through the regulatory agencies (to which they are typically the largest provider of funding through fees), or the politicians, which are likely to act on exit threats.

Capture – transnationally oriented banks – explanation: According to this claim, transnationally active regulatees (I refer to regulatees as an alternative term for banks) should dominate the policy process and their interests should be predominantly integrated into the agreement. More specifically, the banks' global associations, like the IIF and ISDA, should be most influential in pursuing their interests. However, Goodhart (2011, 413–417) reveals that the Committee was keen about keeping its distance from global banking associations, in particular the IIF, until the BCBS, from 1996 onwards, needed to gain the international, technically advanced banks' input on innovative risk modelling techniques. Even then the BCBS officially kept its distance, which does not deny the substantial impact through the national regulators as well as the working groups.[5] Furthermore, recent research indicates that the influence is lower than frequently argued and that it is conditional upon several factors (Young 2012). In light of this mixed evidence, it is crucial to explain under which conditions influence is exercised, and how.

The G7/20 as global political principal of the BCBS

Another potentially influential factor is the G7/20 acting as the Basel Committee's global political principal. According to this argument, the most powerful countries' politicians agree internationally to delegate the task of harmonising banking regulation to the Basel Committee.

As Drezner (2007, 147) argues, 'the United States and European Union ... empowered ... the Basle Committee ... to ensure control over the establishment and enforcement of common financial standards. The G7 countries then pushed to have the IFIs act as enforcement regimes for these new standards, with moderate success'. Moreover, 'the composition of the FSF [Financial Stability Forum] – as well as the standards highlighted for global implementation – was designed to ensure G-7 control over the standard-setting process. ... the FSF promulgated what it considered [were] the twelve key financial codes and standards for the international system' (136–137), which included the standards for global banking regulation.

Extending this argument, the BCBS is a collective agent with collectively delegated authority from the great power concert of the US and the EU, who form a global political principal in the G7 context (see also Büthe & Mattli 2011, 197). Thus, the Basel Committee would adopt harmonised standards according to the G7 directives. In the G20 context, the coalition may have to encompass further jurisdictions.

Global political principal – G7/20 – explanation: This explanation implies that the G7/20 summits and/or their financial ministry meetings decided that the Basel Committee should harmonise regulatory standards among the industrialised nations. Further, it should be expected that the G7/20 sets the broader Basel agenda, while delegating merely the detailing and implementation issues to the transgovernmental regulatory agent.

The domestic regulatory regime and divided authority: political principals and regulatory agents

Another set of explanations relates to factors from within dominant nation states of the financial governance architecture. Basel standards are likely to be affected or even driven by influential actors in the domestic regulatory regimes (Oatley & Nabors 1998, Rosenbluth & Schaap 2003, Singer 2007). The first domestic explanation concerns the influence of national politicians, who force their national regulators to pursue international or national political goals (in favour of particular interests) through the transgovernmental network (Oatley & Nabors 1998, Rosenbluth & Schaap 2003); this is possible due to political control mechanisms that politicians can use. For example, Oatley & Nabors (1998) find that US Congressional Committees dictated the contents of the Basel I Accord by directly controlling their regulatory agencies.

Domestic political principal(s) – US politicians – explanation: Accordingly, the US government and/or legislature can drive global regulation according to their particular interests (I discuss the country selection in the next chapter). Underneath the US variant of this correlation is the well established market-power hypothesis, according to which the United States' political principal should be capable of enforcing its interests vis-à-vis less powerful jurisdictions with smaller markets (Simmons 2001). US Congressional Committees or the Presidential administration would dictate the contents of global standards by directly controlling its regulatory agencies.

Yet, two factors can facilitate substantial influence of actors from less powerful jurisdictions. First, the US might not be able to determine the result alone. It may have to cooperate with other jurisdictions in the BCBS to prevent transnational spillovers while also ensuring the competitiveness of its jurisdiction and banks (which might suffer in the global market place if the US pursues unilateral stricter regulations) (Singer 2007).

The second factor can be explained by applying Institutional Complementarity Theory (Büthe & Mattli 2011). According to this approach, the capacity of jurisdictional actors to wield influence in setting global standards is not only a function of that jurisdiction's market power, but also of the institutional make up of its system of interest representation in the global standard-setting body. In other words, national actors from comparatively less powerful states can affect global standards as a result of beneficial institutional channelling of interest representation (Büthe & Mattli 2011). Thus, whether national institutions can present strategic transnational opportunity structures to channel domestic interests globally also plays an important role in the setting of global standards.

Domestic political principal(s) – German politicians – explanation: As a result, other jurisdictions' political principals can wield influence if the dominant jurisdiction (the US) has considerable interests in pursuing global harmonisation, and if the other jurisdiction has complementary institutions of interest representation. More specifically, the national institutions need to constitute a coordinated system that integrates business interests into finding a national consensus, and that represents these interests through a coherent national position globally (Büthe & Mattli 2011, 42–59). Therefore, I analyse whether Germany's Ministry of Finance and/or the federal parliamentary chamber's (the Bundestag) Finance Committee can integrate their interests (I discuss the country selection in the next chapter).

At the same time, however, several studies have demonstrated the considerable influence of national regulatory agencies in pursuing their domestic interests transgovernmentally (Singer 2007, Bach 2010). Underlying this influence is that regulatory control is not in political hands, but delegated to regulatory agencies who have a crucial role in the banking regulation of industrialised states (Copelovitch & Singer 2008, Busch 2009).

Regulatory agent(s) – US/German regulators – explanation: The crucial difference to the political principal explanations is that the national regulatory agency has considerable room to manoeuvre in creating policies that result in agency losses, i.e. policies that deviate from the principal's interest (or go unnoticed by him). Accordingly, national regulatory agencies should be highly influential in setting global standards. If the US, as the most powerful jurisdiction, succeeds in driving the agenda, Basel standards should be closer to US regulatory preferences. Likewise, German regulators can be influential if the dominant powers prefer global cooperation and German institutions facilitate a unified Basel position.

Domestic–transnational feedback processes

Finally, locally/nationally oriented banks,[6] who fear competitive disadvantages due to the shifting regulations' impact on the national market, can be expected to alert national politicians, who, then, reactivate control over their regulator to intervene on behalf of the influential, alarming actor (Lütz 2004, Eberlein & Grande 2005, Drezner 2007, 59); this results in renegotiations in the Basel Committee, which is likely to change the entire process dynamic.

To increase their influence, such banks need to raise a 'fire alarm' (McCubbins & Schwartz 1984) with the political principals (to be explained in the following sections) – i.e. raising the attention of a parliamentary committee and/or ministerial department to the problem

– of the regulatory agency, which, then, reactivates control over their agent on behalf of the alarming actor. In that case, the principals become veto-players and ensure that the regulatory agent enforces the special interest in the Basel Committee negotiations. The agency's freedom will be restricted for that specific purpose. Therefore, domestic conflicts can switch the international interaction mode from trans-governmental cooperation towards inter-jurisdictional negotiation. In other words, the domestic-transnational feedback mechanism takes place once a domestic bank can activate political representatives to forward their concerns. The parliamentary or ministerial actor, then, would take control over the regulatory agent, convincing him or her to integrate the domestic banks' interests in the transnational agreement. If that is opposed by another country or occurs in several jurisdictions, it will change the interaction mode in Basel from transnational cooperation more towards an international negotiation.

Nationally/locally oriented banks – US/German banks – explanation: Accordingly, one would also expect nationally or locally active banks – like Sparkassen in Germany or community banks in the US – to be influential in the development of Basel standards, if these sub-sectoral interests are capable of mobilising their political representatives.

Combining the outlined explanations, the study's aim in evaluating their empirical relevance is twofold: first, to assess the distinct, relative influence of actors in setting global standards transnationally; second, to analyse them eclectically, i.e. combined and in their interactive nature. This section provided distinct explanations. The aim of the following sections is to reveal, how the transnational governance constellation conditions influence in a manner that benefits national voice coalitions of politicians and banks as well as transnational harmonisation coalitions of transnationally active banks and regulators – while there is, however, no reconciliation of these influences with the protection of financial stability.

3.2 Competition state and opportunity structures of the regulatory regime

My aim is to reveal how the just outlined influential actors and institutions interact in the global political economy of setting harmonised standards. Therefore, I now outline the synthetic theoretical framework that delineates these interactions and how they result in regulatory loopholes being created at the stage of developing transgovernmental standards. Figure 3.1 presents the theoretical framework of the

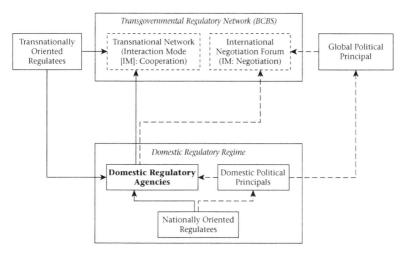

Figure 3.1   Process map of influence in the transnational regulatory regime of banking

Note: Boxes depict collective actors (in bold is the pivotal actor); boxes with dotted lines depict alternative interaction modes of the Basel Committee; continuous arrows depict permanent/regular relations; dashed arrows depict ad hoc/sporadic relations.

transnational regulatory regime of global banking regulation as a process map. The TRR framework refines the two-level game heuristic of international politics (Putnam 1988) by integrating additional intra-level and dynamic inter-level mechanisms, more specifically a transnational network/regime and a domestic regime modification. In sum, it encompasses the state unit-bound mechanisms of a two-level game of international politics – i.e. national intra-level regulatory regime dynamics and interstate G7/20 deliberations – plus transgovernmental and transnational mechanisms as well as dynamic feedback processes between these three arenas. In the figure, the boxes each depict a collective actor capable of affecting global banking regulation. The domestic regulatory agencies are the pivotal actors in this game, as they are the main connection between national and global governance. Arrows depict patterns of political influence that one actor can wield upon another, aiming at affecting the content of harmonised regulatory standards – where the final drafting of the agreement is carried out by the transgovernmental regulatory network of the BCBS. These patterns can be either of a permanent/regular nature (continuous arrows) or of an ad hoc/sporadic type (dashed arrows). The hybrid nature of the Basel Committee is depicted by the alternative interaction modes under the same roof of the transgovernmental network (boxes with dotted lines). All elements of the figure will be defined throughout the chapter. I begin by outlining how influence is conditioned by the opportunity structures within domestic regulatory regimes.

As briefly discussed before, scrutinising the regulatory governance of banking has to start at the jurisdictional authority over financial intermediation. The nation state, in particular at the federal level, still plays a central role in this sphere. However, control is not in political, neither governmental nor parliamentary, hands, but is instead divided between politically mandated principals and administrative organisations that receive considerable delegated authority (conscious delegation) and discretion (unintended delegation) in regulating (i.e. setting) and supervising (i.e. scrutinising) standards of prudential conduct.

In a domestic regulatory regime, as presented by the lower level box in Figure 3.1, supervisory agencies are the pivotal (though not necessarily most powerful) actor. They balance the responsibility delegated by political principals and their political control, on the one hand, and the pressure from (nationally and transnationally) oriented banks to design regulatory standards in their interest, on the other. Therefore, agencies need to carefully balance their own goals, regulatees' interests and their principals' interests; if they fail to work within the policy preference set of regulatees and principals simultaneously, the latter will re-enact control and potentially even impose sanctions (Singer 2007).

Two politico-economic aspects characterise the opportunity structures of the domestic regulatory regime, namely delegation and capture. Accordingly, independent supervisory agencies, as pivots, have substantial influence and authority beyond the formally delegated powers (since politically mandated authorities abdicate their formal control opportunities), while well-organised private interests might capture regulatory policies to some degree. These characteristics facilitate the prevalence of competition state strategies in regulation, i.e. competitiveness-boosting regulation.

Delegation and dispersion of regulatory authority

In all developed countries, a principal–agent relationship between politically mandated authorities and administratively authorised organisations has been established. The crucial role of regulatory agencies in the banking regulation of industrialised states is an established fact

(Copelovitch & Singer 2008, Busch 2009, Jordana, Levi-Faur & i Marín 2011, Jordana & Rosas 2014). Responsibility has been delegated from legislative or governmental (ministerial) principals to agencies which are distant from the principals' direct reach. This transfer of responsibility has been substantial and encompasses, to differing degrees, the design, interpretation and implementation of legislation, oversight of banking markets, individual bank supervision, and regulatory enforcement. In most industrialised nations, and all participating jurisdictions of the Basel Committee, one of two institutional designs is currently in place (Copelovitch & Singer 2008, 666): banks are supervised either by the central bank or by a separate regulatory authority (where the central bank is responsible for monetary policy only). There are several mixed forms in which either banks are regulated by both an agency and the central bank or regulation is further divided among several agencies. Thus, the division of regulatory authority over the banking sector between a politically mandated principal and regulatory agents is common among industrialised countries, though the specific institutional designs vary.[7]

Recent contributions, which generate original datasets of regulatory agencies in general (Jordana et al. 2011) and with regard to the realm of banking regulation in particular (Jordana & Rosas 2014), provide substantial empirical support for the claim that regulatory authority is divided and the autonomy of agencies can be considerable. Both studies demonstrate the widespread mode of delegation to regulatory agencies as well as formal and de facto independence of bank supervisors in industrialised nations.[8] The recently constructed data set of Jordana & Rosas (2010, 7–8, 16–19) reveals that formal and de facto autonomy of bank supervisors have become the widespread modus since the 1980s, and in particular since the 1990s. Their three indicators measuring the autonomy of agencies have, on average, values in the upper third of the scales. Moreover, when isolating the values for industrialised countries with established regulatory regimes in banking supervision (in particular the BCBS members around 2000), these values are even higher (Jordana & Rosas 2010, 36–38).

The tendency is unequivocal and provides comfortable empirical support for the claim that sufficient cross-country homogeneity exists among the BCBS member countries regarding the delegation and division of authority as well as the considerable autonomy of bank regulators from political control mechanisms. These regimes have regulatory agents as separate organisational entities that are either entirely independent, or at least considerably separated, from the governmental and legislative sphere and have formally delegated authority in the regulatory control of banks. Thus, while there are national variations in the institutional authority to control banking regulators, the political control and regulatory delegation principle is comparable. Furthermore, whether it is the government or parliament is less relevant for the present research question than the fact that the considerable delegation of authority to regulatory agents is common. Therefore, the parliamentary and governmental majorities responsible for designing banking regulation are conceptualised as *political principals*, while the bureaucracies authorised to regulate and supervise banks are conceptualised as *regulatory agents*. Singer (2007, 21–35) applies a similar approach and builds the foundation for the present design.

The regulatory agents, however, are not fiduciaries in Majone's (2001) terms, since they cannot freely choose which policy to implement. Rather, they are agents with considerable leeway who, nevertheless, are always latently subject to hierarchical limitation of regulatory authority through potential policy intervention by their principals. Therefore, in banking regulation, as in most other regulatory areas (Weingast & Moran 1983), it would be an oversimplification to postulate regulatory agencies as completely independent fiduciaries. Political principals are still the primary possessors of authority, and merely refrain from wielding their power continuously through 'police patrol' oversight. They continue to have a clear responsibility in fields where regulatory policies – with political and legislative character – are designed. In effect, agencies and principals share authority over banking regulation. Therefore, it is crucial to understand the conditionality of political interventions that limit regulatory agents' authority, as this defines the mechanisms that are fundamental to the division of authority in regulatory regimes.

The political principal's main challenge is to prevent diversion from his or her preferred policies. In complex regulatory areas like banking regulation, the informational asymmetries between delegator and delegatee therefore become a main obstacle to controlling an agent and preventing diversion (Coen & Thatcher 2005, 333–342). The political control of agencies in banking regulation is particularly difficult since the informational asymmetry between regulatory agent and political principal is substantial and actual intervention is costly to political principals (Thatcher 2005). Even though they are subject to disciplinary measures of the principal in cases of deviant policy and resulting agency loss, supervisory agencies are rather unlikely to be tightly controlled, since this is not in the interest of the political principals. It is very costly for politicians to acquire the necessary information about regulation that is adequate to achieve their interests.[9] Moreover, it is more convenient for political principals to resort to 'fire alarm' control of regulatory agencies. Only when alarmed by constituents or other, exogenous, alarming events will the government and/or legislature engage in close oversight of the supervisors (McCubbins & Schwartz 1984). Thus, political control mechanisms work only on behalf of interests capable of raising such an alarm with political principals. In other words, actors need to have sufficient incentives and capacities to impose their influence on political principals, who, in turn, must be sufficiently affected in their interests in order to exercise its authoritative influence and limit regulatory agencies' authority.

The delegation and division of public authority increases the complexity and opacity of the political economy, thereby opening the door for strategic interest intermediation and selective principal intervention. Combined with competition state dynamics, private interests of profitability and competitiveness as well as the preference of voters, consumers and producers for credit-fuelled growth receive disproportionately high attention in banking regulation, since political principals intervene selectively on behalf of these alarming interests, limiting the regulators' authority to set restrictive regulatory standards. For example, Frach (2008, 113–121) shows for the German Federal Financial Supervisory Authority (BaFin, Bundesanstalt für Finanzdienstleistungsaufsicht) that political control mechanisms work mostly on behalf of private interests to ensure banks' competitiveness and generous credit provision.

This setting, then, is conducive to typical collective action problems of asymmetrical organisation incentives and capacities. Well-organised private interests of profitability and competitiveness are more likely to affect the interests of political principals than the diffuse and uninformed support for the public good of financial stability. Moreover, even popular public interests in economic growth and generous credit intermediation are more likely to enter politicians' calculus – if banks' credit stimulus to the overall economy is in danger, it is not in an office-seeking politician's interest to demand tighter regulation (Keefer 2007).

In sum, regulatory regimes of industrialised countries with developed financial systems are characterised by influential regulatory agencies that wield considerable authority in setting regulatory standards. These regimes have regulatory agents as separate organisational entities that are either entirely independent or at least considerably separated from the governmental and legislative sphere. They have formally delegated authority in the regulatory control of banks with substantial room for manoeuvre due to distant political control mechanisms under high information asymmetries between politicians and regulators. This creates abundant opportunities for regulators to enact regulatory decisions with political and legislative character as long as political principals are not alarmed. They are, however, subject to the scrutiny of political principals, which limits their independence. This means that regulatory standards are set in a framework of de facto divided authority, where the responsibility to regulate banks is shared between politicians and regulators. The reach of actual authority and leeway depends on the capacities of and incentives for politicians to invoke their primary authoritative right. Therefore, banking regulation is prone to classic collective action problems of public goods, since the 'fire alarm' type political control mechanisms facilitate the asymmetric influence of well-organised private and popular public interests vis-á-vis the diffused and weakly organised public interest of the provision and protection of the public good of financial stability. In Figure 3.1, the dashed arrow between principal and agent depicts their conditional relationship.

Secondly, as discussed before, regulatory capture is prevalent in banking regulation. Divided authority and deficient political control mechanisms become particularly problematic in the face of industry capture, which provides a fundament for the asymmetric influence of the industry (vis-á-vis the diffuse interests in the provision of financial stability). The likelihood of regulatory capture that achieves the disproportionate regard of the banking industry's competitiveness is increased in the national regulatory regime as a result of the incentives of industry and public officials. Most importantly, opportunity structures incentivise public officials – regulators and politicians – to advance domestically (and transnationally) active banks' competitiveness, while neglecting the provision of financial stability.

Moreover, the potential for capture is substantially augmented, since the political and regulatory institutions are embedded in a regulatory regime where informal rules of networks among politicians, supervisors and regulatees play an important role in the design of regulatory politics. Coleman (1994b, 274) comes to the conclusion that a 'corporatist mode of policy-making' in complex network structures characterises all of the five fairly different regulatory regimes of Canada, France, Germany, the United Kingdom and the United States (although the US has a more pluralist system, it does, however, exhibit a policy community and network ties within its banking sector). The dense networks of this policy community and the resulting opaque regime structures enable uncontrolled regulators and capturing regulatees to pursue interests through well-established channels of the political economy as well as strong connections among politicians, regulators and bankers. I briefly outline how the opportunity structures affect the involved actors' incentives in this manner.

The electorate's inability to assess and affect banking regulation

Banking regulation is not a public, but an opaque, vested interests focused policy. Its highly technocratic nature and complex governance structure make it inaccessible for consumers and voters. Even for highly educated individuals, including most journalists, it is almost impossible to evaluate how a set of regulatory formulas and accounting rules affect personal or social welfare. The costs of informing oneself about appropriate regulatory policies (let alone concrete regulations) are simply too high in relation to the benefits for an individual (Keefer 2007). An institutional environment of deposit insurance, too big/interconnected to fail, and lender of last resort instruments greatly reduces the incentive to inform oneself to a negligible degree. Only in the rare event of a banking crisis is the attention of consumers and voters directed to the issue (Malhotra & Margalit 2010, Crespo-Tenorio et al. 2014).

However, since it is hard to know how much has been redistributed and to whom, the topic still does not provide much leverage for voter mobilisation (Keefer 2007, 607–612, 616–619). Even in times of crisis and open redistribution to banks, due to the complexity of these issues, polls are rather driven by blunt redistributive policy discussions than by complex regulatory issues (that also might be feared to choke the credit engine of growth). *Ex post* policies directed at resolving banking crises and the societal redistribution dominate the debate, while the opaque issue of *ex ante* political measures that are directed to prevent future crises is neglected (Keefer 2007, 616–619). Because people cannot evaluate whether these highly complex policies are based on sound economic reasoning, regulatory politics, and banking regulation in particular, are typically not on the agenda of elections and political summits. Even if they are, as during the recent crisis, the realisation of the general political strategies, i.e. the regulatory policy design, rule adoption and implementation, will again be in the shadows of complexity and opacity, leading producers to be the main motivated actors to organise and lobby, while consumers, taxpayers and voters move on to broad redistributive politics – the Basel III analysis in Chapter 5 will reveal that we witness such a clawback trend in the context of current post-crisis reform struggles. Hence, voters, customers and taxpayers can be excluded from the analysis, as these have a relatively minor impact with regard to negotiating regulatory standards (Scholte 2013). However, they can have an effect on the politicians to be elected, which will be accounted for by indirectly integrating public pressure on domestic politicians (see below).

Capture by nationally and transnationally oriented banks

Referring to the previous discussion of industry pressure, two general patterns characterise sectoral behaviour: first, due to the wider politico-economic settings of explicit state guarantees to protect banking deposits and implicit ones to save troubled systematically important institutions, there is an in general morally hazardous business behaviour that is exclusively directed towards profitability and competitiveness of the banking sector – while neglecting the external effects that a breakdown of one bank might cause to the entire system (Admati & Hellwig 2013); second, and in accordance with the first pattern, there is the attempt to capture regulatory rule-setting and supervisory enforcement.

While the influence of citizens on banking supervision is low, a growing literature, particularly within the realm of international finance, has stressed the importance of private actors and their influence and authority in setting regulatory standards and their international harmonisation (see e.g. Mosley 2009). The channelling of this influence of the banking sector is mostly established along sectoral and sub-sectoral associations (Coleman 1994a, Busch 2009). Thus, the distinction of industry actors needs to build on the sector-specific production factors perspective (Frieden 1991), according to which vested interests are established across sectoral and sub-sectoral lines. In particular, with a view to influence in setting Basel standards, the most significant sub-sectors are those of transnationally and nationally/locally[10] oriented banks.[11] They differ substantially in production factors due to different portfolio and customer strategies. Small local and national banks with predominantly local/national customer bases, local investments and less technically skilled employees (arguably three of the most important production factors in banking) have other factor-related interests than large, internationally active banks with global investment strategies, a widespread customer portfolio, and highly trained experts. Accordingly, it can be expected that nationally/locally oriented banks on the one hand and transnationally oriented ones on the other hand will have partly differing and partly converging preferences.

With regard to the harmonisation effect of global standards, the differences between transnationally and nationally/locally oriented banks is obvious. Sectors or firms with substantial transnational customer bases, global investment strategies, highly trained employees and specific technology will be interested in making the cross-country production and exporting of their services as easy as possible. Among such firms are certainly investment banks, universal banks, financial insurance companies, exchanges, hedge funds and private equity firms. In contrast, opposition to a strengthening of global competition will originate from nationally oriented sectors focusing on local customers and investment: mutual savings banks, thrift institutions, local and state public savings and loans institutions.

Additional regulatory costs stemming from newly created harmonised standards, however, are just as relevant to firms and sectors as the question of transnational harmonisation. Industrial actors weigh the costs from additional or simply new regulation against benefits from access to new markets through harmonisation (Murphy 2005). Provided that financial firms and their agents are devoted to maximising income and minimising costs, regulatory actions depict either additional (lower) costs in cases of additional (less or cheaper) stipulations to be met, or increased (reduced) production volumes with smaller (higher) transaction costs in cases of market establishing (delimiting) regulation. While transnationally oriented actors, which are positive towards harmonisation, and nationally oriented actors, which are against such harmonisation, might have similar positions towards regulation as it enhances/deteriorates both parties' operational costs to a comparable extent, at the same time their evaluation might diverge on another aspect/effect of such rules. Due to their different operational and strategic orientations, they are likely to prefer different regulatory stipulations.

In terms of strategy and strategic political alliances, transnationally oriented and nationally/locally oriented banks pursue distinct pathways. Transnationally active banks can – in principle – exit national markets. While a global market for financial assets suggests that this is easily done, it is less important here, since banks cannot escape a Basel Committee standard if they want to be active in the market of an industrialised nation. Since the Basel Accord of 1988, all important markets' supervisors have implemented these rules, and, as a result, investors benchmark their decisions based on the adherence to these standards (Tarullo 2008, 45–84). Transnationally oriented banks, however, have three natural access points for the application of the voice strategy: the attempt to capture the design of standards by closely cooperating with supervisors can be undertaken either via ties with the home country regulator, or by influencing the transnational network. The third strategy, applicable if regulator–regulatee cooperation results in dissatisfactory results, is to activate national political principals by voicing concerns over competitive disadvantages vis-á-vis foreign competitors and negative repercussions on credit provisioning to the domestic economy.

Nationally or locally oriented banks, in contrast, are more limited in their instruments, since they can only appeal to domestic authorities. Accordingly, after they have exhausted the possibilities of the direct communication with their domestic supervisor, national and local banks have to activate the domestic political principal to pursue favourable or less unfavourable regulation. Nonetheless, this channel might prove particularly promising as their geographical concentration and close ties with political subdivisions might privilege their collective action capacities in assessing a politician (Stigler 1971, 12). Furthermore, the threat of disadvantaged national banks, due to the harmonised standards tilting the competitiveness of national firms, provides for a useful competition state narrative that politicians are unlikely to ignore. Such a coalition among office-seeking politicians and national/local banks is one that can use well established institutions of collective action and provide a succinct political image.

Political principals and competition state concerns

Parliament and government are authorised by the electorate to enable and protect productive credit intermediation and, at the same time, a stable financial system as the backbone of the economy. With reference to the earlier outlined competition state dynamics, however, political principals weigh competitiveness of economic actors in their constituency higher than the financial stability of the economy due to two interrelated factors concerning their concrete decision making situations, namely short-sighted office-seeking orientation and inform-ation/resource deficits to comprehend banking regulation and demand appropriate regulation. Politicians of the legislature and government are under pressure from the special interests of the industry, which can claim unfavourable standards will result in reduced credit and economic growth, and threaten withdrawal of political support. Moreover, the more complex the policy becomes, the less capable politicians will be of actually scrutinising a regulatory policy in terms of its contribution to financial stability. Politicians, therefore, are likely to enforce control over regulatory agencies to ensure the competitiveness of important constituents, but fail to enforce stability issues accordingly. In sum, given these basic elements of politicians' interest, for incumbents the preferences regarding international financial regulation are mainly determined by their influence on the overall economy and influential economic interests.

Accordingly, politicians favour regulation that ensures growth-augmenting credit intermediation, competitive banks, and foreign market access for transnationally oriented banks (Way 2005) – and grant de facto autonomy to regulators and regulatees to set harmonised standards accordingly. They, however, engage in 'fire alarm' type intervention into regulators' freedom, if important (mainly import-competing) constituents are negatively affected. Consequently, nationally elected politicians are likely to support broad liberal harmonisation but intervene on behalf of negatively affected nationally oriented banks. Since financial turmoil occurs less frequently than elections, the upcoming election is more relevant to political authorities than potential financial turmoil. Moreover, the long time lags between weak regulation and crisis as well as the almost inaccessible relation between *ex ante* policy and crisis further weaken the incentives of politicians to pursue strict prudential regulation (Keefer 2007, 617).[12]

Regulatory agents and competition state concerns

The regulatory agencies are authorised by the elected representatives to enable and protect productive credit intermediation on the one hand, and a stable financial system as the backbone of the economy on the other. Regulators' – understood as office-seeking individuals – main interest, however, is to maximise their power and career perspectives (i.e. tenure and reputation for future jobs) as well as the agencies' budget and scope of and autonomy in tasks (Niskanen 1971, 1975). From a policy viewpoint, their task is to ensure the functioning of credit intermediation markets and the stability of the banking system. From a political entrepreneur perspective, however, the regulator has an incentive of keeping the principals unalarmed and the regulatees competitive. The agency needs to implement regulatory practices or suggest new rules that lie within its 'win set', i.e. which satisfy regulatees and political principals simultaneously

(Singer 2007). Otherwise, political principals might reactivate control over them and/or deteriorate career and agency prospects. Regulatees, if dissatisfied with regulation, might activate political principals, reduce career perspectives in the private sector or put pressure on the supervisor through its close inter-organisational ties.

Consequently, regulatory agents tend to weigh competitiveness higher than stability, since they are subject to the two related pressures of industry capture and selective principal pressure. Capture is facilitated through close relationship between regulators and regulatees: they finance large parts of the regulatory agencies through direct fees; they constitute substantial parts of the agencies' advisory boards; informal network-like ties through everyday close cooperation with the industry result in a bias towards understanding common needs; they can choose among regulators (mainly in the US). Even though supervisors are still highly attentive to systemic stability (and fend off disproportionate industry influence), the selective intervention of political principals on behalf of specific interests further weakens supervisors incentives to foster stability, as not giving in to political pressure would likely worsen the regulator's utility. The consequence is banking regulation that comfortably ensures competitiveness of influential sectoral and sub-sectoral interests at the expense of a thorough strengthening of financial stability. Therefore, in light of the somewhat lesser importance of instability risks in the projections of banks and politicians, it is convenient for regulators to keep regulatees competitive and political principals unalarmed (Singer 2007).[13]

Nevertheless, regulators also value stability, which they are mandated to provide, as they will be blamed in the event of a crisis. Thus, regulatory harmonisation across jurisdictions in which transnationally active banks do business is conceived of as highly important, since transnational activity might be out of the scope of regulators authoritative control – and might ultimately result in foreign crises spilling over to one's jurisdiction. As discussed before, introducing harsher regulation unilaterally is a political option which increasingly loses attractiveness given widely globalised financial intermediation. In order to overcome collective action problems and the globalisation of the public good of financial stability, while simultaneously keeping international and national level playing fields, it is attractive to coordinate transnationally (Singer 2007). Nevertheless, while harmonisation is pursued, regulators also want to keep the additional regulatory costs for influential regulatees below rising profits from additional market access as well as the domestic market equilibrium. In the context of these pressures, mock compliance becomes a convenient complementary option to transgovernmental cooperation.

Hence, in response to increases in transnational banking activity and the resulting transnational crisis spillovers, transgovernmental coalitions for the (global) public good of banking stability become an attractive option to regulators. The supervisors utilise the Basel Committee forum to develop new policy strategies to achieve their interests. At the same time, the capture by transnational banks also becomes more likely. Consequently, regulators can exploit the transnational governance structure in order to implement policies either in pursuit of the public good, their own interests, or their predominant economic constituents' interests. They are, however, subject to political control and industry capture.

In combination, capture and delegation result in agency loss due to shirking, i.e. bureaucratic self-interest, and slippage, i.e. institutional incentives causing the agent to divert from the principal and general public's interests. The autonomy and discretion of regulatory agents and regulatees permits this potentially suboptimal regulation (Thatcher 2005, Coen & Thatcher 2005, 333–342). Capture is institutionally fostered by the intensive cooperation of supervisors with regulatees in exchanging information on banks' health, the impact of regulatory standards, and the design of legislative measures. The close cooperation, in conjunction with competition state imperatives, results in interdependence and shared perspectives on regulatory policies. The close ties between national supervisory agencies and banks with primary establishment in their specific national jurisdiction open substantial room for capture of regulatory standards (and the domestic regulator's pursuit of those jurisdictional interests through the transgovernmental network). Figure 3.1 depicts this in the form of a continuous arrow that mirrors the permanent linkage between regulators and regulatees in national jurisdictions (lower left).

Industry capture is, however, also possible through activation of political principals to activate control over the regulatory agent. The threshold of catching the attention of politicians is higher and harder to exceed for banking interests when compared to the responsible regulator's attention (this sporadic relationship is depicted by the dashed line connecting regulatees, political principals and regulators in Figure 3.1; I will return to this soon within the section on domestic feedback processes). Nevertheless, concerns of politicians related to the competition state make them susceptible to banks' mourning about deteriorating competitiveness.

BCBS members' jurisdictions share a common phenomenon of delegated and divided authority and distant political control mechanisms, which are potentially prone to disadvantaging the weakly organised interest in the provision and protection of systemic stability.[14] In sum, given delegation and capture in the national regulatory regimes, it is likely that public officials serve industry interests of competitiveness, rather than the public good of financial stability.[15] Regulators and politicians have relatively lower incentives to enhance the provision and protection of financial stability, than to ensure the competitiveness of specific, well organised industry interests. The accumulation of many regulatory (and supervisory) decisions to the benefit of specific firms raises the probability of negative externalities from imprudent banking on stability and reduces the regulator's capacity to forward stricter regulation that enforces systemic stability.

These competition state mechanisms are augmented through the integration into the global political economy. The TRR interlinks the realms of national regulation and global standard setting. Thereby, it connects competition states with global governance networks/regimes.

3.3   Global governance and opportunity structures of the transnational regulatory regime

Through the transgovernmental cooperation among BCBS regulators, domestic regulatory regimes have become subject to an incrementally increasing degree of regulatory and political globalisation. As a result, in the context of globalising politics, the dispersion of authority and the inherent weakening of political control mechanisms is amplified by the transnationalisation of the regulatory regime through the cooperation in the Basel Committee, i.e. the layering of national and transnational processes and institutions. In other words, the global process layers that evolve through the transgovernmental network, the transnational industry associations, and the global political principal are added to the domestic regulatory regime's national layer of processes. Moreover, domestic–transnational interactions provide an intense new connection that introduces transnational dynamics into the policy process.

Global political principal and ex post crisis stabilisation

An international layer of political processes is constituted by the G7/20 negotiations in the context of either their heads of state/government or their financial ministers and central bankers. Therefore, in light of the internationally shared interest in the global public good of financial stability, politicians might emphasise global cooperation to regulate banking – as global political principal. According to Drezner (2007, 63–64), they might engage in forum shopping, i.e. the most powerful politicians might agree internationally to delegate the task of banking regulation (or part of it) to the Basel Committee. In this case, as Figure 3.1 depicts on the outer right side, the link between the global political principal and the BCBS would subordinate the Basel Committee as a collective agent with collectively delegated authority from an internationally constructed principal, and would adopt harmonised standards according to the G7/20 directives. It is, however, more likely for the G7/20 to focus on ex post crisis policies of macroeconomic crisis management and redistributive measures, and to refrain from active intervention in ex ante regulatory policies designed to pre-empt future crises (Cooper 2010, Knaack & Katada 2013, Viola 2014).

The transgovernmental network and the hybridity of the first transnational layer

In the shadow of distant international politics, two transnational layers of political processes unfold their impact on global standards, namely transgovernmental networking and domestic–transnational feedback mechanisms. With regard to the first, regulatory agencies who initiate the cooperation through the transgovernmental network of the BCBS are in the pivotal position in the global political economy of banking regulation. As discussed in the previous chapter, in order to understand how the Committee wields influence as collective actor as well as how it channels global politics as deliberation and negotiation forum, we have to take its hybrid interaction mode into account. This switches between and balances two interaction mode equilibria: the international negotiation forum among jurisdictions with different and competing interests, and the cooperative network mode that attempts to solve common problems. In Figure 3.1 this dynamic is depicted by the dotted boxes within the transgovernmental regulatory network box. Accordingly, the Basel Committee can function as a cooperative transgovernmental network on the one hand, and an international negotiation forum where competing competition state interests are pitted against each other on the other hand.

This can be characterised as a nested game, which is depicted in Figure 3.2: the outer, nesting (international negotiation) game reflects the problem of cooperation between competing jurisdictions. In Figure 3.2, the italic typeface depicts the attempt to cooperate, which is likely to

Country1		Country 2			
		C		*D*	
		C1	C2		
C	C1	**3 : 2**		*0 : 4*	
	C2		2 : 3		
D		*4 : 0*		*2 : 1*	

Figure 3.2   Nested transnational regulatory standards game with two interaction modes of either international negotiation or transnational deliberation

Notes: Values refer to pay offs (presentational order: country 1: country 2). Country 1 represents a (market power based) relatively dominant jurisdiction, country 2 a relatively less powerful jurisdiction. C1/C2 = cooperation on international standards based on country 1's/2's regulatory setting (or closer to its status quo); D = no cooperation. Assumptions: international competition, international externalities of instability, capital mobility and regulatory arbitrage, explicit and implicit too-big/interconnected-to-fail arrangements. *Source*: Adapted from Genschel & Plümper (1996, 242).

result in mutual defection, and a unilateral move by the most attractive markets to adjust standards, which the less attractive jurisdictions would have to follow in order to sustain access to the attractive market (I will turn to the power-asymmetries of the game constellation in a moment). This is overcome in an institutionalised, cooperative setting, which emerged from previous games and intensifying communication, and which is provided by the BIS and BCBS framework. Repeated games of political interaction enable learning about previously unfamiliar actors, thereby allowing actors to build trust relationships and institutionalise them (Axelrod 1984). Accordingly, actors start to weigh the dangers of cooperation due to the deceitful behaviour of other agents as lower, and the likelihood of cooperation – with previously faithful actors – is evaluated as higher. Cooperation is considered mutually beneficial, and the question becomes rather how to cooperate – here, on which standards to agree upon (Genschel & Plümper 1996, 242). The nested (transgovernmental cooperation) game, accordingly, has a different actor constellation due to altered preferences more favourable to cooperation. It mirrors the purely distributive conflict that takes place in network cooperation, which places emphasis on whose standards to agree upon. This is depicted by the inner quadrant in the upper left of Figure 3.2 and mirrors two possible outcomes, namely cooperating on standards closer to jurisdiction one (C1), or on country 2's rules (C2).

The cooperative, nested constellation is likely to prevail, since incentives for transgovernmental cooperation are provided by the global and transnational characteristics of banking activities. These result in mutual, though asymmetric, interdependence among industrialised countries, since they are not capable of benefiting from global capital markets without incurring the increased risks from (a) foreign banks operating in their jurisdictions and (b) bank failures and systemic crises in other countries' spilling over into their own jurisdiction (Simmons 2001, Drezner 2007, 43–58). Therefore, even though there are considerable power asymmetries, due to differing market size, cooperation is the dominant scenario, since the gains from cooperation are higher for, in terms of market-based negotiation power, intermediate or negligible jurisdictions as well as dominant states, i.e. states with markets of substantial relevance in global financial intermediation.

For non-dominant countries the point is one of a rather obvious nature, since their dependence is rooted in the access of domestic firms to the dominant markets. If no cooperation with dominant nations was reached, diverging regulatory standards would mean relatively higher transaction costs compared to those competitors that have better access to these markets – either domestic firms of the dominant jurisdiction or companies from states that have harmonised their rules with it. Moreover, once a more powerful state changes its stipulations in response to international instabilities, this could mean exclusion from the market or at least rising regulatory costs due to the adjustment to the new rules. Furthermore, the less powerful country's regulatory authorities would certainly prefer to have a mutual cooperation agreement on how to deal with each other's banks' activities in the foreign jurisdiction, since the spillovers from national banking system failures in the dominant state also threaten smaller states heavily.

From the perspective of relatively dominant states, the level of interdependence is less clear, but also substantial. One reason for this is that – while the interest in access to foreign markets is less pervasive, yet with regard to international portfolio diversification strategies certainly not negligible – the threats from potentially less controlled foreign bank branches is actually higher in this market, where many firms from around the globe want to be active. Since foreign banks' branches and subsidiaries are more difficult to supervise, the global attractiveness of a market actually increases exposure to transnational spillovers of financial turmoil. Another reason is related to the profoundly global character of financial transactions, where these can be relocated with relatively low transaction costs. Therefore, adjusting national regulation autonomously could disadvantage domestic banks vis-á-vis institutes from other, less strictly regulated markets, and could lead to firms exiting the country to more lenient foreign jurisdictions. It is questionable, whether a firm would actually leave a market like the United States, but in the face of serious competition from London and other markets, such a scenario at least would provide a solid ground for a viable voice strategy. Sectoral interests would certainly paint such a scenario as part of a voice strategy that could very well gain the attention of public authorities.[16]

Therefore, both dominant and less powerful members in the transgovernmental network have a keen interest in harmonisation. Given the established transgovernmental network, this moves the game to the nested, cooperative endeavour that is concerned with whose jurisdiction's standards to agree upon (Genschel & Plümper 1996, 240–242). Nevertheless, the cooperation is not a policy deliberation among exact equals. Rather, a country's market size tends to be a good indicator of the differing degrees of a jurisdiction's influence on the specific content of standards – and whether these standards will be closer to that jurisdiction's own or another one's standards (Simmons 2001, Drezner 2007).[17] The outcome, however, is still a cooperative agreement, since even the dominant states prefer harmonised standards.

Thus, while a cooperative interaction mode and standard will be pursued by all BCBS regulators, the regulatory content will to a higher degree represent the interests of jurisdictions with relatively larger markets under their authority. In finance, the United States is still the most attractive and relevant market and is widely viewed as having hegemonic power, although its relative power decreases vis-á-vis the EU, and in particular the UK (Simmons 2001, Drezner 2007, Novembre 2009, Posner 2009, Bach 2010). In more recent accounts, the EU – as a cohesive actor in the area of regulatory standards for the global political economy – plays a comparable role, which leads to duopolar theoretical models (see e.g. Drezner 2007). However, in the Basel Committee, the EU is not a coherent jurisdictional actor, but rather the single states pursue their individual interests in the BCBS (see Chapters 4 and 5). The EU was not established as a single jurisdictional actor in the BCBS during the period of the Basel II deliberations (Bundestag Finance Committee 2003a, Tarullo 2008), and it is still not today (Chapter 5). Accordingly, the only other actors with potential relevance in terms of negotiation power based on market size are other BCBS member states with substantial financial centres like the UK, Germany, France and Switzerland.[18]

Despite asymmetric interdependence, the key derivation of Figure 3.2 is that the transgovernmental network of supervisors is likely to deliberate on which standards to harmonise, rather than whether to cooperate at all. Furthermore, they are likely to interact in a cooperative network mode, unless competition state or global governance demands, in particular interventions by global or national political principals, force them to negotiate. The transgovernmental cooperation adds transnational institutional as well as process layers to regulatory governance. Three exogenous influences, however, can alter the basic cooperation game: the already discussed (rather negligible) guidance of the global political principal of the G7/20; the capture, due to dependence on informational support from their primary regulatees, i.e. transnationally active banks; and the national reactions to foreshadowing transgovernmental standards, i.e. domestic feedback from opposed national voice coalitions.

Domestic–transnational feedback processes and the unintended consequences through the second transnational layer

The second transnational layer of political processes, that unfolds its impact on global standards in the shadow of distant international politics, is constituted by domestic–transnational feedback mechanisms. These can alter the transgovernmental cooperation mode into one of international negotiation. In Figure 3.1, this dynamic is depicted by the dashed arrow connections from nationally oriented regulatees, going through domestic political principals, that control their domestic regulatory agencies, to renegotiate in the Basel Committee, which, finally, switches the BCBS interaction mode to international negotiation. The empirical analysis will reveal that the Basel Committee and national regulatory regimes grew together into a more thoroughly connected, politicised TRR through the interventions of domestic political principals – a general mechanism known from the EU (Eberlein & Grande 2005). According to this logic, locally/nationally oriented regulatees in the national arena, affected by the new regulation but with a weaker (than transnationally oriented regulatees) influence in the transnational network, invoke the voice mechanism and push national principals to act as international veto players.[19]

Such mechanisms of domestic political veto to policies of a transgovernmental regulatory network can be delineated on the basis of Hirschman's (1970, 2–4) idea that actors dissatisfied with a certain outcome in a certain segment of a political economy can either exit that segment or voice concerns with the management of that segment. Adapting the Hirschman frame, in a national economy that is integrated into a partially globalised economy, economic actors will activate political opposition through the exit or voice options if the adjustment costs to meet harmonised regulatory standards increase costs disproportionately or reduce a company's market income (Drezner 2007, 59). Put succinctly, banks can either threaten to exit domestic markets or activate political opposition through electoral and/or lobbying channels.

While transnationally oriented banks can voice their concerns within the Basel Committee, nationally/locally oriented ones must focus their efforts towards national regulators and politicians.[20] Their first option is the direct approaching of the domestic regulator. Yet, the regulators might fail to advance all demanded regulatory changes, since they consider these less relevant in the context of the BCBS negotiations during which regulators are more concerned about the international, rather than the national, level playing field. If, then, nationally/locally oriented banks fear competitive disadvantages within their domestic jurisdictions due to harmonised regulatory standards that disproportionately benefit international banks, and find themselves incapable of exerting influence on their design, they will – as a follow-up strategy – appeal to political principals by voicing concern with them.

Once these banks can overcome a certain threshold of political principals' attention, they can reactivate the discussed fire alarm control of political principals over the regulatory agents on their behalf. In this case, the parliament or government becomes a veto player and ensures that the regulatory agent enforces the national specific interests in the Basel Committee deliberations. Agency freedom will be restricted for this specific purpose. I will discuss below in more detail which interests drive political principals' decisions, but I can outline here that office-seeking public officials react to two forms of voice. First, if banks, as a central engine of economic growth, claim unfavourable standards will result in reduced credit provision and, thereby, economic prosperity, politicians tend to become nervous. Second, if politicians fear the withdrawal of political support from influential banking associations, this also enters politicians' calculations considerably.[21]

As a consequence, politicians of the legislature and the government are under pressure from the special interests of the industry (dissatisfied with internationally harmonised regulatory standards), if the latter can credibly claim that unfavourable standards will result in reduced credit provision and economic growth, and/or threaten withdrawal of political support. The resulting domestic conflicts can switch the equilibrium of the BCBS interaction mode back to the inter-jurisdictional negotiation game with less favourable preferences regarding cooperation. Hence, domestic politics play a key role in shifting these equilibria. More precisely, the cause of such shifts in the global interaction mode from transnational networking to international negotiation is located in shifts in domestic principal–agent relationships – from autonomous regulation to principal intervention. These domestic shifts occur when principals are incentivised through voice activities by (primarily locally oriented) regulatees.

This political intervention, as facilitated by a national institutional design to ensure accountability of regulators to elected political authorities, has unintended consequences that affect regulators capability of providing financial stability. This domestic–transnational feedback mechanism is at the root of detrimental layering of national and transnational political processes in the global political economy. It facilitates the competition state layer in the global politics of banking regulation. Together with transnational capture it constitutes the problem of unchecked simultaneous influence that creates global regulatory loopholes.

Transnational capture and the transnational harmonisation coalition

As I discussed before, transnational banking associations have long established, close ties with the regulatory community of the Basel Committee. The Committee, however, was keen about keeping its distance from global banking associations until the BCBS, from 1996 onwards, was in need of gaining the international, technically advanced banks' input on innovative risk modelling techniques (Goodhart 2011, 413–417). Even then the BCBS officially kept its distance. Nevertheless, transnational capture was facilitated through the substantial impact on the BCBS working groups. In light of rising complexity in the regulatory approaches, the harmonisation endeavours of the Basel II and III frameworks forced the regulatory networks to rely more and more on the input from banking associations (Claessens & Underhill 2010, Young 2012). The outer left of Figure 3.1 depicts this relationship.

Moreover, the domestic–transnational feedback mechanism, i.e. the political pressure to integrate certain national demands, leads domestic supervisors and the transgovernmental network to take these threats to their independence into account, and attempt to counterbalance and pre-empt these interventions. As the empirical analysis will reveal, they intensify the cooperation with the transnational banking community through the detailed technical work in working groups and task forces, where this transnational harmonisation coalition hammers out complex solutions that satisfy transnational banks' as well as national competition states' influential interests. In other words, regulators and bankers seclude themselves in a transnational network in order to pre-empt political intrusion.

These two channels foster the transnational process layer and the influence of the transnational harmonisation coalition. Together with the national voice coalitions they simultaneously affect the content of transgovernmentally harmonised regulatory standards. This creates regulatory loopholes that are, then, transnationally diffused. This is the origin of global governance gaps. It could be countervailed through national or global political control mechanisms. As this chapter aimed to demonstrate, however, global political principals do not carry out this function, while national politicians actually advance loopholes in favour of their preferred constituents rather than demanding the provision of financial stability.

To conclude, the transnational connection between regulatory regimes adds new layers of regulatory politics. The outlined structural elements of delegation, opaque policy community ties in regulatory regimes, and capture are manifested across the levels and the changing logic of collective action alters the potential for successful coalitions.

In sum, the dispersed authority between political principals and regulatory agents, and the weak political control mechanisms on behalf of financial stability, increase the probability of regulatory standards that do not regard stability to a sufficient degree. Moreover, the layering of national and transnational processes and institutions in the TRR deepens this tendency, as it enables the influence of specific well-organised interests through diverse channels, but disables proper regard of the public interest of stability in the everyday decision making of public officials. The probability of public officials providing public goods is significantly reduced by the dispersed authority and layered processes/institutions in the governance constellation of domestic and transnational regulatory regime structures.

In abstract terms, we can delineate the following politico-economic process: (1) an endogenous or exogenous initiation of harmonised rule-setting; (2) the transgovernmental network sets standards that change the domestic market equilibrium; (3) national coalitions of private interests raise their voice and achieve a selective fire alarm intervention by politicians; (4) transnational coalitions raise their voice with the transgovernmental network (and in addition with domestic regulators and politicians) and achieve integration of their private interests into the global framework; (5) the combined influence weakens the regulators' capacities and incentives to provide regulation that protects public goods.

Thus, the opportunity structures of the transnational governance constellation condition the policy process of setting globally harmonised standards in a manner that entrenches asymmetric influence of national voice coalitions and transnational harmonisation coalitions. The following empirical chapters demonstrate that the preferential influence by the private interest coalitions as well as the missing counterbalancing for public good provisioning reduce the protection of financial stability. In effect, the TRR raises the possibilities for organised special interests to integrate their preferences into policy outcomes, while at the same time decreasing the incentives for, and capacities of, public officials to protect the public good of systemic stability and regulate externalities.

4
Global Banking Regulation Before the Great Recession: The Dynamics of Basel II

This chapter presents a measurement of influence in the global politics of regulatory standard-setting, and how this influence translates into the content of regulatory policies. I conduct a systematic empirical assessment of the policies and politics of the Basel II agreement during the period 1998–2008. Departing from the two previous Basel II studies (Wood 2005, Tarullo 2008), I simultaneously investigate the degree of influence exercised by international, transnational and various domestic actors and trace the global political dynamics underlying the regulatory outcome.

Accordingly, the study combines a correlational content analysis of actor positions and their integration into the Basel II framework to measure influence in transnational standard setting with a process tracing to identify which political channels of influence were underlying these outcomes. The first enables me to assess how the Basel II policies reflect the success of distinct national, transnational and interstate actors, which allows interpretations about influence in transnational policy processes. The second, by tracing the underlying political processes within the G7, the Basel Committee, transnational banking associations, parliamentary committees of both U.S. Congress chambers, and the financial committee of the German federal Parliament, provides insights into the mechanisms that drive the global political dynamics of banking regulation.

The findings can be summarised into two groups, namely policy-related results of the Basel II standards and process/institution-related insights concerning the TRR in global banking. Regarding the first group, I find that Basel II operated as a diffusion device of regulatory practices that were at the root of the Great Recession. The development of new standards, in particular the risk measurement and management paradigm based on internal banking systems, was spearheaded and diffused through the Basel II exercise and the Basel Committee's transnational network. Hence, while not the primary cause of the regulatory failure, the transnational endeavour certainly failed to reduce the likelihood of financial turmoil and its spreading through transnational spillovers. Moreover, it even contributed to the spread and development of rules prone to regulatory gaps. Excessive risk taking and regulatory arbitrage were not pre-empted and in several cases even facilitated.

The second group of findings demonstrates that underlying this policy failure was the asymmetric influence of national and transnational coalitions, which both could introduce their preferred aspects into the Basel II framework. The empirical analysis reveals that coalitions at both the domestic and transnational levels focused on the competitiveness of the banking sector or certain sub-sectors (e.g. small, local banks), but failed to prudently consider negative externalities threatening systemic stability. This asymmetric influence can to a considerable degree be traced back to the layered processes and institutions in the TRR. Due to the complex dynamic of layered or dispersed authority in the TRR, the issue of systemic stability was substantially weakened at the expense of the sector's, sub-sectors' and several specific national stakeholders' concerns regarding competitiveness.

I proceed in four steps, where the first section outlines the research design, while the second section summarises the final contents of Basel II from a policy-analysis viewpoint. The latter section will present the main technical standards of the negotiated agreement as a basis for the political evaluation of how these relate to actor interests. The subsequent, main section analyses in detail the four episodes of the Basel II process. Each of the public consultation rounds are investigated separately, with a view to the relative successfulness of the actors as well as the political mechanisms that led to the results. The fourth section combines the episode-specific insights into an overall evaluation of the Basel II policies and processes.

4.1   An approach to assess influence in the global political economy

To analyse who is influential in global banking regulation, I assesses empirically which interests are incorporated into a globally harmonised agreement and which are rejected. I analyse in detail the crucial regulatory effort to harmonise financial regulation prior to the recent financial crisis: the Basel II framework. It was not only the most important element of the global financial regulation architecture. Basel II is also a typical case for projects of global harmonisation of regulatory standards.

Analysing Basel II, as discussed above, necessitates to investigating actors organised within international, transnational and domestic fora. To gauge international factors, the G7 are included in the analysis, since neither the IMF nor any other international organisation or forum has any direct impact on the harmonisation between industrialised nations.[1] More precisely, the G7 governments' interests were measured by coding the preferences regarding banking regulation voiced within the publicly available documents of the summits.[2] Transnationally, the Basel Committee's interests and the associations IIF and ISDA (as well as transnational banks' domestic activities) are analysed by referring to their position papers during the negotiations.

To investigate the domestic actors' influence, actors are chosen from two different jurisdictions. The selection criteria are sought to maximise variation on two dimensions, namely relevance in the transgovernmental network (in terms of market share and negotiation power), and institutional and collective action characteristics of the domestic political economy. Accordingly, from the set of all BCBS member jurisdictions, the United States and Germany were selected. The selection of the United States and Germany provides a high degree of necessary variance along the characteristics of the domestic political economies. This reduces the probability that the main study results are driven by these national polity aspects. First, as outlined in the preceding chapter, the two nations differ in international negotiation power – conceptualised via Simmons's (2001) market-based power concept, according to which a nation has a rising degree of international negotiation power with an increasing domestic market size, to which other countries' firms want access without high legal transaction costs. The US as the most powerful country is a natural choice for the high end of the scale, while the EU was not established as a unitary actor in the Basel Committee during the period under investigation. Germany is also an attractive case as it is not entirely without market-related power, but certainly with much lower values than the US, as well as the UK and Japan with their financial centres in London and Tokyo.

Second, the type of authority division and delegation also differs considerably between the two cases. Germany and the United States clearly diverge with regard to the setting of responsible political principals: while in the US, Congress is the primary responsible principal, although this responsibility is shared with the President and

Secretary of the Treasury in several instances, in Germany the main regulatory agency, BaFin, is subject to the formal, hierarchical scrutiny of the Ministry of Finance. At the same time, the number of regulatory agents and their division of labour varies substantially, where the US is characterised by at least four agencies that have responsibility in the regulation of banking (plus several other regulators responsible for securities firms, insurance, exchanges etc.),[3] and Germany is characterised by a twofold division between an encompassing financial sector regulator, BaFin,[4] and its independent central bank, the Bundesbank.

Furthermore, the two political economies provide maximum difference on the dimension of the style of interest intermediation in the political system and economy. This difference has been identified by Büthe & Mattli (2011) as one particularly important factor affecting the capacity to negotiate internationally on how to design regulatory standards. While the US is an example of a pluralistic, highly fragmented political system (Coleman 1994a, 49; 1994b, 286–287), as well as of a liberal market economy (Busch 2009, 16–19), Germany is a very clear case of a corporatist, consensus-oriented political system (Coleman 1994b, 286–287) and coordinated market economy (Busch 2009, 16–19).

Finally, the two political economies differ considerably in the importance of the banking sector in the calculations of public authorities. Whereas the United States is a clear market-based case, where banks are – relatively – less relevant since financial intermediation is strongly carried out on public capital markets, Germany is a classic example of the credit oriented system. It relies more on the banks' credit intermediation role, since the majority of credit is intermediated via established bank–firm relationships (see e.g. Busch 2009, 75–98). German banks are particularly powerful and its interest intermediation system is highly developed (Coleman 1994a, 32).[5] This dichotomous differentiation also correlates with the US as a type of a liberal versus Germany as a coordinated market economy, according to the Varieties of Capitalism approach (Hall & Soskice 2001, Busch 2009, 16–19).[6]

If these countries' actors submitted positions directly to the BCBS, these were included in the analysis. The major part of the domestic analysis is based upon the industry's position papers with national regulatory agencies as well as the extensive discussions in specialised parliamentary committees (for details see Table 4.1). The positions of industry, national regulatory agencies and political principals (parliamentary and ministerial authorities with power over the supervisors) are mainly drawn from the committee hearing documents of both

Table 4.1 Operationalisation of actors' interests

Actors	Operationalisation	Data sources	Analysed/coded documents
Global political principal, G7	G7 Heads of State/Government and Finance Ministers	G7 summit and ministerial meeting declarations (G8 Information Centre Website, University of Toronto)	16/4
Basel Committee	BCBS joint or chairman positions	Official publications of the BCBS; public speeches of high-ranking regulators; starting with episode 2, the prior episode's consultative proposal of the BCBS was coded as their position in the new episode	41/8
Transnationally oriented banks	Influence in domestic jurisdictions, US: Financial Services Roundtable (FSR), American Bankers Association (ABA)	Comments on consultative papers (to domestic supervisors and the BCBS); positions in Congress hearings	9/3
	Influence in domestic jurisdictions, GE: Zentraler Kreditausschuss (ZKA, represents the entire German banking industry), Bundesverband deutscher Banken (BdB)	Comments on consultative papers (to domestic supervisors and the BCBS); positions in Bundestag hearings	12/6
	Transnational banking associations: Institute for International Finance (IIF), International Swaps and Derivatives Association (ISDA), Group of Thirty	Comments on consultative papers (to BCBS); positions in Congress hearings	13/4
Domestic political principals	US Politicians: Congress (Senate and House of Representatives) committees; Department of Treasury	Hearing Documents, committee websites; no sources revealed participation of the Department of the Treasury	22/6

Category	Actors	Documents	Analysed documents
	GE Politicians: Bundestag (Federal chamber) committee; Ministry of Finance	Non-public hearing documents of the parliamentary finance committee (special access); ministerial position papers included in the hearing documents	34/13
Domestic regulatory agents	US federal banking regulators: Fed, Office of the Comptroller of the Currency (OCC), Federal Deposit Insurance Corporation (FDIC), Office of Thrift Supervision (OTS), Conference of State Bank Supervisors (CSBS)	Position papers; public speeches of high-ranking regulators; congressional testimonies	35/14
	GE federal regulators: Bundesanstalt für Finanzdienstleistungsaufsicht (BaFin) and Bundesbank	Position papers and statements included in the Bundestag committee hearing documents; public speeches of high-ranking regulators	21/8
Nationally/locally oriented banks	US: American Community Bankers (ACB), ABA, Financial Guardian Group (FGG)	Comments on consultative papers (to domestic supervisors and the BCBS); positions in Congress hearings	10/4
	GE: ZKA, Deutscher Sparkassen- und Giroverband (DSGV), Bundesverband der Deutschen Volksbanken und Raiffeisenbanken (BVR)	Comments on consultative papers (to domestic supervisors and the BCBS); positions in Bundestag hearings	13/4

Notes: 'Analysed documents' gives the number of all documents that reported positions by the respective actor on global regulation. All of these were analysed concerning qualitative information on the political process and the agreement's content. Coded documents is the subset of documents that were included into the correlational content analysis since they revealed the most substantial information regarding actor positions.

Congressional chambers and of the German Bundestag (including newly discovered confidential hearing records from the influential Finance Committee).

To obtain a detailed measurement, I disaggregate the Basel II agreement and the actors' policy preferences and analyse influence at the level of single integrated or rejected interests. In order to quantitatively assess, on the basis of the identified documents, to which degree actor preferences were or were not incorporated into the Basel II agreement, I build integration and rejection rates for all actors. Put succinctly, the indicator of the integration rate measures for each actor the ratio of successfully pursued interests in relation to all policy issues included in the Basel II agreement.[7] The rejection rate relates for every actor the number of preferred policies not integrated into the agreement to the total number of proposals that were rejected from integration into Basel II.[8] In other words, the rejection rate measures how many of the issues proposed for, but were not included in Basel II, were those of the respective actor. Therefore, the integration and rejection rates provide relative measures of success and failure comparable across actor categories. The indicators are built on the basis of coded actor positions and the comparison with the coded policy issues in Basel II. First, for each actor position papers are coded according to their positions on Basel II topics – e.g. transnational banks demand lower regulatory requirements on securitised mortgages.[9] Second, the Basel II agreement is coded to indicate the policy outcomes. This leaves us with three types of policy issues: those proposed by one or more actors, but not included in Basel II; those proposed and included; and those that were included without proposal. Every policy issue provides a dependent variable realisation (integrated in Basel II or not) and has independent variable values for each actor type (nine actor positions concerning the issue; three more than the six introduced categories, since US and German actors are presented separately). Then, for every issue, dyads for each 'policy outcome – actor position pair' are derived. The outcome for each dyad is binary, i.e. actor a's interest was integrated or rejected.[10] Building a simple sum of the integrated issue dyads of the G7 and relating them to the sum of all issues integrated in the Basel II agreement delivers the G7 integration rate. Summing all rejected suggestions of the G7 and relating them to the overall number of rejected proposals delivers the G7 rejection rate. In that manner, nine integration and nine rejection rates were constructed for the nine analysed actors. They measure each actor's relative success and failure and provide a differentiated analysis of the political implications of all issues in the Basel II framework.

Just measuring the final negotiation outcome, however, is insufficient, since global governance agreements are achieved through a multi-stage process (Avant et al. 2010, 17). Likewise, the Basel II agreement was incrementally built through three intermediate and a final negotiation stage with each separate and additive outcomes. The BCBS issued three consultative papers (CP) to the public before the final agreement was rendered, and solicited comments on each. Every CP reflected the current opinion of the Committee at that time and included the Basel II elements negotiated during that stage. The CPs and subsequent comment periods are constitutive of the political process of setting and harmonising regulatory standards. They structure its development and affect which actors can integrate their interests how and when. Therefore, the analysis of the Basel II negotiations is better approached by the disaggregation into four negotiation episodes and their individual assessment. The separate analysis, combined with the aggregation of the intermediate negotiation outcomes, is a more accurate description of actor success and failure than one which analyses only the final outcome. This is due to the latter approach omitting adaptation strategies of actors and intermediate successful or failed propositions. Accordingly, the results will be discussed in five steps: first, each of the four episodes will be analysed in a separate analysis, and then these results will be aggregated and evaluated in sum. Each episode's dependent variable has a value that can be measured by the content of the episode's consultative paper. It also has distinct independent variable values, because during each episode preference formulations of all relevant actors are measured prior to the agreement.

Tables 4.2 and 4.3 describe in detail the data basis for the analysis. Table 4.3 presents the frequencies and distribution of coded policy issues. It provides a quantitative description of the relative importance of issues during the entire process as well as during the single episodes. For example, during the first episode, 15 policy issues that fall under the category 'credit risk calculation' were discussed. 'Operational risk calculation' was a hot topic during episode 3, when 22 issues of that category were debated. Table 4.2 describes the distribution of incorporated and rejected interests for all actors during all episodes of the analysis. The integration and rejection rates of the following analytical sections can be drawn from this table. In the table, the reader can find the absolute number of integrated and rejected interests for each actor during each episode and in sum: each block of rows describes the results of the coding analysis for a specific actor. The five columns provide the results for the entire analysis and the four separate episodes.[11]

Table 4.2 Data description: frequencies and quotas of integrated and rejected policy issues

Actors	All episodes	Episode 1	Episode 2	Episode 3	Episode 4
No. of issues	369	86	109	138	36
G7					
No. of integrated issues	17	15	2	0	0
Percent of integrated issues	59%	71%	25%	–	–
No. of rejected issues	12	6	6	0	0
Percent of rejected issues	41%	29%	75%	–	–
Basel Committee					
No. of integrated issues	46	28	7	10	1
Percent of integrated issues	40%	62%	30%	29%	8%
No. of rejected issues	69	17	16	25	11
Percent of rejected issues	60%	38%	70%	71%	92%
Transnational Banks					
No. of integrated issues	67	17	32	16	2
Percent of integrated issues	36%	40%	51%	23%	20%
No. of rejected issues	119	26	31	54	8
Percent of rejected issues	64%	60%	49%	77%	80%
US Politicians					
No. of integrated issues	9	–	–	–	9
Percent of integrated issues	56%	–	–	–	82%
No. of rejected issues	7	–	–	5	2
Percent of rejected issues	44%	–	–	100%	18%
German Politicians					
No. of integrated issues	13	–	9	4	–
Percent of integrated issues	41%	–	53%	31%	–
No. of rejected issues	19	–	8	9	2
Percent of rejected issues	59%	–	47%	69%	100%
US Regulators					
No. of integrated issues	32	18	2	8	4
Percent of integrated issues	41%	50%	22%	31%	50%
No. of rejected issues	47	18	7	18	4
Percent of rejected issues	59%	50%	78%	69%	50%
German Regulators					
No. of integrated issues	19	9	7	1	2
Percent of integrated issues	46%	56%	47%	17%	50%
No. of rejected issues	22	7	8	5	2
Percent of rejected issues	54%	44%	53%	83%	50%

(Continued)

Table 4.2 Continued

Actors	All episodes	Episode 1	Episode 2	Episode 3	Episode 4
No. of issues	369	86	109	138	36
US Banks					
No. of integrated issues	11	–	–	5	6
Percent of integrated issues	30%	–	–	18%	67%
No. of rejected issues	26	–	–	23	3
Percent of rejected issues	70%	–	–	82%	33%
German Banks					
No. of integrated issues	47	2	17	26	2
Percent of integrated issues	42%	67%	49%	41%	18%
No. of rejected issues	65	1	18	37	9
Percent of rejected issues	58%	33%	51%	59%	82%

Notes: No. of integrated/rejected issues = number of integrated/rejected positions of actor i; Percentage of integrated/rejected issues = actor i's integrated/rejected positions in relation to all positions of actor i; based on coded policy issues, where only those issues are integrated that were coded at least twice.

For three reasons, the quantitative analysis was complemented by a qualitative process tracing. First, the conducted analysis cannot qualify and weigh the importance of different issues (the outlined exclusion of once-only coded issues, however, leads to the exclusion of rather irrelevant topics). It is important to identify highly salient and rather secondary issues, which can be achieved by following the political debates closely. Second, in instances of equifinality, i.e. where the rates do not offer clear answers regarding the crucial influential actors, the additional empirical information can clarify the correct interpretation. Third, and most importantly, while the empirical insights on correlations between actors' positions and policy outcomes provide an important systematic portfolio of information, they are insufficient for assessing how the global governance structure conditions influence. Applying a process tracing technique for the purpose of triangulating empirical relations provides additional information about the developments that caused the policy outcome. For these three purposes, the processes were traced through a careful reading of all coded documents and those considered for but excluded from the coding analysis.

Accordingly, the processes within the TRR of global banking that led to the Basel II framework are chronologically traced along the structures of the theoretical framework and among the relevant actors. For this

Table 4.3 Data description: frequencies and distribution of coded policy issues

Policy issue: Issue description	All eps	Ep. 1	Ep. 2	Ep. 3	Ep. 4
Credit risk calculation: Calculation of credit risk capital requirements (including standardised approaches, internal models, and internal ratings)	112	15	41	49	7
Operational risk: Calculation of operational risk capital requirements	41	3	7	22	9
Legal and statistical basis for capital calculation: All basic stipulations underlying capital calculation: legal and accounting parameters/variables; capital definition; whether and how financial conglomerates should be evaluated as one consolidated or separate entities	38	10	10	12	6
Credit risk mitigation: Regulatory recognition of hedging of credit risks via derivative products and accounting strategies	35	7	11	17	–
Pillar 2, Supervisory review: Requirements for (a) banks regarding internal risk management procedures, and (b) for regulatory agencies to supervise banks	31	15	9	4	3
Pillar 3, Information disclosure: Requirements for disclosure of information to supervisors and the public (to enable market discipline)	29	16	7	4	2
Securitisation: Rules relating to the administration of securitising assets and the resulting risk and capital calculation	20	1	5	13	1
Mode of supervisory cooperation: Discussions about the general mode of global cooperation among regulatory agencies	14	10	4	–	–
Emerging market harmonisation: Diffusion of regulatory approaches to the financial markets of emerging market countries	9	7	2	–	–
Interest rate risk: Calculation of interest risk capital requirements	7	–	6	1	–
Other: All other issues that do not belong into any of the major issue areas	33	2	7	16	8
Sum	369	86	109	138	36

Notes: Number of coded policy issues, where only those issues are integrated that were coded at least twice; each category encompasses families of several sub-codes, which each reflect specific policy issues.

purpose, empirical evidence was gathered from different, heterogeneous sources, which ensures data reliability (Gerring 2007, 172–173): first, the documents analysed in the content analysis are simultaneously investigated as to whether they reflect strategies; second, further documents are integrated that did not reflect an actor's position but rather constituted a report on significant events; third, the chronological sequence, and the location in terms of political fora/channels, were interpreted with reference to the TRR framework outlined in the previous chapter. In sum, 300 documents were integrated into the detailed tracing, and each document was categorised to a specific actor-institutional channel typology and then summarised with a description of positions, events and an interpretation where plausible. The resulting empirical information is chronologically listed in an appendix on the author's website (romangoldbach.wordpress.com).

In the next section, I begin the analysis of global banking regulation before the Great Recession by outlining the policies of the final Basel II agreement. This is a necessary basis for the interpretation of how these contents reflect influence and regulatory failure.[12]

4.2 Basel II policy analysis

The Basel II framework, as finally agreed upon in June 2004 and amended in 2005 (Basel Committee on Banking Supervision 2006), is an agreement of highly detailed character – consisting of 350 pages, which include complex formulas and stipulations for internal bank capital requirement calculations and management, plus extensive complementary documentation.[13] It was designed as a response to the increasing globalisation of financial intermediation, in particular the transnationalisation and conglomeration of banking groups, and the threats these developments posed for global financial stability. Supervisors, meeting in Basel, developed the framework to overcome these challenges, thereby attempting to solve the problems of regulatory arbitrage associated with the old Basel Accord. At the same time, the inception of the process that eventually resulted in the Basel II framework was a continuation of transgovernmental harmonisation of risk weighted capital adequacy regulation (Tarullo 2008, 87–92).

The effect on national adoption: optionality and framework character

Overall, Basel II is a highly complex regulatory framework, which integrates a diverse set of preferences into a detailed set of rules. The framework did widen the scope and depth of regulatory standards harmonised through the transnational network. At the same time, however, it softened the character of the harmonised standard by deliberately augmenting national freedom in adopting the rules. Two major aspects have contributed to this softening, namely optionality and the loose *framework* character.[14]

First, the agreement established optionality/modularity as a governing principle, whereby national jurisdictions can choose which options to implement; moreover, in some cases, banks obtained the freedom to choose among options for compliance. Accordingly, national agencies can build jurisdictional solutions consisting of particular modules, and individual banks can build their modular solutions within the jurisdiction's limits. Optionality became a trend during the process, as, step by step, many decisive issues were put into differentiated solutions that encompassed the preferences of several key actors.

The second factor increasing the potential for deviant domestic adoption that serves special national interests was the further softening of the agreement's character as a 'Framework'. Even though the deliberations set out to achieve an 'Accord' like Basel I, in contrast to the first Accord, Basel II was eventually designed as a 'Revised Framework' in order to mitigate US opposition by introducing more domestic leeway in its implementation.[15]

Nevertheless, as the empirical analysis will reveal, the Basel II process strengthened the Basel Committee's influence on the harmonisation of regulatory standards via more indirect diffusion mechanisms. Therefore, the presented regulatory standards are of considerable importance in the regulation of banks, but only subject to complex diffusion patterns. In sum, the extensive range and detailed character of the Basel II provisions had a significant effect on how banks manage risks and supervisors scrutinise their prudence (see also Tarullo 2008).

Two major paradigms are fundamental to the hundreds of technical pages documenting Basel II: first, encompassing supervision of banking groups (the 'scope of application' of the rules), which aims to prevent regulatory arbitrage through transactions among entities within such a conglomerate that undermines prudential regulation; second, an encompassing approach towards measuring and controlling banks' risk profiles through the *three pillars*. I will begin by outlining the general three pillar logic, followed by the scope of application, and will then discuss the major issues of the Basel II framework.

The Three pillar structure

Even though it is of soft legal character, for the supervisors and banks to which the rules are applicable, the agreement has caused a paradigmatic shift in organising and supervising banking activities. The developed standards are based upon the confidence in three paradigms, namely market forces detecting and penalising imprudent banks, the calculability of risk and risk-based regulation, and regulation building substantially on private authority, more precisely internal bank capacities to measure and manage risk thoroughly.

These principles were entrenched in the fundamental structure of the three pillars, which reflects the purpose of strengthening risk regulation through a complementary approach. The first pillar constitutes the maintained basic concept of capital adequacy regulation. It is substantially refined in order to increase the precision of risk measurement and management. The Basel I approach of simply putting a broad-brushed standard risk weight on a few, internally diverse, categories of assets is fine-grained through increasing the number of regulatory risk measures, which is supposed to mirror the economic risks more accurately. This is achieved by enhancing the capture of credit risks in regulatory capital measures, as well as newly incorporating adequate measures and capital charges of market, interest rate and operational risks.[16] The resulting need for an increased scope and depth of information is achieved through regulatory reliance on banks' internal organisation of risk management (organisational structures that ensure portfolio and institute-wide control of the banks' risks) and internal statistical and data resources to estimate the risks of assets and portfolios. The approach for managing and regulating risks is targeted at making regulatory capital charges more sensitive to the actual risk of specific assets in individual institutions. While providing substantial freedom to banks in estimating risks and capital charges, the supervisors maintain decisive roles in setting several parameters and minimum levels, which limit banks' freedom substantially.

Second, the capital-charging approach to banking regulation is complemented by two new pillars. These are paradigmatic shifts within the transnational coordination of banking regulation, which transferred developments in national jurisdictions and large banks (both mostly in the US) into the transnational arena. Pillar two complements the complex internal risk calculations with a qualitative-quantitative supervision of the internal organisational and estimation-related instruments through the increasingly individual supervisory review of single banks. It means that supervisors, rather than merely controlling the fulfilment of regulatory requirements ex post, now undertake individual bank reviews that ex ante scrutinise the adequacy of banks' internal instruments to regulate risks in a prudent manner.

The other complementary element, pillar three, aims to standardise and enforce disclosure of capital level, risk type, and risk management information to the general public, so that market forces can be strengthened in controlling the prudential risk management in banks. The underlying logic is that investors will demand risk premiums, or even withdraw funds, from those banks that do not, or relatively worse than competitors, adhere to the best practices of risk measurement and management.

In effect, this general approach of the Basel II framework implied increased reliance on three complementary mechanisms: the internal organisational and estimation capacities of banks (pillar one), the individual direct supervision of banks through regulatory agencies (pillar two), and the market's disciplining forces of efficient information processing (pillar three). These regulatory paradigms were merged with another crucial principle, namely that all parts of diversified, complex financial conglomerates with banking activity were supervised and no arbitrage could be exercised through the legal, yet imprudent movement of capital within such a group. This scope of application is one of the cornerstones of Basel II.

Scope of application

The framework's scope of application covers all internationally active firms that are predominantly engaged in banking activities.[17] These banking groups were identified as a source of global instability, as their complex legal and operational structures enabled regulatory arbitrage through double-gearing of capital.[18]

As a result, internationally active banks have to report their capital levels on a globally consolidated basis, as well as on a sub-consolidated account for all significant subsidiaries. This encompasses all banking, as well as the majority of other financial entities (securities firms, etc.).[19] Hence, capital surveillance is now, in principle, carried out in a globally consolidated manner, while at the same time scrutinising sub-consolidated activities.

In practice, however, this consolidation is more limited due to problems under pillar two: since there is no global supervisor, the consolidated supervision depends on the successful coordination of supervisors from home and host countries. This is particularly challenging with regard to the complex advanced internal estimation techniques in globally connected banking groups, i.e. internationally linked capital adequacy calculations and management systems that cover business units in more than one jurisdiction. Moreover, the consolidation with regard to pillar three is similarly limited, as neither a harmonisation of accounting standards, nor a development to one global report has been achieved. I now turn to the detailed discussion of the content of the individual pillars.

Pillar one: credit risk measurement

Pillar one, and in particular the estimation of, and capital charges on credit risk is naturally the most important issue (and also the most encompassing one in terms of extent and development effort), as it covers the biggest share of bank activities. The first pillar covers the rules outlining how banks have to derive the capital charges on their portfolios, most importantly on credit risks.

Three options, the standardised approach and
external credit ratings

How banks can estimate these risk-weighted capital charges is of crucial relevance as it directly effects the costs of a credit. Risk measurement approaches became highly complex and differentiated, since they had to encompass the models for large, internationally active banks, as well as the techniques of smaller, less technically advanced banks. Three credit risk calculation approaches were introduced as options for banks. They differ in complexity and reliance on banks' internal capacities (and, vice versa, a decreasing reliance on supervisory parameters): a simple standardised approach for banks with less complex operations and systems; an advanced internal ratings based approach (A-IRB) for the banks with the most sophisticated techniques; as well as an intermediate internal ratings approach (foundational internal ratings based approach, F-IRB), that deliberately opens the door for using internal estimation capacities for institutes who compete with the most advanced ones without being capable of producing the same degree of estimation detail. The three-tiered model was the first element of optionality, which became the role model for many other optional modules throughout the negotiation and development process.

The standardised approach increased the risk sensitivity of capital charges for banks without advanced estimation and management techniques by increasing the number of detailed credit risk categories (so-called 'buckets') with a more fine-tuned risk-weight differentiation. In order to enable banks to provide the detailed categorisation (i.e.

rating) of their assets in the absence of internal capacities, they had to use external credit(-worthiness) assessments (ECAs, commonly referred to as external ratings) from credit rating agencies (CRAs, in Basel II jargon external credit assessment institutions (ECAIs)).[20] Under this approach, a debtor has to solicit a rating from a CRA, based on which the creditor bank can categorise the credit to the debtor and risk-weigh it accordingly. The regulatory demand for such ratings increased their importance for debtors to banks that applied the standardised approach.[21]

Internal ratings based (IRB) approaches

The internal ratings based (IRB) approaches are the core of the Basel II framework as they mirror its main purpose, namely the enhanced adequacy of measuring and controlling risks in the most sophisticated internationally active banks. To this end, the IRB approaches draw on banks' internal risk assessments and translate the banks' estimations into capital charges, while refraining from leaving the capital calculation entirely to banks' internal models. The recognition of internal port-folio models as the sole source of adequate capital level calculations – without regulatory parameters or other interventions in the banks' models – was the starting point of this debate and was pushed by the international banking community.[22] Supervisors, however, refrained from this entirely self-regulatory proposal and followed a path that introduced less freedom for banks and more regulation say regarding the basic parameters of the calculations.

Basically, the IRB approaches are a combination of formulas and parameters stipulated by the regulator on the one hand, and inputs generated via internal bank information to be included into these formulas on the other. A bank might calculate certain default risks via historical data and internal calculation models, but the derived values are then entered into the supervisory formula in order to come up with the risk-weighted capital requirement for the specific position. Before using any of these techniques, banks must achieve supervisory recognition of their internal approaches. This is exercised under the supervisory review process of pillar two and formulates extensive requirements on the banks' internal risk management organisation and risk calculation/data quality – these need to be met in advance and on a continuing basis.

To offer IRB application to a wider range of banks besides the largest global players, typically with the most advanced technical capacities, a bifurcated IRB approach was installed: the F-IRB approach, where supervisors provide most of the input parameters, but banks have the important freedom to internally assess the probability of default (PD) for a specific credit. The A-IRB approach differs from the simpler version in that banks can provide their own estimates of four additional risk components: loss given default (LGD), exposure at default (EAD), treatment of guarantees/credit derivatives, and maturity-related riskiness.[23] The A-IRB elements can be recognised individually and in an evolutionary manner, while banks have to speed up the implementation of the remaining elements once a first element has been recognised by the supervisor.

In other words, the two approaches differ in the level of a bank's freedom to use its own data and calculations as the basis for risk assessments and capital requirements. While F-IRB banks can calculate the crucial credit risk variable, i.e. the probability of a credit defaulting, they predominantly have to use formula parameters provided by regulators. In contrast, A-IRB banks can apply their internal data and estimations to calculate variable values and integrate them into the capital formulas, while the F-IRB banks have to use the regulatory parameters.

For all approaches, in comparison to Basel I standards, a substantially more differentiated risk categorisation is introduced with distinct risk weights under the standardised approaches, and risk weight functions under the IRB versions (here at least 11 different portfolio types are identified).

Small and medium-sized enterprise credits and retail portfolios

Two newly introduced portfolio categories (among the several portfolio categories defined) are particularly noteworthy as they reflect a new concept of treating small firms' and private customers' credits favourably through reduced capital requirements. First, so-called retail credits were upgraded to a portfolio status, with a simplified administrative procedure, as well as a specific (lower) risk-weight function. Retail credits can be calculated on a cumulative basis (i.e. do not each have to be funded by an individual capital charge), whereby capital is calculated for the entire portfolio of eligible retail exposures. This reduces charges on such credits (like small business loans and consumer loans), and simplifies the administration for banks, in particular those with their predominant activity in this area. Moreover, credits to small and medium sized enterprises (SMEs) also receive preferential treatment by permitting categorisation into either the retail portfolio (for very small credits to small business customers), or a portfolio with an intermediate risk weight function that is lower than the risk weights for comparable large-scale corporations. Both retail and SME portfolio specifics are available under standardised and IRB approaches.

Level of minimum capital requirements

As already mentioned, prima facie the overall level of capital is held constant, i.e. at 8 per cent minimum capital of risk weighted assets. Since the risk-sensitivity of the new measures is supposed to adjust the capital that banks hold to the real economic risks in their portfolios, the guiding principle refines the capital requirements for most assets, bringing them more in line with the actual risks, while the sum of the adjustments should be capital-neutral from the banking system's perspective. Thus, the crucial element is the relative adjustments of the risk-weights, which de facto reduce capital charges in several areas, while increasing them in other segments.

As a result, capital levels remained largely constant for banks applying the standardised approach, while sinking substantially for those institutes applying the IRB, in particular the A-IRB, approach (Tarullo 2008, 160–166; Buchmueller 2008, 119–120). This is due to the reductions in capital held to cover credit risks, which is only partially offset by the new capital charge on operational risk. The reductions for A-IRB banks are advanced through a technical solution at the very basis of the regulatory approach: the adaptation of the underlying assumption about how adequate amounts of capital should be provided in relation to credit losses, as well as the concurrent partial capital redefinition. The very basic parameter of the risk-weighing capital adequacy regime is the definition of threat against which capital has to be provided – in other words, how is the credit loss defined against which risk-weighted equity has to be provided. This is crucial in the determination of the level of capital requirements, since it defines the type of loss which banks have to provide equity for. Basically, the question is whether banks only need to have capital against unexpected losses (UL), i.e. those losses that are not already reflected in the credit conditions (interest rates) of a loan, or also for those latter expected losses (EL).[24] Capital requirements based on the combined recognition of UL and EL result in substantially higher equity demands.

The credit risk calculations of banks using the standardised approach are based upon unexpected *and* expected losses. Technically more advanced banks that apply one of the IRB approaches to credit risk, however, can separate their capital calculations for unexpected and expected losses, and base their capital adequacy calculations solely on UL, while being subject to a complex provisioning framework. The latter allows banks to use separate provisioning for expected losses, and even add certain surplus provisions to their tier two capital.[25] This enhanced recognition constitutes a de facto partial modification (and dilution) of the capital definition that integrates a wide diversity of various debt instruments and provisions as equity surrogates.

These adaptations eventually lowered capital requirements for A-IRB banks to a degree that caused countervailing limitations, namely a scaling factor and transition floors. The scaling factor multiplied capital requirements of A-IRB banks by 1.06 to make sure that reductions did not go too far, and the transition floors set a maximum reduction of capital over the first three years.[26]

Pillar two: bank internal risk management and qualitative supervisory review

While the first pillar took up the major part of the supervisors' work and debate (which is reflected in its share in the final document of more than 250 of the 350 pages), pillar two mirrors the increased importance devoted to qualitative supervision by regulatory authorities, i.e. the supervisory process. The basic idea is that banks themselves, under the scrutiny of market forces, are better prepared to evaluate the specific risks of their operations and assets. Accordingly, it is considered more promising for supervisors to focus on the risk management capacities of a bank, and the evaluation of whether these are suitable to deal with the bank's risks. Buchmüller (2008, 176–198) describes the supervisory review process as qualitative supervision of banks that aims to enhance the interaction between supervisors and banks and incentivise banks to implement sophisticated internal risk management systems. For this purpose, pillar two defines principles that guide the supervisory process, thereby strengthening risk evaluation.

In the Basel II framework, the result is four basic principles: first, banks need to have internal risk management processes (internal capital adequacy assessment process, ICAAP) in place;[27] second, supervisors shall adopt a qualitative review process in which they monitor and control the internal risk management systems on an individual basis, also adjusting capital requirements if necessary (supervisory review and evaluation process, SREP);[28] third, supervisors should expect banks to hold capital above minimum requirements (i.e. 8 per cent as an absolute minimum, which banks should meet comfortably); fourth, supervisors need to be capable of intervening in banks at risk at an early stage.

The importance attributed by other Basel II evaluations to the second (and third) pillar is typically much lower relative to the first (see e.g. Claessens & Underhill 2010). While this assessment is sensible for the most part, it fails to take into account that the changes in qualitative supervision (as opposed to pure number checking or evaluation of external audit reports) mean a substantial alteration in many jurisdictions' approaches to banking regulation. Moreover, with reference to the impact of Basel II, it has to be understood that one major concern of supervisors – the dangerously weak risk management in globally active banks, as revealed throughout the emerging market and derivative trading crises in the 1990s – is addressed through the improvement of banks' internal risk management systems (Buchmüller 2008, 176–199).[29] In this regard, pillar two is a major innovation, which was primarily diffused through the transnational supervisory network.

Pillar three: disclosure requirements and market transparency

The basic idea behind the third pillar is to strengthen control through market forces, where supervisory agencies are simply overwhelmed by the amount of information to be monitored (Buchmüller 2008, 200–227). Therefore, the Committee decided early on in the agenda setting process that market discipline should be strengthened via disclosure stipulations for banks, forcing them to make equity and risk positions, as well as risk management strategies/systems, publicly accessible.

The disclosure requirements encompass qualitative (descriptive) and quantitative information: capital positions and conditions, risk measurement system, risk positions according to pillar one (credit, market, operational) and pillar two (interest rate), and the risk management system ICAAP. According to Buchmüller (2008, 200–227), however, the information to be disclosed is not clearly specified and leaves considerable room for individual supervisory and bank decisions. Buchmüller (2008, 200–227) comes to the conclusion that the overall structure of information disclosure is diffuse, since the information is different from accounting related information, is not clearly defined in most instances (which reduces comparability and accessibility), and, in many instances, is not provided as aggregated data.

Operational risk

The introduction of an operational risk capital charge as a new regulatory risk category is another major innovation of the framework, which is directed at reducing risks from banks' operational mistakes in their daily banking and trading activities. Banks have to provide the operational risk charge in addition to the credit risk charge, and it is designed as a combined approach along all three pillars. Under pillar one, a capital requirement for operational risk is introduced, where banks can choose from three approaches in accordance with their internal capacities. The Basic Indicator Approach (BIA) simply stipulates a 15 per cent capital charge on the bank's gross income (averaged over three years); supervisory recognition is not necessary. The standardised approach is similar to the BIA, but the capital requirement is calculated as a sum of eight separate business line calculations that each have a capital requirement between 12 per cent and 18 per cent; as a precondition, an internal risk management system supervised under pillar two has to be implemented in the bank.

The advanced measurement approach (AMA), which is mandatory for internationally active banking groups using the A-IRB approach, is strongly principle-oriented, and based substantially on internal banking capacities to provide inputs. The very vague, principle-oriented manner of the AMA reflects a compromise between proponents of a pure quantitative capital charge and those of a purely qualitative supervisory review. Accordingly, while supervisors provide the basic parameters, the banks can collect the relevant calculation data themselves and have considerable freedom in inputting the necessary information into the calculations. Furthermore, operational risk insurance is accepted for AMA banks to reduce capital requirements (subject to a maximum of 20 per cent of the bank's total operational risk capital requirement). This approach allows institutes to apply internal risk calculation capacities to a considerable degree. The operational risk capital requirement is reduced with increasing complexity from the BIA to the standardised approach and to the AMA version (Buchmüller 2008, 87–163).

Securitisation

Securitisation was already a rapidly increasing financial technique to distribute risks from otherwise rather immobile assets, like residential mortgages or credit card lines, when the Basel II talks began, and its spread accelerated during the negotiations. US mortgages and credit card lines especially were securitised by banks, i.e. they were bundled and transferred into the form of a tradable security. It allowed banks to reap profits from these businesses without having to keep the unattractive risk profiles on their books (Hellwig 2009). The Basel Committee integrated the capital requirement calculation into the credit risk framework by mandating to calculate required capital amounts either via external or internal ratings. Basel II provided rules for investing and originating/sponsoring banks.

Basically, all 'investing banks', i.e. banks who buy securitised tranches, had to calculate capital for securitised assets that had an external rating from a CRA based on this rating – irrespective of the investing institute's credit risk approach. IRB banks can take some additional information into account. For non-rated tranches, IRB banks had to use an (even for Basel II standards) extremely complex supervisory formula, but could input their internally derived data. Institutes using the standardised approach had to deduct non- or low-rated assets entirely from capital.

The approaches regulating the 'originating banks', i.e. those where the underlying asset originates and is securitised, was modelled closely to US market practices in the early 2000s. To calculate the capital requirements on their retained tranches of securitisation, these banks were also allowed to use the external rating based approach. Moreover, the internal assessment approach and several other features allowed the large, internationally active 'originating banks' to use internal capacities to calculate capital requirements for the important credit and liquidity facilities of securitisations.[30] Put succinctly, standardised banks have to use the external ratings based approach, F-IRB banks the supervisory formula (SF), and A-IRB banks their own internal calculations to calculate credit and liquidity enhancements, which are important in the profitability of securitised assets.

The capital requirements on securitised residential mortgages and securitised credit card lines were kept low through the Basel II approach and the approaches were diffused transnationally.

Credit risk mitigation techniques

Another important credit risk-related issue is the widened regulatory recognition of *credit risk mitigation* instruments. Throughout the 1990s banks developed many new instruments to hedge against risk positions in order to optimise portfolios and reduce capital loss risks. Until, however, the Market Risk Amendment in 1996, these were only recognised in a very modest manner, and thereafter there was still only very limited recognition in the banking book. Basel II introduced a detailed and complex framework to widen the scope of recognised credit risk mitigation instruments – which reduces banks' capital requirements for hedged positions considerably.

For collateral (i.e. some form of security that is deposited elsewhere and secures a transaction in case of default), a haircut model[31] is introduced which reduces the capital requirement for a hedged position according to the quality of the hedge. Again, three approaches of different sophistication are offered, where the basic one is simple and the most sophisticated version allows for the use of elements of banks' internal models – with decreasing capital requirements for increasing sophistication. The range of eligible collateral is widened substantially to many financial and physical (real estate etc.) assets. Repo transactions, short-term refinancing instruments of high importance in daily financial trading and hedging are recognised favourably. Guarantees and credit derivatives are subject to similar Basel II treatment as collateral.

Another widely used credit risk mitigation instrument that received widespread recognition in the Basel II framework are netting arrangements. These are legal arrangements between creditor and debtor to net multiple contracts between the two parties, so that in case of a default of one party, the other party is legally permitted to net the defaulting positions with other transactions with that party and thereby reduce losses. After some negotiations, banks obtained substantial freedom in combining very different positions, even between on- and off-balance sheet positions.

Summary

Most of the issues discussed during the Basel II deliberations belong to one of the broader topics outlined above. For the sake of brevity, not all details are included in the in-depth discussion, while all of these technical issues, however, are included in the correlational analysis.[32]

In sum, the 'Revised Framework' is a capital adequacy based approach to harmonise banking in BCBS countries, in order to reduce the possibility of banks engaging in morally hazardous credit and trading activities. The principles and rules developed in Basel II reflect a regulatory model that largely delegates supervisory scrutiny to regulatees and markets, and puts the regulatory agencies in a managing position. In other words, supervisors stipulate certain goals and give regulatees considerable leeway in how to achieve them and, moreover, base the regulatory model upon banks' private authority to provide crucial inputs. Furthermore, these new standards are attempting to increase public scrutiny of market participants as a complement to the limited capacity of supervisors to control and enforce all details of the complex rule set (Tarullo 2008, Buchmüller 2008). The fine-tuned and technically advanced Basel II framework embraces the three regulatory paradigms described initially: first, efficient markets that detect and penalise imprudent banks; second, calculability of risk and risk-based regulation; third, private authority, or more precisely, internal bank capacities to measure and manage risk thoroughly. These are fundamental elements in the regulation of financial intermediaries.

Based on this policy description, two aspects are emphasised which are central for the following analysis: first, the widespread use of technical complexity to integrate many sectoral interests and, second, the extensive integration of optionality, i.e. different options and modules to adopt and implement the Basel II rules. The following empirical analysis reveals that the combination of complexity and optionality is reflective of regulatory standards that recognise a multitude of sectoral interests in competitiveness. At the same time, the design of these standards is less devoted to the public good of systemic stability. The remainder of this chapter puts the described regulatory standards into a politico-economic context. The following section analyses the four episodes of the Basel II process to reveal to what extent these regulatory standards are the result of asymmetric influence. The combined evaluation of the episodes' results in an overall analysis completes the chapter.

4.3   The global politics of the Basel II process

In this section, the four Basel II episodes are individually assessed through a triangulation of process tracing and correlational analysis of the integration and rejection of the different actors' interests. The periods are analysed as four single, though not independent, observations of deliberations in the TRR. These four distinct episodes (Table 4.4 presents an overview) provide four cases of political deliberation, policy design and decision making in the TRR. Their separate evaluation offers the opportunity to scrutinise mechanisms in four instances.

Each episode's section begins with the tracing of the political processes on the basis of the qualitative empirical substance. The focus is to reveal the causal mechanisms behind actors' success and failure to integrate their preferences into the framework through different political channels.[33] The political processes are delineated along specific threads that dominated the episode, and are mostly presented in the context of one of the four main arenas of political discourse and negotiation – namely the transnational networks around the Basel Committee, the US congressional committees, the Bundestag's finance committee, and the G7 summits. The procedural descriptions and analyses refer to the process map of theoretical framework (Figure 3.1). Each episode's section is then concluded by a summary of the key

Table 4.4 Four episodes of the Basel II process

Episode, Time period	Episode description with inception and finalisation
Episode 1, June 1997–June 1999	Launching the process and issuing the first consultative paper
Episode 2, June 1999–January 2001	Reactions to the first consultative paper and process up to the second consultative paper
Episode 3, January 2001–April 2003	Reactions to the second consultative paper and process up to the third consultative paper
Episode 4, April 2003–December 2008	From the third consultative paper until implementation (including agreement on the Revised framework in June 2004, refinements, recalibration and renegotiation until November 2005, and implementation)

policies rejected or integrated, the influential actors during the specific period, and the mechanisms underlying the patterns of influence.

These four chronological steps accrue to an extensive political process of 12 years, in which shifts and postponements became the norm. The agenda setting episode was characterised primarily by discussions among the regulatory and banking industry communities between at least June 1997 until the decision to craft a new Accord in September 1998 and eventually the first draft in June 1999. The two following proposal amendment episodes offered a broader discussion in terms of involved actors. This complicated the process to such an extent that it took from June 1999 until January 2001 to adapt the first draft, which was interrupted by many bilateral negotiations and Basel Committee meetings. From January 2001 until April 2003, the process was transformed further into constant evaluation, negotiation, and redrafting – the BCBS working groups issued several working papers to channel the highly technical discussions around the globe, carried out two impact studies, and adjusted the agreement's content accordingly. Finally, the last episode was an even more opaquely multifaceted process, including agreement on the Revised framework in June 2004 (instead of an 'Accord'), further refinements, recalibration and renegotiation until November 2005, and, eventually, domestic adaptation and implementation.

Episode 1, June 1997–June 1999: inception and first consultative paper

The inception of the process that eventually resulted in the Basel II framework was, on the one hand, a continuation of the transgovernmental harmonisation of risk-based capital regulation, and, on the other hand, the response to cumulating crises with international repercussions in the 1990s and particularly between 1994 and 1998 (Tarullo 2008).

Episode 1 dates from June 1997 and the G7 Summit in Denver, just before the Asian Crisis peaked, until June 1999 when the Basel Committee issued the first consultative paper (CP-1).[34] This agenda setting phase was characterised primarily by discussions among the regulatory and banking industry communities. While it took some time to come to the decision to create a new Accord in September 1998, the first draft was developed over a short time by April 1999 (while it was made public in June 1999).

Political process

The US supervisors, in particular the US Fed led by the New York Fed president McDonough, realised their ambitions through the transgovernmental Basel network. Nevertheless, even though this episode revealed the agenda setting power of the dominant regulatory actor in the dominant member state with the highest market power, it also demonstrated the conditioning role of the transgovernmental regulatory network on which the US supervisors relied to forward their preferences globally. While the Basel II policy agenda originated in the US regulatory regime, with the Fed as its main process carrier, the position of main driver was shared: by the US supervisors uploading their regulatory style as well as by the pressure from US-based, internationally active banks.

Antecedent to the Basel II process, US regulatory agencies perceived a twofold problematic: first, the US branches of foreign banks were increasingly threatening financial stability, without giving American supervisors an opportunity for prudent supervision of these branches;[35] second, the trend of growing financial conglomerates, which was made possible through the repeal of Glass-Stegal regulation,[36] in combination with the more and more complex risk operations within these large organisations.[37]

As a response, the agencies started initiatives to adapt supervisory rules in their jurisdiction. In November 1997, several months before the Basel Committee group for the revision of the Accord took up its work, US regulators issued a proposed rule-making, combined with a solicitation for comments, to enhance credit risk capital requirements via rating agencies' credit assessments, and suggested developments in the direction of applying bank internal risk measurement models. Both elements would later be part of the first Basel II proposal. Furthermore, the three-tiered approach to banks' risk measurement (i.e. three options: standardised, F-IRB and A-IRB) was discussed in the United States in November 1997 – also long before the Basel Committee negotiations.[38]

Moreover, Fed Governor Meyer (2001) outlined that the regulatory approaches of the supervisory review process (pillar two) and market discipline via disclosure (pillar three) were developed and applied by the Fed and the Office of the Comptroller of the Currency (OCC) as early as 1999 and reflect the preferences and agendas of those agencies (dating back to the supervisory policy statement SR 99-18). Meyer recognises the substantially higher burden for other nations' supervisors in adapting to this supervisory approach.

Simultaneous to these supervisory concerns, US-based internationally oriented banks also aimed at amending the Basel I Accord to recognise internal models for supervisory purposes as early as June 1997 (when the working group on capital adequacy of the IIF decided that it was time to suggest such changes and started to work on appropriate solutions).[39] Moreover, the international banking community was concerned about the inherent risks originating from their own staff (operational risks), as well as the counter-party and systemic risks stemming from the potential failure of one of their fellow core institutions (due to previous experiences during the Peso Crisis in the early 1990s and specifically the 1995 Barings Bank failure). Now they aimed for a framework that strengthened their security without disturbing their business practices too much. But, at the same time, they pursued reduced regulatory costs from the divergent domestic regulatory frameworks that these global institutions had to cope with.[40]

While it is not possible to overcome equifinality concerning the cause of the US push, the pressure stemming from its banking community – the domestic regulatory regime of the dominant market power – clearly resulted in the onset and initial agenda of the Basel II development. Ergo, the US supervisors pushed ideas that had emerged in the community of international bankers with its then predominant basis in the US centres of New York and Chicago (MacKenzie 2006), where regular job changes between industry, supervisory, and political positions result in dense, personal connections (Sorkin 2010).

While the US, however, had been promoting a new Accord for some time, most other members of the Basel Committee were opposed to the swift revision of the old Accord, instead favouring an incremental adjustment.[41] Agreement with the other BCBS jurisdictions was not achieved before New York Fed president William McDonough took over the chair of the Committee, which enabled him to substantially direct the agenda (while the Asian Crisis provided a welcome functional argument). At a meeting in July 1998, the BCBS decided that it was time to review the Basel Accord, and on 23 September 1998 the Committee group, chaired by Claes Norgen, began to revise the Accord.[42] US prevalence, combined with the newly acquired chairmanship, gave the US sufficient power to start a complete Accord revision, even though several member states (like Germany and the Netherlands) were in favour of a more incremental progress.[43]

Nevertheless, the US had to meet fellow regulators' reservations and accommodate other jurisdictions' preferences: the introduction of IRB instead of internal model approaches; no introduction of market discipline via subordinated debt; no pre-commitment approach; the introduction of an operational risk charge (see discussion in the following section on the policy outcomes of this episode). The reason behind these compromises was the perceived need of the US to pursue a globally harmonised approach in order to ensure a global level playing field for its transnationally oriented banks (this argument has also been advanced by Singer 2007). At the same time, other BCBS countries' ability to withstand US power was low due to the home industry's crucial access to the central global financial market place.[44] Moreover, all BCBS regulators shared the interest of reducing the dangers from banks' capital arbitrage strategies spilling over transnationally and threatening (global) financial stability. The combined interests in stability and US market access outweighed the interests opposed to a new Accord. Thus, as this early negotiation process demonstrates, the harmonisation of regulatory standards is a game of distributive rather than conflictive dimension – i.e. the actor constellation concerns which standards to agree upon, rather than on whether to agree at all. Furthermore, it reveals that it is crucial to find a solution that is compatible with all relevant partners' domestic standards. Accordingly, the US gave in to opposed claims, particularly to those of the German delegation. Two compromises are of particular importance and supportive of this claim, one being a broader Basel Committee agreement, another being a specific US-German compromise.

First, the case of the internal rating based (IRB) approach was a broad compromise with several Basel Committee members.[45] It emerged as an agreement between the US, which promoted a bifurcated approach of internal portfolio models and a standardised approach based upon external ratings, and European countries whose banks for the most part did not have internal modelling capacities comparable to those in the US (and were highly sceptical regarding the reliability of such risk estimations) or external ratings. Therefore, the majority of Basel Committee members favoured the internal ratings based methodology as the 'only solution not affecting competitiveness in a disproportionate way' (Bundesaufsichtsamt für das Kreditwesen & Deutsche Bundesbank 1999, 16, author's translation). The bargaining result was the bifurcated IRB and standardised credit risk measurement approach.

Second, a compromise with Germany was found as it threatened to use its veto option – which, until then, had not been used by any member during the 25 years since the Committee's creation – if its request for a generous capital treatment of corporate bank credits was disregarded.[46] This threat in March 1999 delayed the issuance of the first consultative paper until June of that year. In the following two months, the United States launched an intense media campaign that culminated in lead articles in *The Economist*. Individual, two-party transnational negotiations between the US and Germany led to a conclusion close to the German position (the US negotiators had no disadvantages from this, but were opposed to such loans since similar credits had caused the Savings and Loans Crisis in the early 1980s; once a publicly communicable solution was found, the US delegation overcame its opposition). This substantial German influence can be traced back to the domestic regulatory regime, where supervisory agencies and their regulatees formed a coalition to protect the key German bank activities. Through the regulator-industry ties, the initial divergence among German actors' positions was overcome. The agencies and ministry struggled hard to achieve a unified bargaining position that encompassed all sub-sector associations, but once it was achieved, this strengthened the German negotiating position in Basel.[47]

The G7 did not precede or intervene in the Basel efforts, but accepted the forum chosen by the supervisory agencies. While the Basel II endeavour was broadly in line with their interests, the global leaders' preferences were so unspecified that the regulatory agents were almost free to adopt policies. Moreover, it was the regulatory agencies who decided to harmonise regulatory standards through the transgovernmental network – i.e. they initiated the process and set the agenda. Two relatively separate discourses took place: the G7 discussed at their regular summits and finance minister meetings in Denver (June 1997), Birmingham (May 1998) and Washington (October 1998) how to control international externalities from emerging markets and create transparency in global financial markets;[48] in the meantime, the BCBS could elaborate on the rules of international banking supervision in a relatively autonomous manner – bank regulation of developed nations was not debated within political circles, but rather endorsed by the G7 summits without any issue-related guidance.

Rather, the biggest industrialised nations strengthened the World Bank and in particular the IMF in order to increase scrutiny and control over developing and emerging country financial markets, so that crises from these less regulated jurisdictions could not spill over. This was to be achieved via the increased diffusion of the Core Principles for Effective Banking Supervision, a set of standards aimed at enhancing regulation in emerging markets.[49] On the one hand, these standards were to be diffused through the intensified cooperation between supervisors from developed and developing countries.[50] On the other hand, the G7 aimed at strengthening the control of emerging and developing markets via IMF and World Bank programmes. They were calling upon the two institutions to integrate the regulatory standards into their monitoring of countries that received funds from them.[51]

While transparency and emerging market monitoring were promoted, however, issues of banking supervision in developed nations were merely touched upon and left to the Basel Committee.[52] No call for a revision of the capital Accord was voiced.

Neither political principals nor small, locally oriented banks in domestic spheres participated in the process during that early stage.[53] German banks are an exception since they affected their regulators indirectly at the end of the first episode. The effect, however, was rather small and substantial influence on the regulatory standards would only be achieved in later episodes.[54]

Policy outcomes and influential actors

Overall, the first episode reflects the crucial influence of US supervisors, in particular the US Fed, in setting the agenda. The analysis indicated that much of the initial Basel II blueprint originated in the US regulatory regime, and that the Federal Reserve was the main process carrier.[55] Figure 4.1 measures the agenda setting power in the global harmonisation of banking regulation by way of presenting actors' capability to integrate their interests into the first consultative paper of the Basel II agreement. The black/grey bars reflect the percentage of the specific actor's integrated/rejected positions in relation to all integrated/rejected positions of episode 1; the values in brackets depict the absolute number of integrated and rejected proposals of the respective actor. Referring to the influence of the US regulators, this means that 20 per cent of the policy issues integrated into the first consultative proposal coincide with the supervisors' preferred policy options, while 24 per cent of all issues not integrated into the proposal were those preferred by the agencies (these shares are equivalent to 18 of 89 integrated and 18 of 75 rejected issues).

Yet, to overcome potential misinterpretations from this quantitative assessment, I differentiate salient from rather less important policy issues. Therefore, the crucial topics of high salience were reconstructed on the basis of the qualitative process tracing. The result is Table 4.5, which is derived as an extract of the *crucial/key* policy issues. Accordingly, Table 4.5 lists for each actor the crucial integrated and rejected positions – i.e. those topics that were important as regulatory elements in the agreement as well as to the specific actor. The presented content provides a succinct snapshot of crucial policies, where the selection is based upon a qualitative weighting (on the basis of the process tracing) of all relevant regulatory policy issues.[56] For example, Table 4.5 reflects the asymmetric influence of US regulators in setting the agenda of the Basel II deliberations, where several key issues were integrated into CP-1 due to pressure by US agencies. The fact that many position fields are empty does not necessarily mean that an actor was incapable of integrating any preferences or that none of his or her positions were rejected, but rather that the issues were not among the crucial topics. In order to assess whether an actor was either not related to one of the key issues, or not involved at all, one can consult the integration and rejection rates on the right-hand side of Table 4.5. A non-involved actor is reflected by zero integrated and rejected issues.

In contrast to the selective key issue approach, the indicator values in the columns of the outer right of Table 4.5, refer to the entire data of that episode. The primary values for each actor type reflect the integration/rejection rates of Figure 4.1. The first value in brackets refers to the specific actor's integrated/rejected positions in relation to all positions of that actor, i.e. an actor-specific success rate – for the US supervisors, a 50–50 rate. The second value in brackets depicts the absolute count of integrated/rejected positions of each actor.

The table reveals the Fed's (the main US regulator during this episode) success as an agenda setter; many of the integrated policy issues coincide with its preferences: the development of a new Accord; the introduction of the three-pillar approach that added supervisory review, and disclosure requirements; the increased reliance on sophisticated bank risk measurement techniques; the introduction of external rating based risk weights.

Notwithstanding the substantial US influence, however, the BCBS as a transgovernmental network clearly limited its impact. The high values

Table 4.5 Actors' integrated and rejected interests in Basel II, episode 1

Actor type	Crucial integrated positions	Crucial rejected positions	Integration rate	Rejection rate
Global political principal (G7)	– Development of 12 key financial standards – Policy diffusion to emerging markets via IFIs		17% (71%; 15)	8% (29%; 6)
Transgovernmental network (BCBS)	– Credit risk calculation via internal rating rather than with internal portfolio model approaches – Constant capital requirement levels – Interest rate risk capital charge	– Incremental Basel I adaptation, instead of a new Basel II agreement – No introduction of external ratings	31% (62%; 28)	23%(38%; 17)
Transnationally oriented banks	– New Basel II agreement	– Portfolio model instead of the IRB approach	19% (40%; 17)	35%(60%; 26)
Domestic political principals				
US Politicians			–% (–%; 0)	–% (–%; 0)
GE Politicians			–% (–%; 0)	–% (–%; 0)
Regulatory agents US Regulators	– New Basel II agreement, no Basel I adaptation – Introducing three pillar structure along US practices with internal bank self-regulation, qualitative individual supervision and market surveillance	– Pre-commitment approach – Subordinated debt as additional market surveillance instrument under pillar three	20% (50%; 18)	24%(50%; 18)

GE Regulators	– Introduction of external ratings as cornerstone of standardised approach and securitisation – No internal portfolio models – No pre-commitment approach – Operational risk capital charge	– Incremental Basel I adaptation, instead of a new Basel II agreement – No introduction of external ratings	10%(56%; 9)	9%(44%; 7)
Nationally/locally oriented banks				
US Banks			–% (–%; 0)	–% (–%; 0)
GE Banks			2% (67%; 2)	1%(33%; 1)

Notes: Integration/Rejection rate = first value depicts percentage of actor i's integrated/rejected positions in relation to all integrated/rejected positions of episode 1; values in brackets: first value describes actor i's integrated/rejected positions in relation to all positions of actor i; second value depicts the absolute count of integrated/rejected positions of actor i; based on coded policy issues, where only those issues are integrated that were coded at least twice; in sum 86 issues.

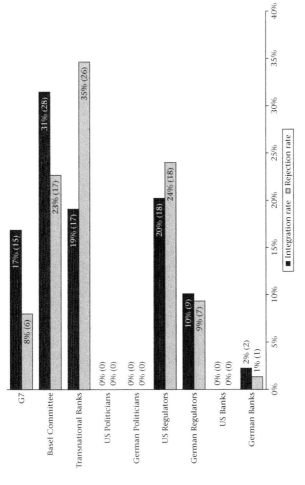

Figure 4.1 Integration and rejection rates in episode 1

Note: Integration/Rejection rate = percentage of actor i's integrated/rejected positions in relation to all integrated/rejected positions of episode 1 (89 integrated, 75 rejected); values in brackets = number of integrated/rejected proposals.

Source: Own calculations based on correlational content analysis.

in both Table 4.5 and Figure 4.1 reflect that the US had to accommodate a considerable number of compromises within the supervisory network, in order to achieve an agreement with fellow BCBS members to develop a new Accord. Yet, the very high rates of the BCBS are, in part, due to the fact that William McDonough's speeches – the then New York Fed chairman – as chairman of the Basel Committee are coded as positions that represent the common interest of the Committee (McDonough 1997, McDonough 1998, McDonough 1999). This is in part not accurate, since McDonough strongly pushed principles that were in line with current US practice and preferences.[57] Therefore, the BCBS score suggests a higher transgovernmental network influence than the US, even though the latter was clearly dominant. Nevertheless, the BCBS network, as discussed, also played an important role in limiting US power in making decisions single-handedly. The process tracing and qualitative review of the documents supports this interpretation.

As both Table 4.5 and Figure 4.1 also reveal, transnationally oriented banks vividly pursued their interest in the renewal of regulatory harmonisation, which was served quite well. The high rejection rate, however, demonstrates that their success was by far not an absolute capture of the process. The clear-cut rejection of internal portfolio models by the BCBS, for example, was a major failure.

There was no conscious delegation strategy by G7 governments, but rather the silent acceptance of their regulatory agents' activity. Against the backdrop of the turmoil caused in emerging markets by the Asian Crisis and the spilling over into the industrialised world, the G7, at its summits in Denver, Birmingham and Washington, mainly aimed for the stabilisation of these markets and the prevention of future spillovers. It was pursued through the inception of the process that led to the 12 key financial standards and their enforcement via the International Financial Institutions (IFIs) of the IMF and World Bank. The global political principal, however, neither initiated the harmonisation of developed countries' banking standards, nor engaged in substantial issue/goal specific delegation or control of the Basel II agenda.

The first episode is characterised by two core findings: the agenda setting impact of the US Fed demonstrates that the power of an influential domestic supervisor in uploading its regulatory ambitions can be tremendous within a transgovernmental regulatory network. Second, after the launch of the Basel II process had been enforced by the US, the actor constellation in the Basel Committee was that of a distributive game – i.e. all supervisors had an interest in cooperating, and conflicts only emerged regarding the distributional consequences of choosing one or another set of standards. This shared interest resulted in a first consultative paper that mainly reflected supervisory interests. To a limited degree it was subject to capture by transnationally oriented regulatees. Domestic regulatory regimes, however, played an early role as competition state coalitions among domestic supervisors and regulatees were relevant in setting the agenda (US) and influencing negotiation positions (GE).

Episode 2, June 1999–January 2001: negotiating the second consultative paper

Episode 2 ranges from July 1999 until the second consultative paper (CP-2)[58] in January 2001. It was characterised by substantial critique, with about 250 industry comments in response to the last period's CP-1.[59] Criticism was widespread as sectoral and political opposition emerged. Three patterns characterise this episode: a US (Fed) push for swift reform, German opposition, and the changing balance between BCBS and transnational banks.

Political process

The second episode was characterised by a continuously broadening discussion in terms of involved actors. This complicated the process to such an extent that it took from June 1999 until December 2000 to adapt the first draft, which was interrupted by many bilateral negotiations and Basel Committee meetings. The unintended, prolonged process was a result of the shift from secluded network cooperation towards international negotiation in the Basel Committee, which, in turn, had its origins in domestic regulatory regimes.

On the one hand, the Federal Reserve, through their continued chairmanship in the Committee, pushed to achieve an agreement on a new Accord in a short time. This happened against the US domestic background, where supervisors experienced substantial pressure from Congress, as well as from sectoral actors, to adapt their regulatory implementation of the Gramm-Leach-Bliley Act – in particular to apply it on a globally consolidated financial holding level to foreign universal banks. This, in turn, led European regulators threatening to abandon the negotiations on the new Basel Accord, since it would have heavily impacted on all European banks active in the US, which were almost entirely universal banks.[60] Basel II remained the Fed's attempt to solve national and global problems simultaneously. On the other hand, however, in order to build a coalition, considerable concessions to other Committee members, Germany in particular, were necessary to ensure the ongoing progress of the negotiations. German veto threats arising from domestic parliamentary deliberations shifted the development of the process and the outcome substantially.

The substantial resistance at the national level in Germany depicts the first of two main patterns during this episode. It was initiated by a coalition of locally oriented public banks, who activated domestic principals, thereby achieving substantial changes in the framework's design.

In this context, the deliberations of the internal rating based approach, which resulted in the bifurcated IRB approaches, are revisited. These present a fitting example of the procedural pattern of how domestic principal activity shifts the interaction mode in the Basel Committee from transnational network cooperation to an international negotiation forum.[61] The initial push to recognise internal portfolio models for regulatory capital calculations was due to transnational banks, especially US-based ones (supported by US supervisory agencies), which promoted an internal entire-portfolio-wide model calculation for the most advanced banks. In contrast, German supervisory agencies (and other BCBS members) strongly rejected the internal modelling approach, but were less opposed to the regulatory application of external ratings. This led to the interim outcome that within the first consultative paper, a rather sophisticated IRB-approach for technologically advanced banks, and a standardised approach for remaining banks, with the refinement of risk weights via external ratings from rating agencies, was envisaged.

In response to CP-1, however, both the sophisticated IRB and the standardised approach based on external ratings were heavily criticised. Since regulatory capital would have been substantially lower for banks using the IRB approach, several members of the Committee pushed for a simple IRB option that the majority of banks in their jurisdictions could implement quickly and apply easily. The CP-1 proposal was expected to result in large financial conglomerates with the most advanced internal modelling capacities – mostly US institutes – outbidding its competitors in serving large international creditors. Consequently, Germany, in union with several other countries, signalled that they could not consent to an IRB approach unless a simpler entry version would be introduced. The Basel Committee therefore asked the *Models Task Force*, one of its working groups, to develop a simple and an advanced option, which ultimately led to the bifurcated approach of foundational F-IRB and advanced A-IRB.[62]

Furthermore, several Committee members also realised that the external ratings based credit risk calculation of the standardised approach would distort the level playing field to their banks' disadvantage. Consequently, Germany suggested using it solely for highly rated addresses (AAA to AA-rated debtors) and found a compromise with most other members, since these highly rated European corporations already had external ratings for the most part. Since, however, most US firms were B-rated (in the US many medium-sized firms with lower creditworthiness have to refinance on public bond markets), the American negotiators quickly agreed upon the internal ratings version.[63]

The German process of deliberation and interest intermediation highlights the domestic roots of this transnational compromise. In response to CP-1, a unified national position was formed to block the proposals that were conceived of as putting its small and medium-sized banks, as well as SME businesses as these banks, primary customers, at a severe international disadvantage due to relatively increased capital costs.[64] It was these locally and nationally oriented banks who initiated the unified national bargaining position, encompassing parliament, government, supervisory agencies, and all three banking industry sub-sectors. German negotiators subsequently pursued – successfully – the objective of an approach to credit risk calculation that avoided any disadvantages for the small- to medium-sized and rather less transnationally oriented banks, thereby altering the Basel Committee's approach significantly. The successful position ensured that external ratings were used only in a less encompassing manner, and a second IRB approach was introduced, which allowed almost all German banks its application (the F-IRB approach).

The actors achieved the unified German position via three domestic channels: first, the regulatory agencies, in particular the BaKred,[65] where regulatees voiced their demands in personal meetings;[66] second, the federal ministry, which also conducted a series of personal meetings, and to which formal written correspondence was directed;[67] and, thirdly, via the finance committee of the German Bundestag.[68] The supervisory authorities responded to this pressure and altered their bargaining position in Basel. Moreover, especially the DSGV (Deutscher Sparkassen- und Giroverband, German Association of Savings Banks), the national association of local, public banks (Börsen-Zeitung 1999a, b), but also other associations contacted members of parliament from the conservative parties CDU/CSU,[69] which then put the topic on the committee's agenda – ultimately resulting in a joint decision by the Bundestag that strengthened the position of German negotiators in Basel.[70] In sum, the widely attributed feature of consensual decision making in German politics (see e.g. Busch 2005) resulted in a distinct political process that had far-reaching international implications. The long established formal integration of all banking associations into the parliamentary committee's decision making processes on all legislative activity directed at the banking sector has created established bonds and informal rules (Busch 2009, 89–99, 111–123). Therefore, in light of a regulatory activity like the Basel II consultations, even though the parliament has no formal authority, the committee was instrumentalised as a forum for the crafting of a consensual, unified German position.[71]

Three other important Basel II issues were changed as a result of the above dynamic. First is the preferential 50 per cent risk weight for commercial collateralised loans;[72] this privileged treatment met strong opposition in the Basel Committee, but was insistently demanded by the Bundestag, as this form of financing was considered essential for the functioning of the SME or Mittelstand[73] business model, which has a crucial role in the German political economy.

Second, German banks, supported by their supervisors and the Ministry of Finance, successfully opposed the suggested capital deduction of equity investments in commercial entities from the regulatory capital measure.[74] Since it was a common feature of the 'Deutschland AG' that banks hold cross-investments on a long-term, continuous basis (Höpner 2003, Höpner & Krempel 2004), the deduction (in contrast to a rather mild risk weighted capital charge on such investments) would have resulted in considerable additional capital needs for German banks. In response, the Basel Committee developed an alternative approach, where only such commercial investments would be deducted that surpass a certain 'materiality' level, while all investments below that threshold would receive a 150 per cent risk weight. Nevertheless, German actors, which opposed both elements of this proposal, upheld their opposition, and succeeded partially: the risk weight for investments below materiality levels was reduced to 100 per cent, while the less favourable deduction was introduced for those assets above materiality levels.[75]

Third, German small and medium sized banks successfully aimed for supervisory recognition of the higher level of granularity within their portfolios (many smaller credits) through a risk weight adjustment for portfolios with high granularity, as well as the introduction of a separate portfolio for retail credits.[76]

In sum, BaKred and the Ministry could report the success in enforcing German positions – in particular the foundational IRB approach, the

50 per cent risk weight for commercial collateralised loans, and a consideration of introducing a beneficial capital treatment for banks with highly granular portfolios – to the parliament's committee. The agency and Ministry both emphasised the crucial role played by the Bundestag's resolution in strengthening Germany's position in the Basel Committee negotiations.[77]

Thus, due to German – as well as other European countries' – domestic opposition, US supervisors had to retreat from their initial position in a twofold manner: first, they had to abandon the internal models approach and to agree on the IRB option preferred by the majority of Basel Committee members. Second, with regard to the standardised approach, instead of the sole reliance on external ratings from credit rating agencies, the additional F-IRB approach, which permitted medium-sized European banks to apply internal ratings, was introduced as well.

The second main pattern during this episode was the changing balance among regulators and regulatees in the transnational network. Transnational banking associations accepted previously opposed rules that were favoured by regulators, and adjusted their positions in order to achieve at least a partial supervisory recognition of their sophisticated risk management techniques. The IIF, however, had a substantial influence on the outcome of the second consultative paper. Its original suggestions of a threefold approach to credit risk calculation, as well as a threefold credit risk mitigation approach, are largely resembled in the Basel Committee's compromise proposal. ISDA also attempted to reconcile its interest in the supervisory recognition of its members' advanced risk management techniques with the BCBS proposals. The association promoted its evolutionary approaches to the recognition of internal portfolio models for credit risk calculation, and further advanced instruments concerning internal rating and credit risk mitigation techniques – the BCBS integrated these approaches rather modestly.[78]

The success of introducing compromise proposals is clearly visible in the table on this episode's main policy outcomes. Beyond the evolutionary IRB approach, the integration of optionality for the calculation of capital reductions through credit risk mitigating effects from collateral can be seen as a major success – which can also be found in the suggestions of the Institute of International Finance (2000). The increased recognition of collateral and derivatives as capital requirement reducing instruments mirrored the voiced interests of the sector in general, and the transnational banks in particular. These outcomes reflect considerable capture by internationally active banks.

Nevertheless, in sum, the second draft of the Accord still reflected the supervisory community's compromise more than it did the preferences of the banking community. The many issues designed in accordance with the supervisors' interests support this claim: the rather restrictive credit risk mitigation rules on netting arrangements and guarantees, as well as the denial of double default recognition;[79] the explicit rejection to recognise internal portfolio models, instead sticking to internal ratings based methods; the globally consolidated supervision (including sub-consolidation) without a lead regulator model for transnational banks; the retaining of unexpected and expected losses as the basis for capital calculations; the extensive pillar three requirements for mandatory information disclosures to supervisors and the public.

Policy outcomes and influential actors

CP-2 exhibits a compromise between the interests pushing for transnationally harmonized innovation and those aiming for protection of domestic competitiveness: the US push for a quick agreement was blocked by a concerted German veto position in the BCBS. Therefore, a substantial amount of very specific German demands were integrated into the second consultative proposal. At the same time, several compromises were negotiated in the Basel Committee's working groups that reflected the general preferences of the supervisory community and integrated the suggestions for compromise by the international banking groups. These encompassing and complex compromises were the dawn of widespread optionality and technological depth.[80]

Overall, the second period is characterised by a high number of newly introduced issues that were integrated into the second consultative paper. This is reflected in the many topics in Table 4.6. Table 4.6, like Table 4.5 for episode 1, lists the crucial integrated/rejected issues for each actor. As in the previous period, the episode's table reports the integration/rejection in this specific episode, and not in the entire process. Accordingly, an actor can be highly successful during this amendment stage, but be defeated in tough negotiations during the final episode of reaching an agreement.

In sum, this second episode has demonstrated how the Basel Committee became a transnational pivot – balancing pressure from national competition state coalitions led by the respective political principal on the one hand, and the influence from transnationally oriented banks as important cooperators, but also opponents, on the other. This is, however, less reflected in the integration and rejection rates of the BCBS in Figure 4.2, which is rather indicative of the

Table 4.6 Actors' integrated and rejected interests in Basel II, episode 2

Actor type	Crucial integrated positions	Crucial rejected positions	Integration rate	Rejection rate
Global political principal (G7)	– Consolidated supervision of conglomerates – Diffusion of regulatory principles to emerging markets through IMF and World Bank	– Higher capital charges on emerging market firms	3% (25%; 2)	6% (75%; 6)
Transgovernmental network (BCBS)	– (Sub-)consolidated supervision of conglomerates – Operational risk capital charge – Market discipline via mandatory pillar 3 disclosure – Encompassing IRB eligibility criteria	– No favourable credit risk weight for commercial collateralised loans (50%) – Interest rate risk capital charge	9% (30%; 7)	17%(70%; 16)
Transnationally oriented banks	– Enhanced recognition of internal risk measurement techniques – Enhanced recognition of credit risk mitigation techniques	– Encompassing eligibility criteria for IRB application – Lesser extent of mandatory disclosures – No sub-consolidated supervision	42% (51%; 32)	33%(49%; 31)

Actor	Policy issues	Value 1	Value 2
Domestic political principals			
US Politicians		–% (–%; 0)	–% (–%; 0)
GE Politicians	– Parallel partial employment of all credit risk measurement approaches	12% (53%; 9)	9% (47%; 8)
	– F-IRB introduction (reduced focus on external ratings)		
	– Favourable credit risk weight for commercial collateralised loans (50%)		
	– Exception clauses for banks' commercial shareholding		
Regulatory agents			
US Regulators		3% (22%; 2)	7% (78%; 7)
GE Regulators		9% (47%; 7)	9% (53%; 8)
Nationally/locally oriented banks			
US Banks		–% (–%; 0)	–% (–%; 0)
GE Banks	– F-IRB introduction (reduced focus on external ratings)	22%(49%; 17)	19%(51%; 18)
	– Exception clauses for banks' commercial shareholding		
	– Risk weight reductions for portfolio granularity		

Notes: Integration/Rejection rate = first value depicts percentage of actor i's integrated/rejected positions in relation to all integrated/rejected positions of episode 2; values in brackets: first value describes actor i's integrated/rejected positions in relation to all positions of actor i, second value depicts the absolute count of integrated/rejected positions of actor i; based on coded policy issues, where only those issues are integrated that were coded at least twice; in sum 109 issues.

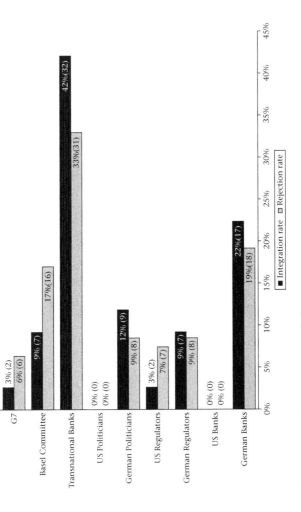

Figure 4.2 Integration and rejection rates in episode 2

Notes: Integration/Rejection rate = percentage of actor i's integrated/rejected positions in relation to all integrated/rejected positions of episode 2 (76 integrated, 94 rejected); values in brackets = number of integrated/rejected proposals.

Source: Own calculations based on correlational content analysis.

many compromises that had to be made. The Basel Committee's continued influential role is revealed by the qualitative evidence of Table 4.6; the Committee's success is mirrored in the high amount of the crucial policy issues that the BCBS kept in the second consultative paper. The consolidated and sub-consolidated supervision of financial conglomerates (i.e. the encompassing risk and capital calculations for large financial conglomerates) as well as the introduction of capital charges for operational and extreme interest rate risks were introduced despite the industry's opposition.

At the domestic regulatory regime level, US supervisors were facing pressures to adapt regulation, which they were capable of enforcing through the transgovernmental network. US success is mirrored in its ability to maintain the overall three pillar structure and the corresponding basic supervisory principles as cornerstones of a new Accord as well as the deepened reliance on banks' internal risk management and measurement capacities.

Germany's competition state coalitions, however, provided a countervailing force: German actors, at odds during the agenda setting episode, were capable of crafting a unified position to be negotiated in Basel; this was achieved through coordination within the parliamentary finance committee, where positions were openly debated among supervisors, ministerial staff, parliamentarians and the industry. The driving interest behind this unifying force was the German Mittelstand and the importance of the banking sector, which led to a unified national position that encompassed highly detailed proposals for the new Accord, that, moreover, were successfully pursued in Basel. As a result, the German negotiating position was very strong and achieved its key goals. Both, the relatively high integration, but also rejection, rates of German nationally/locally oriented banks and political principals in Table 4.6 and Figure 4.2 reflect their active role and substantial success. Within the transnational regulatory network, supervisors had to accommodate the emerging domestic pressures.

At the same time, however, the transnational banking community was able to capture the process by providing technologically advanced compromise solutions, designed according to those regulatees' preferences. They set the agenda for the technical implementation of the IRB approaches as well as the framework for credit risk mitigation instruments, as Table 4.6 outlines. The high integration (but also rejection) rates in Figure 4.2 represent the many technical issues of substantial impact that were developed by the transnational associations of large, internationally active banks. The supervisors, who, as a network, had to steer through these pressures, maintained many of their initial regulatory approaches, but integrated a wide variety of options and specificities. Nevertheless, as Table 4.6 documents, the second draft of the Accord was still closer to the supervisory community's compromise than to the preferences of the banking community. In sum, the Basel Committee became a transnational pivot by balancing pressure from domestic coalitions led by the respective political principal as well as the influence exerted by transnationally oriented banks as important cooperators and opponents.

The global political principal, the G7, maintained its distance from the regulation of banks in developed jurisdictions. Instead, the G7 politicians focused on the stabilisation of the world economy, while promoting the diffusion of best practices in financial regulation to emerging markets. The focus described in episode 1 was further advanced: at their summits in Cologne (June 1999) and Okinawa (July 2000), the G7 decided to strengthen the capacity of the IFIs to exercise the diffusion of regulatory practices to, and control of, emerging markets.[81] As outlined in Chapter 2, this implied the global separation of tasks between the IFIs as supervisors and the BCBS (and others) as regulatory standard setter. Therefore, the IFIs monitor the implementation of the 12 key financial standards, which are developed by several transgovernmental and transnational regulatory networks (Mosley 2009). One of these standards was the Basel Core Principles on Bank Supervision.[82] Thus, the G7 promoted the use of these instruments to diffuse regulatory principles and reduce international financial instability due to spillovers from emerging markets.

Episode 3, January 2001–April 2003: process up to the third consultative paper

Throughout the course of episode 3, from January 2001 until the third consultative paper (CP-3)[83] in April 2003, the transnational supervisory network attempted to immunise itself against domestic interference by secluding the technical work in the BCBS working group structure. Thereby, it integrated most of the potential veto positions in domestic and transnational arenas to satisfy veto players and rescue the overall goal of a new Accord. Consequently, CP-3 would grow to 226 pages (an increase of more than 50 per cent compared to CP-2), with unprecedented technical formulas and options.

During the third episode, the process in the Committee transformed even further into one of a global policy process: constant evaluation, negotiation, and redrafting. The BCBS working groups issued several working papers to channel the highly technical discussions around the globe, carried out two impact studies, and adjusted the agreement's content accordingly. Three phases can be identified. The first, lasting until June 2001, was the realisation of opposition in many jurisdictions and the international banking community, and the consequential extension of the timetable, adding yet another consultative paper. Even after the relaxation of the timetable, the second phase depicts the stagnation of the negotiations, in December 2001 leading to the further postponement of CP-3 to an unspecified date later than the former early 2002 deadline. Especially during this period the BCBS working groups had to elaborate highly technical solutions to overcome the road blocks to agreement.[84] In July 2002, the standstill was overcome when the Basel Committee presented a compromise solution with a refined timetable. From July 2002 until April 2003, secluded work was undertaken in the transnational network of supervisors with considerable assistance from international banks. To make sure that opposition to the third proposal would not be as severe as before, preparation, realisation and evaluation of a quantitative impact study, as well as the resulting recalibration of the Accord's parameters, were discussed in these groups.

Overall, episode 3 witnessed the simultaneous increase in pressure from domestic and transnational stakeholders. On the one hand, it revealed the same pattern regarding the intervention of domestic principals as episode 2, but in an intensifying manner: with repeated opposition from the German principal-regulatee coalition, as well as the parallel emergence of such a coalition in the US. On the other hand, the transgovernmental network increasingly integrated the transnationally oriented banks and attempted to isolate them from domestic intervention.

Political process

I begin by outlining the German processes, followed by those in the US, and those in the BCBS. Even though, in the meantime, some disputes had emerged among the actors of the national regulatory regime, they were able to return to a unified negotiation position – which the German delegation pursued decidedly.[85] A four-step process underlay this dynamic: as during the first two episodes, the domestic regulator-regulatee coalition already ensured the integration of several national industry specific interests into the negotiation process; second, after this proved to be unsatisfactory for the banking sector, the nationally oriented regulatees reactivated their coalition with the domestic political (informal) principal, i.e. the parliamentary committee, which, thirdly, mandated the regulatory agent to increase engagement in the Basel negotiations on behalf of German banks and the Mittelstand; fourth, the supervisory agencies, while following this demand to a great degree, counteracted the principal's engagement by warning that further insistence on specific German positions would threaten the successful adoption of Basel II in its entirety.

The banking industry was highly supportive of the currently negotiated state of the Accord, and agreed that most of the initial disadvantages in earlier drafts were removed. In particular, problems for the German Mittelstand were evaluated as being nullified. Nevertheless, banks were still concerned with several currently contested issues and demanded unmitigated negotiation regarding these positions. The banking sector continued to follow a strategy that aimed at reactivating political principals by convincing them of the devastating competitive disadvantages on German banks and industry structure, due to national industry specific repercussions of the Basel rules.[86]

Accordingly, politicians were still concerned about disadvantages for the German Mittelstand, and some parliamentarians voiced scepticism regarding the willingness/ability of supervisors to effectively pursue German banks' and SMEs' interests, had the parliament and government not intervened in the process. Already at an early stage, in May 2001, a consensus was achieved among parliamentarians and industry: a compromise on several issues aimed at protecting the German banking structure, in particular small and locally oriented banks, and preventing negative repercussions on SMEs.[87]

Nevertheless, discontent remained between supervisors on the one hand, and industry and parliamentarians on the other. While the banking sector, supported by the parliamentary committee, demanded even more favourable conditions for small banks and SME-related lending, the German negotiators, BaKred and Bundesbank were opposed to this. They explained that the future capital charges for SME businesses would already be beneficial (compared to German rules in place at that time) rather than having negative repercussions.[88] Throughout a series of meetings,[89] regulators and regulatees, as well as the Bundestag finance committee, developed a unified German position once again, with only minor differences among the actors. This is reflected in a two-tiered explication of unified German interests: a business associational compromise with a highly detailed position paper that integrated all German banking associations and their positions (Zentraler Kreditausschuss 2001);[90] and a political compromise explicated in the Bundestag's motion for a unified German negotiation position (which was supportive of the main positions of the banking sector).[91]

The supervisory agencies, while following this demand to a great degree, counteracted the principal's engagement by warning that further insistence on specific German positions would threaten the successful adoption of Basel II entirely – which the supervisors argued would not only mean less international financial stability, but would also hurt German interests. In March 2002, the BaKred negotiator reported that Germany was aiming for a quick agreement on the Accord before momentum was lost. Jochen Sanio, the BaKred president, reported that changes in the supervision of German banks were already under way, which is why the implementation of Basel II was considered particularly important. This shows how the diffusion from transgovernmental networks into domestic politics is transmitted through network cooperation rather than formal agreements.[92]

The high level of political attention towards the claimed negative repercussions on the German economy, and the consequential activation of the political principals' attention and control over regulatory agents, was demonstrated by the direct intervention of Chancellor Schröder in 2002: the meeting of Gerhard Schröder and then BCBS chairman William McDonough in July 2002 finally convinced the other BCBS members about the seriousness of the German political veto threat. Less than one week later, the Basel Committee agreed on the compromise, integrating most of the German Mittelstand-related demands into the Accord proposal.[93] BaFin president Sanio is cited,[94] and repeats this evaluation in the Bundestag finance committee, as saying that the Chancellor's intervention clarified the seriousness of the German veto threats, which had been doubted in the BCBS prior to the intervention since political lobbying had not occurred in any other Basel member state at that time.[95]

Accordingly, the intermediate negotiation compromise in July 2002 reflected most of the crucial German positions.[96] The consensus among Basel Committee members on the treatment of SMEs mirrored almost exactly the German position:[97] all SME borrowers below 50 million euros in annual sales received reduced risk weights different from those of larger firms – the exposures to SMEs were charged with capital requirements that were, on average, 10 per cent lower relative to credits to larger firms; below the threshold of one million euros of the overall exposure to one SME borrower, such credits could be treated under the IRB retail portfolio treatment; furthermore, this portfolio treatment was made available under the standardised approach. A further point where

German interests were met was the introduction of a second type of retail portfolio category, with a distinct risk weight scale which was specifically directed towards including small SME credits (single loans below one million euros to one SME).

Moreover, the compromise agreement on maturity add-on charges[98] comfortably accommodated the German position as well: first, while A-IRB banks had to apply it, F-IRB banks' obligations were made subject to the domestic supervisor's discretion whether to implement this requirement within his jurisdiction; second, another domestic choice between options was provided by the permitted exemption of smaller domestic firms (with sales and assets of less than 500 million euros) from the maturity framework – in these jurisdictions, all exposures would be assumed to have an average maturity of 2.5 years (as under the F-IRB approach).

Putting the pieces of the extensive German deliberation during this third episode together reveals the success story of a consensus-oriented political economy and the resulting unified jurisdictional position in global standard-setting. German consensus was encompassing and pervasive. The detailed position papers integrated all bank associations and their positions. With very few exceptions, the German banking sector was capable of crafting a unified position on a very detailed basis.[99] The extensive level of detail and specificity of the 150 page compendium of ZKA recommendations – almost every single paragraph of the consultative document is subject to comment and suggestions for improvement – depicts the coordinated German policy process. Every single sectoral interest was included to achieve a unified position, which is in stark contrast to the US industry, where three banking organisations, plus several other banking-related business associations and several individual banks have provided separate, comparatively brief and general statements (most around 10 to 20, but all below 50 pages).[100] Moreover, as outlined above, the Bundestag (2001) issued a unified political position of all authorities, based on which unequivocal negotiations were pursued.

In contrast, the domestic process in the United States reveals a pluralist dynamic. There, broad political deliberation and congressional interference began more than two years after the German process. Moreover, US politics had not been interested or involved in the process before mid-2002 – as pointed out by the German negotiator of the Bundesbank, referring to discussions with the US Fed. The Fed had expressed considerable concern that active participation by Congress in the process, and consequently Basel becoming part of the political agenda, would make an agreement improbable.[101]

This attempt at protecting its regulatory turf against political intervention was not successful in the end. The US process moved the regulatory regime from the shadow of hierarchy into the brighter light of congressional politics and underwent three main steps: first, after rising bank concerns with the new proposals, the Fed, the OCC and the Federal Deposit Insurance Corporation (FDIC) started an active campaign to integrate this criticism through regulator-regulatee consultations; second, some dissatisfied banks – a coalition opposed to the operational risk charge and a group of community banks – activated the principal (congressional) attention, in which, third, an inter-agency conflict became obvious. As the coming paragraphs demonstrate, the US process in episode three meant the inception of intense conflict in Congress that would determine most of the remaining Basel II negotiations.

Since the US banks became concerned with several of the suggestions made in CP-2, their national supervisors started a broad discussion with the industry after the second consultative paper in January 2001. A week after the release by the Basel Committee, the three federal agencies of the Fed, OCC and FDIC issued a common questionnaire to the industry, in which they urged attention and solicited feedback. They directed the focus to some specific issues by addressing several particular questions that were mirrored in the banks' comments on CP-2. The Office of Thrift Supervision (OTS) followed this approach a few days later by sending the above questionnaire to their regulated entities and calling OTS regulatees to attention concerning the ongoing discussions about the second Basel Accord, and that this process might have a substantial impact on them.[102]

Yet, it proved impossible to advance the Basel II agenda at the Fed's preferred speed while integrating all industry interests at the same time. Accordingly, the agencies eventually accepted another consultative episode in Basel, rather than pushing the Accord through in this second round. American supervisors extended the negotiation deadline in the Basel Committee in order to mitigate conflicts directly with the industry, without integrating politicians.[103] While this strategy had worked since the beginning of the Basel II negotiations, with increasing clarity and encompassing character, the proposal created more substance for contention among US regulatees, who then voiced concerns with congressional members.

Two coalitions activated the House of Representatives: first, a broad coalition rejected the design of the operational risk capital charge, because they preferred a pillar two instead of pillar one approach – the only issue rejected by all industry associations.[104] Second, small and local banks, as well as the OTS, were concerned that the application of the Basel II rules would result in competitive advantages due to lower capital requirements for Basel II banks (i.e. those few banks that were expected to be capable of and forced to applying the Basel II rules).[105] The fear was that this could lead to further sector consolidation due to the Basel II banks' ability to offer cheaper products, as well as the excess capital (due to lower capital requirements) these banks had ready for the acquisition of smaller banks.[106]

Political awareness evolved through two House hearings, the first taking place in October 2002 and the second in February 2003. The first hearing documents a discourse among political, regulatory and industrial actors about the EU's Financial Services Action Plan (EU-FSAP) and the resulting consequences for US financial markets and firms. Although not on this hearing's agenda (and until then Basel II had not been considered by Congress in any documented manner), the meeting mirrors the rise of political awareness concerning potentially negative consequences of the renewed capital Accord on US banks and securities firms. The emergence was mainly due to the conflict surrounding the operational risk capital charge, which in the US would have applied to banks but not securities firms, and therefore would have tilted the domestic level playing field in markets where banks and securities firms compete.[107] The domestic competitive disadvantage for US banks vis-á-vis their competitors from the securities industry gave rise to the Basel II political discourse within US Congress.[108]

The driving actors formed a coalition strongly opposed to the operational risk capital charge. The allegedly independent commentary of the consultancy firm Federal Financial Analytics gave rise to concerns from the New York representative Mrs. Maloney that

> these international standards ... are putting our very strong, high-performing capital markets at a disadvantage. And I guess this is a question I probably should be asking the Fed or the Comptroller, what steps are we taking in our overview to make sure that our businesses are not put at a disadvantage, and our financial institutions?

The argument appears to be a pretext since the discussed facts point rather in the contrary direction, as was clarified by an expert in the same meeting. This hearing reflects the starting point of US political discourse on Basel II. The emergence was due to strategic agenda setting by the affected industry.[109]

Two considerable developments in the aftermath of the meeting support this perspective: first, Carolyn Maloney, a representative from the Wall Street district New York, raised the issue and investigated whether US supervisory agencies are protecting the interests of American banks and securities firms. This eventually resulted in a series of political debates that started with congressional committee meetings in February and June 2003;[110] second, Federal Financial Analytics represented the Financial Guardian Group, a group of banks opposed to the operational risk capital charge methods, during the remainder of the Basel negotiations (in domestic as well as transnational context – position papers were introduced with Congress as with the BCBS).[111]

The coalition opposed to the operational risk charge was capable of activating Representatives in the House to voice their interests that were not heard by the supervisors, which resulted in a second hearing, a Subcommittee hearing devoted entirely to the Basel II issue.[112] In this meeting, chairman Bachus outlined that several industry stakeholders were calling on Congress to control the regulatory agencies:

> Nonetheless, some of the banks have indicated to me, through their representatives, that they are in fact tremendously concerned about Basel. I understand that banks that have reservations about the U.S. position are hesitant to object openly to a regulatory agency that exercises power over them.

The emerging congressional scrutiny is, again, demonstrated by the New York representative Carolyn Maloney, who, in the same Congress meeting, said:

> This is tremendously important to me. The financial system is the main employer in the district that I represent. And they are domestic banks, international banks. And I am concerned that there be some type of way, that either with this capital charge or the operational charge or whatever, we could be placed or even with regulatory, more severe regulatory oversight, placed at a disadvantage.

She even threatened the supervisory agencies in a letter, saying that the opposition to the operational risk charge could be numerous in Congress and result in a considerable delay of the process.[113]

In sum, Congress was beginning to use its control powers over the regulatory agencies due to domestic regulatees' ability to overcome the threshold of political attention. Once on the agenda of the House of Representatives, however, the Congressmen proved their non-existent familiarity with the Basel Committee: the specialised members of the finance committee were unaware of procedural and institutional features concerning the BCBS and its work.[114]

Surprised about the substantial meaning of the Basel II initiative and the diffuse US regulatory process, the first hearing in the House was mainly concerned with action to clear up ineffective intra-agency governance issues and stop illegitimate agenda setting by the Fed, in particular the New York Fed. Committee members Frank and Oxley voiced tremendous concerns over the disagreement between the supervisory agencies on several policy issues within Basel II, as well as the domestic process for developing the US position. In this regard, the Federal Reserve's supremacy, and particularly the agenda setting role of the New York Fed, not being legitimised by President or Congress, was criticised. Especially concerned was representative Frank:

> [T]his is a profound issue for me. You three [the agencies Fed, FDIC, OCC] are appointed by the President of the United States and confirmed by the United States Senate. The New York Fed, as capable a technical institution as it is, is, as are all the regional banks, a self-perpetuating institution with no democratic involvement in the appointment of the head.[115]

A particularly fierce controversy developed between Congressman Frank and Fed Board Governor Ferguson, where the former even pointed towards deception by the Fed. Along with this suspicion, Frank voiced concerns over the exclusion of the positions of other supervisors (OCC, FDIC and OTS), and the consequential disadvantage for smaller and regional banks. In sum, the congressional committee was generally in favour of an enhanced Basel agreement to regulate international banks and it commended the agencies, in particular the Fed and the New York Fed (the last explicitly by the committee chairman Oxley), for having 'spearheaded the reforms of the Basel Accord'. Nevertheless, several concerns were voiced, mostly over the competitiveness of and regulatory burden for US banks as well as the separated negotiation position of the US agencies.

During the heated debates in the House of Representatives, the divide among US supervisors was brought to the surface. A conflict between the Fed, as regulator of internationally active banks, and the supervisors of domestically oriented banks, in particular the OCC, became apparent.[116] While the Fed was pushing its domestic agenda through the Basel Committee by using its predominant positions in the transgovernmental network and the US regulatory regime, the OCC opposed the high speed and overall character of Basel II as it had emerged from transnational compromises. The conflict had begun prior to this hearing, but it surfaced here and became a major US domestic conflict that would alter the dynamic of the US political process and, as a result, postpone the transnational negotiations. The fourth Basel episode will shed more light on this.

In summarising the emergence of domestic political conflict in the United States and the activation of the political principal, it is important to highlight why the US responded so late. The Fed had pushed for internationally harmonised, improved regulation of internationally active banks, mainly as a response to national problems with these institutions' activities – circumventing domestic disputes. This led to opposition in other BCBS jurisdictions, where the proposed rules would have negatively affected profitability. As a result, in order to integrate non-US banking system characteristics, the agreement became increasingly complex and encompassing, which then put the US industry in an unfortunate situation. In response, the disadvantaged American actors activated the US-based veto options at their disposal.

In many respects, US preferences were successfully integrated into CP-3, of which two concerns were of crucial relevance: first, the operational risk capital charge realisation through a pillar two instead of pillar one approach – the only issue rejected by all industry associations – was de facto achieved; while the AMA was officially designed as a pillar one approach, the final design of CP-3 and the latter framework revealed more pillar two characteristics, i.e. internal risk management and individual qualitative supervision, than quantitative pillar one restrictions. Second, the now proposed securitisation rules, the refinement of which was a major innovation of this consultative episode, largely reflected US market practices. It already met several of the previously voiced criticisms of the American industry, which feared the slowing of the development of this, at that time crucial innovative, market segment in the United States. US banks, however, were less successful in achieving other goals, namely reducing the overall level of capital charges and adjusting the approach of consolidated supervision through a functionally based building block approach,[117] instead of extending the 'predominantly engaged in banking' definition of the BCBS to all firms in a financial conglomerate with substantial banking activities.

It is noteworthy that no political executive intervention by the President or Treasury is reported until the very end of Basel II (see implementation discussion). Furthermore, the active political principal, Congress, intervened comparatively late. For a long time, regulatory agents were successfully playing their principals and attempting to solve the conflicts with regulatees without the activation of politicians. Nevertheless, the evolution of domestic opposition was becoming a main road block for transnational coordination.

In response to the dissatisfaction with the second Basel II proposal in many jurisdictions and the international banking community, the BCBS had to adapt its strategy. In response to more than 250 received comments on CP-3, the Committee, after an initial evaluation, announced in June 2001 that significant adjustments were considered necessary,[118] which included major cornerstones of the new Accord: the overall calibration of capital was to be kept unchanged for the average banks (applying the standardised approach), and aimed at providing incentives to apply IRB approaches – which implicitly meant reduced capital charges for such institutes; capital requirements for credit risks of F-IRB banks and operational risk charges should be reduced; risk weights on SME-credit exposures were to be lowered. Most importantly, a new timetable was envisaged, that introduced a further, third, consultative paper for early 2002, which adjusted the deadlines accordingly: finalisation during 2002 and implementation in 2005.[119]

In a later, second response, as the aforementioned domestic politicisation and simultaneous protest among international banks threatened the entire endeavour, the Basel Committee began, again, to craft another compromise solution. By further stretching the timetable and incorporating crucial concerns of domestic veto players, it calmed opposition on these fronts. By isolating work on the Accord's design within its dense working group structure and strongly including the international banking community in this structure, the transnationally oriented regulatees were integrated.

As a result, the transgovernmental supervisory network deepened its role as coordinator of conflicting domestic interests and transnational stakeholders. After identification of the key challenges, these were delegated to different working groups and task forces, each of which was constituted by a mix of employees from national supervisory agencies and coordinated its work with input from the banking community. The division of labour among the numerous working groups of the BCBS is mirrored in a Committee's statement, according to which the groups

> have been exploring the potential implications of several possible modifications to the Committee's proposals ..., and are now seeking

to obtain feedback from the industry about the potential impact of [the newly proposed] modifications.[120]

The working groups designed regulatory standards for crucial aspects of Basel II, which would be merely adopted by the Basel Committee itself later on. Technical capacity played an important role in defining the outcomes on such decisive issues as operational risk, information disclosure (pillar three), securitisation, credit risk calibration, etc.[121]

The two international banking associations IIF and ISDA were particularly influential in affecting the supervisory work. The BCBS and IIF especially proved to be a network with a combination of epistemic and capture-like strings. Corresponding empirical support is delivered by the adoption of the modified spectrum approach as suggested by the IIF – regarding which the association reports the intense cooperation of supervisors and industry in detailing the Accord:[122]

> In particular, the Basel Committee's adoption of a modified 'Spectrum Approach' for constructing an internal ratings based approach to regulatory capital as recommended by the IIF last year is particularly welcomed and represents a very substantial step in the right direction of developing a risk-based regulatory capital framework.

Moreover, ISDA and IIF represented an industry network in which a separation of the information provision to supervisors among internationally active financial institutions was exercised. This is reflected in the specific working groups established to provide recommendations to the BCBS. The ISDA – which mostly includes banks, but is focused on trading-related interests, rather than traditional banking business – had working groups on trading book and counter-party risks in derivative transactions, while the banks, represented by the IIF, worked on credit and operational risk issues (two working groups, one on capital adequacy, one on operational risk). Where the ISDA focused strongly on those aspects that were related to their core business, namely derivative markets, the IIF represented interests in issues related to banking business.[123]

Thus, the Basel Committee worked increasingly as a forum that coordinated the work of several working groups, each carrying out specific technical deliberations to achieve compromises on contested issues. As the OCC's Comptroller of the Currency Hawke (2002, 10) explained:

I am concerned about the enormous complexity of the proposal. With great respect for the various task forces and working groups that have conscientiously produced extremely thoughtful papers, I would be amazed if every member of the Committee has been able to plow through the details of every paper. I'm frank to say that I have not. I suppose it's a character flaw of mine that as soon as I see the symbol for an indefinite integral on a page, my attention starts to flag. Unfortunately there are many pages of complex formulas in the Committee's recent work.

An important example for the Basel Committee's effort to find a compromise with the industry on contested cornerstones of the agreement is provided by the *Joint Accounting Task Force: Models Task Force Working Group*, which elaborated whether capital charges should be based upon unexpected and expected losses (UL and EL) (supervisors' position) or solely unexpected losses.[124] Their proposed solution was a compromise that had initially been suggested by several associations of the banking sector as a second best solution, given that supervisors would not support the industry's favoured position of sole UL based capital charges: it maintained basing the new capital Accord on UL *and* EL, but increased the range of provisions that were recognised as eligible capital.[125] This meant reduced capital charges, but in a manner that allowed for the adjustment of the Accord without changing accounting rules and capital definitions, which was a major interest of supervisors. Furthermore, supposedly it kept the reductions smaller than under the option promoted by the industry.

Even though the transgovernmental network and bank associations worked intensely, nevertheless the new timetable still proved to be too ambitious when the BCBS negotiations stagnated again in November 2001.[126] The results of the second Quantitative Impact Study (QIS-2)[127] revealed that the current calibration would place a burden on internationally active banks to an unexpected degree, which led to widespread resistance.[128] Moreover, contrary to the BCBS's announced commitment to keep capital requirements in total at a constant level, the QIS-2 indicated that for all three approaches (standard, F-IRB, A-IRB) the capital charges would increase significantly, which was particularly pronounced for institutes applying the F-IRB-approach – 'it [the BCBS] did not seem to understand the effects of its own proposals' (Tarullo 2008, 112).

In response to the QIS-2 results, the unintended and unexpected results, which came as a shock to the supervisors (Tarullo 2008, 112), the BCBS decided that the Accord needed substantial recalibration. It announced an additional QIS-2.5, and outlined three starting points for recalibration that should be evaluated within this study: a modified risk weight curve, an increased recognition of physical collateral and receivables, and modified risk curves for retail exposures, in particular residential mortgages.[129]

Furthermore, reacting to the unexpected QIS-2 outcomes and the widespread criticism, the Basel Committee once more chose a strategy of immunising the work of the transgovernmental network from threatening criticism, while simultaneously incorporating the main stakeholders from the international banking community to re-draft the compromise. For this purpose, the Committee solicited industry feedback on the suggested starting points for adaptation. Furthermore, it announced the postponement of CP-3 to an unspecified date later than the early 2002 deadline.[130] This 'quality assurance phase' (Basel Committee on Banking Supervision 2001j) reflected a further intensification of the consultative strategy to rely on the network of working groups, with their particular supervisor-industry connections: now, a complete detailing of specific issues should be undertaken, followed by a QIS-evaluation, and only then followed by the final consultative paper. Moreover, the creation of the Accord Implementation Group (AIG) was announced, in order to begin the strengthening of information exchange about implementation strategies between supervisors.

The QIS-2.5 results that were announced on 25 June 2002, however, still showed a minor increase in overall capital levels to about 10 per cent, with low levels of variance.[131] Further detailed work in the Committee's working groups and a new impact study, QIS-3, was announced to test several approaches across a broad portfolio of banks – supervisors wanted to be clear about the results of their proposed new rules. Based upon the adjustments, QIS-3 was designed to provide clarity on the consequences of the Basel II proposals, but this time results were to be evaluated within the Committee, and only then should the new consultative document be published.[132] Therefore, between July 2002 and April 2003, the transnational network of supervisors and transnationally oriented regulatees intensified technical cooperation to reach an agreement satisfying both sides. Preparation, realisation, evaluation of QIS-3 and the resulting recalibration were kept closely within this structure, in order to reduce public intervention. Even though QIS-3 was published in May 2003, shortly after the issuing of the third consultative paper, the insights were already incorporated into the proposal through recalibration of several specific parameters and variables.[133]

In sum, isolation was possible within the network of working groups and task forces, where specific elements of the negotiation were each delegated to a separate, specialised group. This strategy was deepened through the extensive back-testing efforts within the supervisor-industry network, ensuring that no premature consultative proposal was issued – which could have halted the process through raised national opposition, that could have activated domestic veto players. While the collaborative network structure of the transnational community existed beforehand, and deepened during the second episode, throughout the third period the intensity and depth of collaboration increased. Conflict with stakeholders was integrated into this structure, rather than left outside, where domestic veto player activation would have made their work more complicated.

The solutions in CP-3 were compromises that in many instances reflected the abandonment of several positions by the Basel Committee that it had embraced in CP-2. These technical solutions, developed in the working groups and in close collaboration with the international banking associations, included issues of securitisation, credit risk mitigation instruments, calibration basis of capital requirements (UL/EL or UL) and mandatory disclosure requirements. Transnationally active banks, after having to give up several maximum demands like internal portfolio models, were able to capture the process incrementally during this episode. This partial success is exemplified by the creation of the Accord Implementation Group (AIG), designed to strengthen the information exchange about implementation strategies among supervisors. On the one hand, it reflects the interest of transnationally active banks that demanded globally consolidated supervision by a lead regulator.[134] On the other hand, given its highly informal nature, the clear exclusion of a lead regulator approach in Basel II, as well as the rejection of an ombudsman role for regulatory conflicts, CP-3 was by far not congruent with the transnationally oriented regulatees' positions. As episode four will show, however, this would move further towards the banks' interest, as pressure and challenges on the transnational network increased further.

A final word on G7 involvement summarises their inactivity on the matter: between July 2000 and July 2001, the previously reported activities (G7 2000) went on without a significant change in focus – IMF-based codes and standards and their institutionalised diffusion to emerging markets, offshore finance, and criminal abuse of the financial system. The supervision of G7 financial markets was not discussed in detail. Development topics were more prominent on the agendas of the heads of state/government and finance ministers. Between July 2001 and April 2003, the G7, and in particular their finance ministers, were preoccupied with the 'Combating Financing of Terrorism' agenda in response to the terrorist attacks of 11 September 2001. The comparatively low relevance of banking regulation is mirrored in the mere reference to vague principles, the emphasis on individual national action, and the complete exclusion of banking supervision from the agendas.[135]

Policy outcomes and influential actors

In sum, during episode 3, Basel II was altered and expanded tremendously as a result of the simultaneous pressure from competition state and transnational harmonization coalitions. While the German voice dynamic intensified during this period, the US domestic discourse began on a broad political basis, due to a simultaneously emerging, twofold conflict: first, nationally/locally oriented American banks became increasingly dissatisfied with the proposals, and therefore activated congressional principals; second, a conflict began between the Fed, as supervisor of internationally active banks, and the supervisors of domestically oriented banks, in particular the OCC. Since the attention of both Congress chambers was activated, they forced their regulatory agents to negotiate on behalf of the US banking system's competitiveness, which shifted the transnational interaction mode from network cooperation to international negotiation. In other words, the conflict between regulatees and supervisors, as well as among the federal agencies, altered the dynamic of the US political process and, as a result, delayed the transnational process by shifting the interaction mode in the Basel Committee further towards international negotiation.

On the other hand, the transgovernmental network increasingly integrated the transnationally oriented banks and attempted to isolate them from domestic intervention. Throughout the third period, the intensity and depth of collaboration in the BCBS working groups was increased and conflict with stakeholders was integrated into this structure. This mirrors the fear of additional domestic veto player activation complicating the deliberations even more.[136] The Basel Committee network developed more towards the pivot position of balancing the opposition of multiple jurisdictions and the international banking associations – in order to achieve an agreement at all. The result was an agreement full of options and risk calculation approaches

– suited to consider all national veto threatening positions, as well as the demands of transnational banks (in exchange for providing crucial information on how to draft the Accord).

The substantial participation of the Bundestag's parliamentary committee in the transnational regulatory process was unprecedented and turned out to be highly influential. In other words, Basel II's substantial impact has resulted in the adoption of preferences of domestic political actors that intervened in transnational regulatory politics.[137] This is mirrored in the high number of crucial integrated interests of Germany's nationally/locally oriented banks and politicians, as reported in Table 4.7; accordingly, CP-3 incorporated a substantial number of highly important issues related to beneficial conditions for SME-credits and small/local bank credit portfolios.

While German negotiators, with a unified national position as backup, were successful in integrating many of their very specific interests, US opposition emerged and activated principal scrutiny. The diverse activities in the pluralist political system took substantially longer to achieve a coalition that triggered the attention of politicians.

Then, however, the US domestic discourse emerged on a broad political basis. This was due to the dissatisfaction of actors in the US financial sector and their activation of political principals in Congress. Simultaneously adding to the initial political attention, a conflict between the Fed, as supervisor of internationally active banks, and the regulators of domestically oriented banks, in particular the OCC, invoked the attention of political principals. The integration rates of the US principals and American national banks depicted in Figure 4.3 do not reflect this process yet, since the inception of the opposition was too late to affect the third consultative paper in April 2003 substantially. The impact of the shifting political dynamic in the dominant BCBS jurisdiction did not take effect before episode 4 (see the following section). Yet, the conflict altered the dynamic of the US political process, which changed the transnational interaction mode more towards conflict, thereby delaying transnational negotiations.

In terms of policy, the number of deliberated and contested issues is remarkable. Even the politicised issues were high in number and the outcomes far from benefiting only one or two actors. Broad integration of most actors' crucial preferences is mirrored in the integration of most actors' crucial positions as reported in Table 4.7. The use of optionality was widened substantially in order to integrate specific national demands. Furthermore, the classification of risk weight functions and categories was widened, which also allowed for the

Table 4.7 Actors' integrated and rejected interests in Basel II, episode 3

Actor type	Crucial integrated positions	Crucial rejected positions	Integration rate	Rejection rate
Global political principal (G7)			–% (–%; 0)	–% (–%; 0)
Transgovernmental network (BCBS)	– Capital requirements on the basis of UL and EL – Strengthened institutionalisation of BCBS (AIG-group)	– Enhanced recognition of general provisioning reserves as tier 2 & 3 capital	14% (29%; 10)	14% (71%; 25)
Transnationally oriented banks	– Enhanced recognition of internal risk measurement and management capacities – Widened recognition of credit risk mitigation instruments and elimination of remaining risks floor (w-factor) – Strengthened institutionalisation of BCBS (AIG-group) – Enhanced recognition of general provisioning reserves as tier 2 & 3 capital	– Capital requirements solely on the basis of unexpected losses – Lead regulator – Harmonisation of accounting rules – Increased freedom in the management of internal capital calculations – Double-default effect recognition	23% (23%; 16)	31% (77%; 54)

(Continued)

Table 4.7 Continued

Actor type	Crucial integrated positions	Crucial rejected positions	Integration rate		Rejection rate
Domestic political principals					
US Politicians			–%	(–%; 0)	3% (100%; 5)
GE Politicians	– Beneficial treatment of SME and retail credits (SME retail portfolio; favourable SME risk weight formula)		6%	(31%; 4)	5% (69%; 9)
	– Exceptional clause allowing refraining from maturity capital charge on long-term credits				
Regulatory agents					
US Regulators	– Advanced Measurement Approach to operational risk		11%	(31%; 8)	10% (69%; 18)
	– Securitisation framework close to US market practices				
GE Regulators	– Beneficial treatment of SME and retail credits (SME retail portfolio; favourable SME risk weight formula)	– No Advanced Measurement Approach to operational risk	1%	(17%; 1)	3% (83%; 5)
	– Exceptional clause allowing to refrain from maturity capital charge on long-term credits				

Nationally/locally oriented banks				
US Banks	– Widened recognition of credit risk mitigation instruments and elimination of remaining risks floor (w-factor) – Enhanced recognition of general provisioning reserves as tier 2 & 3 capital	– No high complexity of the framework – Predominantly engaged definition for consolidated supervision – Capital requirements solely on the basis of unexpected losses	7% (18%; 5)	13%(82%; 23)
GE Banks	– Beneficial treatment of SME and retail credits (SME retail portfolio; favourable SME risk weight formula) – Exceptional clause allowing to refrain from maturity capital charge on long-term credits – Widened recognition of credit risk mitigation instruments and elimination of remaining risks floor	– 'Master scale' of risk weights, equal for all three credit risk approaches – High number of detailed adjustments of the Accord	37%(41%; 26)	21%(59%; 37)

Notes: Integration/Rejection rate = first value depicts percentage of actor i's integrated/rejected positions in relation to all integrated/rejected positions of episode 3; values in brackets: first value describes actor i's integrated/rejected positions in relation to all positions of actor i, second value depicts the absolute count of integrated/rejected positions of actor i; based on coded policy issues, where only those issues are integrated that were coded at least twice; in sum 138 issues

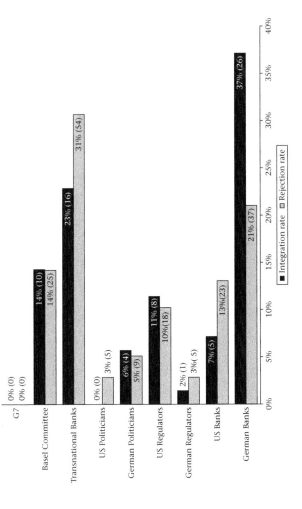

Figure 4.3 Integration and rejection rates in episode 3

Notes: Integration/Rejection rate = percentage of actor i's integrated/rejected positions in relation to all integrated/rejected positions of episode 3 (70 integrated, 176 rejected); values in brackets = number of integrated/rejected proposals.

Source: Own calculations based on correlational content analysis.

integration of additional specific interests. Several menu-for-choice approaches reflected compromises between US and German negotiators as well as with other jurisdictions (e.g. IRB equity exposures treatment).

Yet, the increasing reliance on internal risk management and measurement capacities of banks, the approaches for which had been developed in collaboration with the industry, strengthened the international banks vis-á-vis the supervisory network. A growing number of items of the agreement reflected banks' interests, while the supervisory positions incrementally shifted. The information and coalition-based dependence on international banking associations was important in this regard. Their increasing influence, however, was enabled through increasing pressure from domestic principals, whose interventions complicated the process by promoting the integration of further specific, private interests. The transnationally oriented banks' success finds its recognition in the relatively high integration rate in Figure 4.3. Nonetheless, they also experienced a very high rejection rate due to the large amount of details not integrated. In other words, while internationally active banks were capable of integrating a rising number of their positions, regulators still opposed many crucial issues, like capital redefinition or the further adjustment of securitisation rules to established market practices.

All attempts to preserve the supervisors' common goal of a harmonised regulatory standard, and to do so in due time, were of merely temporary success. The awakened US opposition would change the outcome and prolong the timetable of Basel II during an extensive fourth episode.

Episode 4, April 2003–December 2008: from CP-3 to the revised framework and national adoption

From April 2003 until the final framework in November 2005 (and also considering domestic adoption until December 2008), episode 4 revealed how the 'Accord' became a 'framework'. The last episode is another prolonged, multi-layered process, which includes: negotiation until preliminary adoption of the 'Revised Framework' in June 2004 (with deliberately open agenda points); further assessment, refinement and recalibration until November 2005; and, eventually, domestic adaptation, which resulted in ex post changes of the framework's character.

Accordingly, the episode is characterised by three broad (partially overlapping) sequential phases. In response to the issuance of the new consultative paper, opposition was again voiced, particularly from US community banks and international banks. Political principals in the United States became so concerned, that even a complete failure to reach an agreement on Basel II seemed a realistic possibility. The main veto player in the US was finally convinced of the agreement in October 2003, after which the second phase, the negotiation of the details of the final framework, began. Until June 2004, over many meetings and supervisor-industry exchanges, a preliminary framework was devised. This, however, became subject to some significant adjustments until the final version was derived in November 2005. Together with post-adoption struggles in the US, it constitutes the third phase.

Political process

From April 2003 onwards, US domestic veto players intensified their pressure on the federal supervisors to ensure national interests.[138] American politics only now, as a result of lobbying efforts to activate Congress, began to regard the Basel process as politically relevant. Substantial parts of the sectoral lobby opposed the agreement as meeting too many of the non-US banking sector interests.[139] Again, the two aforementioned industry coalitions activated the House and Senate: the operational risk pillar two coalition, and small and local banks. The first of these groups was concerned that the operational risk charge would disadvantage US banks in competition with US securities firms (to which the rules would not have applied, which was projected to leave them with lower capital requirements for the same business transaction). This coalition was, furthermore, worried about competition with international firms, since the United States already had plenty of operational risk regulations in place that would not have been accounted for under the Basel II regime – instead, banks would have had to provide the capital charges in addition. The second industry coalition of small and local banks (which were not targeted to become subject to the new standard, i.e. they were expected to become non-Basel II banks) was concerned about the negative domestic repercussions on their competitiveness vis-á-vis Basel II banks. This was rooted in the expectation that Basel II banks would have to bear lower capital requirements, compared to the banks not subjected to the new Accord, for offering identical products in several market segments where community and international banks were competing directly (in particular real estate mortgages and credit card commitments).

In other words, the domestic discourse evolved around the concerns that US banks could be at a disadvantage on international financial markets, and that small and local banks could suffer disadvantages vis-á-vis the large, internationally active banks that would apply Basel II rules. Both concerns, but in particular the US opposition of nationally/locally oriented regulatees, were rooted in the conjunction of Gramm-Leach-Bliley legislation and Basel II: while the adjusted US legislation permitted doing business across federal state borders, and accordingly for big banks to buy small ones, the advanced Basel II approaches were expected to provide them with additional resources to buy such small banks. In turn, it was feared by politicians and community banks that this would lead to further sector consolidation.[140]

Consequently, supervisors had to balance (a) demands to implement Basel II in order to maintain the international level playing field, (b) postulations to introduce Basel IA for small, locally oriented banks as an equaliser of domestic competitive disturbances, and (c) demands for maintaining the capitalisation levels in the US banking system, in particular among the Basel II banks.[141] The OCC became the main carrier of US domestic opposition.

A congressional committee meeting mirrored the growing opposition and conflict in US domestic politics early in 2003, at the same time as the third consultative paper was issued. The financial services committee was concerned about the economic repercussions of Basel II on US banks, and confronted the Federal Reserve as they were receiving mixed signals as to whether the Fed would be willing to change parts of the Basel II agreement in US implementation in the case when the application would turn out to have negative effects. Fed chairman Greenspan stated that elements would be changed if such negative repercussions would emerge. The House committee aimed at improving control over the agencies and in particular the Fed's ability to make transnational commitments that did not take the overall US interest into account. Interestingly, while there was considerable divergence in opinions between different supervisory agencies, as well as between supervisors and several parts of the industry, these actors did not favour any formal institutionalisation of domestic deliberation. While leading committee members (Bachus, Oxley, Frank, Maloney) introduced a legislative proposal (H.R. 2043) that would have mandated all regulators to coordinate a unified position under the chair of the Secretary of the Treasury, and would have to report to Congress, neither supervisors nor the industry supported this proposal. In the Congress hearings, these actors instead favoured flexible control by the parliament. The legislative proposal did not receive any support from the agencies, which, given the dominance of the Fed, supports the view that the other considerably weaker agencies were concerned about political intrusion into their regulatory turf – they rather worked out inter-agency agreements in the shadow of hierarchy. Accordingly, the legislative proposal never overcame proposal status.[142]

US supervisors, however, gave in to opposing demands in the domestic regulatory regime in order to pre-empt the emergence of a prolonged political conflict and, therefore, now departed from the initial agreement of applying the Accord to all significant internationally active banks, limiting the scope to a hand-picked group of ten to twelve banks only.[143] This was perceived as the American supervisors' intent to force those internationally active banks into the Accord that would profit from it, while other banks – also internationally active and significant – would be excluded, since they might be disadvantaged through the new rules, in particular through the operational risk charges.[144]

The German lead negotiator, Jochen Sanio of BaFin, reported to the Bundestag's finance committee on 22 October 2003 how the intra-American dispute had resulted in a phase of discontent within the BCBS and almost in the breakdown of negotiations between April and October 2003. He outlined that the domestic conflict within the US had spilled over into the Basel Committee, where the Comptroller of the Currency John Hawke blocked the finalisation of the negotiations for half a year. This, Sanio argues, had been initiated in the US by the combined constellation of several factors, which resulted in heightened political scrutiny and a rather negative attitude to the current Accord proposal. The operational risk opposition of two medium-sized US banks and one European institute with substantial US activity had gained prevalence in the process and activated Congress. This had been possible since congressional committee chairmen had shifted (also the Senate majority had shifted from Democrats to Republicans), and the Enron aftermath had kept other pro-Basel actors, mainly the internationally active banks, otherwise occupied. The Comptroller of the Currency John Hawke had emerged as the main carrier of the initiative, who had taken the conflict into the Basel Committee where he blocked a final agreement. Within the BCBS, Sanio stated, Hawke had changed his main concerns several times, so that it was difficult to integrate him through the accommodation of his demands – which the Committee had attempted to do. The agreement on the further Accord agenda towards final adoption had been an intra-American compromise among the involved supervisory agencies, which had then been integrated into the agenda for final adoption, as agreed in Basel on 11 October

2003: at this meeting, all BCBS members had agreed to finalise the Accord by mid-2004, and work on an explicitly limited list of items until then. The main issue, which mirrored the bargain with Hawke, was the adjustment to base IRB bank capital requirements separately on unexpected losses, while separating expected-loss related requirements and subjecting them solely to provisioning rules. This, BaFin and Bundesbank stated, was considered a windfall for German negotiators as they had demanded this in the very beginning of the Basel II negotiations, but had been blocked by a US-led opposition in favour of a combined UL/EL approach.[145]

The giving in to US demands demonstrates once more how interdependence in the BCBS and domestic opposition can strengthen one negotiating party. Accordingly, OCC, FDIC and OTS appreciated Congress's involvement strongly as it solved domestic discontent and strengthened the transnational negotiation position. Comptroller Hawke made this plainly clear in a June 2003 Congress hearing:

> the Financial Services Committee's involvement has been very healthy for this process. It has certainly strengthened our hand in the Basel discussions. Some of the other countries that are participating in this process have had their legislatures involved from the very outset. And some members of the Basel Committee were constrained in the positions that they could take in the Committee by their parliaments right from the beginning of the process. We were not. We have worked together as a group of regulators and participated in that process. But I welcome the oversight and the interest of the Committee in the process. I think the Committee's continued dialogue with the regulators is important. I think ultimately, it will strengthen our position vis-á-vis the Basel Committee.[146]

While US opposition grew, among the EU members of the Basel Committee, and particularly German supervisors, the main interest was in ensuring a global agreement that could be transmitted into EU law without further renegotiation. Supervisors and banks in Germany wanted the global framework, as both had already started to prepare their institutions for the new environment, and they feared a unilateral American move as it might have unlevelled the playing field and even forced them to prepare for yet more US-dominated approaches.[147] And, since German negotiators had achieved an agreement strongly in line with its political and economic interests, it wanted to avoid new deliberations at the EU level, which is why German authorities preferred to seal the deal in Basel (where Germany had a stronger negotiation position due to the non-unified EU members, and because the EU decisions would be subject to qualified majority voting), and pushed for an EU adoption without much adaptation.[148]

This laid the ground for giving in to the pressure from US domestic opposition. As BaFin president Sanio pointed out, the United States still had the option to exit the process (due to the US dominance in the Committee), while no other jurisdiction could have afforded such a move. Moreover, he outlined that the possibilities to negotiate on further specific German interests were very dim. According to his explanation, there would be no willingness of the Committee members to accept yet another round of specific German demands, and he expected the BCBS chair to notify consensus among the other members, while Germany would be left outside – which he urgently wanted to avoid.

Since Sanio expected the Basel Committee to only consider those industry proposals for amendment that had global resonance, he advised German banks to seek influence via global coalitions; for example, he suggested that the large, internationally active banks should utilise the IIF channel for their purposes. The transnationally oriented regulatees, which expected disadvantages in capital level changes – according to QIS-3 – vis-á-vis smaller German banks, were very disappointed about this refusal to bargain further on their behalf.

The conflicts in the Basel Committee were finally brought to a solution with the so-called 'Madrid Compromise' – a 'watershed moment' that put the negotiations back on track, by giving in to major domestic political pressures in the US, while keeping a tight schedule for the adoption of the Accord, as preferred by Germany and other BCBS members (Tarullo 2008, 121). It outlined five broader areas of modification, for which detailed solutions would be worked out by January 2004. The crucial compromise was the move towards an unexpected loss basis for IRB banks, as pushed by the US OCC. It had been demanded by the industry since January 2001 and constantly resisted by the supervisors, although substantial adjustments had already been integrated, which incorporated specific demands and suggestions of the banking sector bit by bit. Now, however, the clear-cut separation of unexpected (UL) and expected losses (EL) was outlined, where capital charges would be based on UL, but a provisioning ratio would be introduced to ensure incentives for banks to maintain high levels of provisions for expected losses.[149] EL under-provisioning would have to be deducted from capital, and over-provisioning could be accounted for as tier two capital, subject to a 20 per cent maximum, although the specific level should be at the discretion of domestic supervisors. The new approach reflected a clear change in the position of regulators, since de facto capital definitions were altered, an aspect previously excluded from change. These proposals were again made public, and the BCBS solicited comments. Interestingly, the standardised approach was not subject to any UL/EL adjustments, regarding which the Committee explicitly asked for opinions.[150]

As paramount as this issue was for the entire Basel II framework, the other four compromises were just as important: the simplification of the securitisation framework, in particular replacing the supervisory formula with a simpler approach; the revisiting of the treatment of credit card commitments and related issues; the revisiting of the treatment of credit risk mitigation techniques; and the agreement on a post-adoption phase, which allowed specific re-calibrations to respond to unintended outcomes, and in particular to unacceptable capital requirement results that might be revealed through the national QIS-4 studies in the US (as well as in Germany and Japan). These broad compromises and their detailed design in the final framework were intended to keep the United States on board.

The altered actor constellation in US domestic politics shifted the interaction mode in the Basel Committee more towards its state of a negotiation forum. The supervisory network dealt with the pressure in the twofold manner already experienced in the last two episodes. On the one hand, it integrated the veto players' main points into the framework by adding further optionality and other items benefiting US markets. On the other hand, it delegated the detailing to the working groups, which, in a series of meetings, crafted the technical solutions needed to keep all stakeholders on board.[151] Thereby, internationally active banks, after initial pronounced opposition, could be integrated into the transnational coalition with the BCBS through repeated refinements (securitisation, credit risk mitigation) and recalibration.[152] The importance of the web of working groups is documented during a hearing of the Bundestag Finance Committee (2004), which took place simultaneously to the Basel Committee's Capital Task Force finalisation of an important negotiation round.[153] BaFin president Jochen Sanio was not at this meeting, but instead participated in the parliament's committee meeting and therein reported just-in-time information about the working group consultations – that he received during the hearing – to the parliamentarians. Crucial negotiation roadblocks of the regulatory harmonisation project were overcome via technical solutions developed by a transgovernmental task force of regulatory experts.

Based on the working groups intermediate negotiation results, in January 2004 the Basel Committee reported its progress in elaborating on the items of the Madrid Compromise agenda.[154] Within three months the BCBS had received 52 industry comments on its October 2003 proposal concerning the UL/EL treatment, and was explicitly responsive to the demands by incorporating substantial adjustments into the Accord. Repeatedly, it stated that the Committee changed its functional evaluation, 'agreed with industry comments', 'agreed to re-fine rules ... in response to industry comments' or '... in order to reflect industry practices'. The adjustments suggest a strategy of integrating important stakeholders and potential influential opponents. The Committee had simplified the securitisation framework through substantial adjustments that largely reflected the US-based big banks' positions, in particular towards the market practices of originating banks. Furthermore, regarding credit risk mitigation techniques, enhanced re-cognition of such instruments in line with developing industry practice, specifically with regard to double default effects, was announced (which the industry had demanded to be recognised as a mitigating aspect for a long time, but without supervisory consent) – which reduced capital requirements.[155]

Another key progress was the intensifying cooperation in Accord implementation, specifically concerning the global coordination in supervising consolidated and sub-consolidated global banking groups. In line with previous BCBS reports,[156] the Committee indicated the incremental progress its members, particularly through the AIG, were making in establishing a cooperative understanding that moved closer to the lead regulator approach. According to this approach, transnational banks would report solely to the supervisor in the jurisdiction of the institute's incorporation (the home country), while this lead regulator would carry out the bank's consolidated supervision of the bank (and coordinate with the other involved agencies around the globe). In contrast, the intensified cooperation through the AIG means that the home country supervisor of a global banking organisation becomes the central linchpin, who merely coordinates work with host country supervisors and the senior management of the banking groups on the consolidated oversight of the A-IRB and AMA approaches. Several case studies were exercised to establish principles of enhanced cooperation in the surveillance of internationally active banks. The AMA approach played a particular role in this regard, as it involved a new area of cooperation and related to one of the core purposes of the BCBS efforts, namely the enhanced supervisory control of dangerous transnational spillovers from the failure of an internationally active institute through the control of its internal operational risks. Thus, while the lead regulator principle is not mandated or formally codified in the Basel II agreement, it receives increased relevance through the informal Basel Committee's orientation towards this idea. This does not meet the demands of the global banking associations IIF and ISDA, but it moves in this direction.[157]

On 11 May 2004, the supervisors in the Basel Committee finally achieved consensus on the three remaining contested issues, on which they had elaborated upon since October 2003: first, the modifications of the above issues were finally agreed upon – securitisation, credit risk mitigation, capital charges on credit card commitments; second, the overall capital charges to ensure constant capital levels for standardised and lowered levels for IRB banks were obtained through re-calibration and fine-tuning; third, the supervisors agreed to deepen consultation on implementation issues of the framework and in particular home-host regulator cooperation in supervising internationally active banks' advanced credit and operational risk approaches. Even though not explicitly announced, this date documents the official softening of the Basel II status from Accord to framework. While in the January documents the frame of reference had been the 'Accord', as it had been for the last six years, suddenly the document of the final agreement did not once refer to the future Accord, but to the 'framework'. This permitted the post-adoption freedom of adjusting to domestic conflicts, whilst the EU countries could continue with the European adoption.[158]

Whilst transnationally oriented regulatees found many of their interests integrated into the final framework, as before, capture was limited by counteracting supervisors. Many items the banks opposed were kept in the final framework. The IIF demanded reductions of the pro-cyclicality repercussions and the integration of credit risk models to the very end – both demands were rejected by the Basel Committee. More importantly, the introduction of an overall risk floor through the introduction of the scaling factor (which multiplied capital requirements by a factor of 1.06) – to ensure that capital could not fall below certain thresholds – was kept against the industry's strong resistance.[159]

On 26 June 2004, the governors and heads of supervision (GHOS) endorsed the publication of the Basel II framework at a meeting one day after the Basel Committee approved its submission to the GHOS for review. The adjustments developed since October 2003 added up to capital reductions for IRB banks, in particular those applying the A-IRB approach, as well as specific adaptations to bring the framework's rules more in line with US market practices. Opposed US supervisors were satisfied so that at least a 'Revised Framework' became possible, and large, internationally active banks were won over by decreased capital requirements and beneficial modifications to securitisation, credit risk mitigation, consolidated supervision and the trading book.[160]

Simultaneously to the Basel II agreement in the BCBS, however, the domestic conflict in the US escalated shortly after the above compromise. While the EU used the new framework as the basis to progress quickly with EU adoption and national implementation,[161] the US implemented a selective sub-set of rules for a selected sub-set of banks, while failing to adopt the new Basel II regulation for all other banks (which, in terms of numbers make up more than 95 per cent of firms, but less than 20 per cent of assets).

In November 2003, congressional members had already intensified the conflict with the supervisors, when 11 members of the financial services committee of the House of Representatives sent a 13-page letter to the four main bank regulators, saying that the proposed Basel II Accord must be reviewed by Congress prior to any final agreement that might significantly affect US-based firms.[162] During the next round of congressional hearings on the topic in April and June 2004, the diverse positions in domestic politics surfaced even more pronouncedly.[163] The banking sector was divided into three factions, the community banks, mainly represented by the association of America's Community Bankers (ACB), the large, internationally active (nationally chartered) banks, represented by the Financial Services Roundtable (FSR) and several individual bank initiatives, as well as the operational risk opposition integrated by the Financial Guardian Group (medium-sized banks which were competing in several markets with securities firms). While international banks wanted the framework and operational risk pillar one solution, community banks aimed for a Basel 1.5 solution that would offer them comparatively beneficial capital charges to those which A-IRB banks received under Basel II approaches, and the medium-sized national banks wanted a pillar two operational risk approach. Furthermore, the securities firms, in particular the investment banks, entered the discourse since the Consolidated Supervised Entities (CSE) programme of the Securities and Exchange Commission (SEC)[164] would make them subject to the Basel Accord. This programme, while being a voluntary one, was of relevance for the investment banks as it could have functioned as the seal of 'equivalent consolidated supervision', which had to be accepted by the EU in order to operate in its market without additional EU supervisory control.

Securities firms (including investment banks) and medium-sized nationally chartered banks had previously not been integrated into the regulator-regulatee collaboration to include their interests in Basel II. Several statements document that the supervisor-industry cooperation, in developing the details of the new framework, rather focused on two groups of banks: first and foremost, the transnationally oriented regulatees, with which the Fed as the process driver interacted; second, the other banks that were eventually not subjected to the new standards. The excluded actors and those that expected negative repercussions on the national level playing field now used Congress to pursue their interests.

As a result of the US deadlock, many actors did not consider the forthcoming Basel II agreement as being the final word, but rather that it merely offered sufficient specifics for domestic processes to move ahead. In particular, Comptroller Hawke explicitly rejected the idea that the agreement was binding, and claimed that the US could change the Accord after its national impact assessments.[165] The Senate hearing on the condition of the US banking sector in April 2004 depicts how the domestic conflict between supervisory agencies, banks and congressional members transformed into a compromise to proceed with Basel II in a very US-specific manner. After accepting a Basel framework agreement in June 2004, the American agencies would undertake several assessment exercises – including the national QIS-4, the proposed rule-making, and economic impact analysis, as well as continued communication with both chambers of Congress and the industry – in order to estimate the effects on US banks. Thereafter, re-calibration and even re-negotiation in Basel were considered as potentially necessary. Accordingly, while all political and regulatory actors wanted Basel II, they claimed their ability to modify it in accordance with US necessities.[166]

Then, in May 2005, the highly surprising results of the US QIS-4[167] confirmed the worst concerns of politicians and initiated the selective American implementation of Basel II. The national US QIS-4 revealed unintended repercussions of Basel II on the domestic level playing field, where the big Basel II banks received considerably reduced capital requirements, and furthermore, capitalisation levels of institutes with allegedly similar risk profiles dispersed substantially. Consequently, the regulatory agencies had to delay the Note for Proposed Rule-making

(NPR)[168] and return to domestic deliberations with Congress and industry.[169]

Congress members were concerned that the Accord would unduly favour the large, internationally active US banks, thereby resulting in further consolidation in the banking sector (which had already been on the rise due to Gramm-Leach-Bliley-legislation). Moreover, the reduction in capital itself was contested by several members as an imprudent occurrence. Accordingly, they urged the supervisors, in particular the Fed, to postpone adoption until more clarity about the effects on US banks existed and necessary re-calibration and negotiation had been undertaken. One crucial concern of Congressmen was the repercussion on the real estate market (which is mainly subject to securitisation), since Basel II – as QIS-4 suggested – would heavily reduce capital charges for the big Basel II banks on (securitised) real estate mortgages. This was viewed as potentially altering the domestic competition among small banks, big banks and non-banks on this market – potentially to the considerable disadvantage of small, local (non-Basel II) banks vis-á-vis large, internationally active (Basel II) banks. The Committee members' stake in protecting locally/nationally oriented regulatees (and preventing further consolidation), and the feared negative repercussions on local credit markets (in particular real estate, commercial lending, credit cards and securitised real estate), is mirrored in the insistent statements by chairman Frank and ranking member Oxley of the full committee of financial services.[170]

Big banks, however, considered it would be problematic if the United States failed to adopt and implement Basel II on time, as this would have implied considerable supervisory divergence in their operations due to the Basel II implementation by most other BCBS members. The US conflict can thus be described succinctly as between the Basel II supporters that feared international competitive disadvantages from US delay and specific approaches, and a diverse coalition of actors that wanted to slow Basel II implementation in order to achieve a national level playing field before the international one.[171] In response to this twofold pressure, the federal supervisory agencies agreed on a two-tiered simultaneous strategy, which was deemed to be regardful of both domestic and international level playing field concerns: on the one hand, as announced on 30 September 2005, the Basel II implementation time frame in the US was adjusted – it was agreed to begin in January 2008 with a parallel trial run followed by a three-year transition period from 2009 to 2011. On the other hand, as announced a few days thereafter in October 2005, it was decided that

Basel IA would complement Basel II – i.e. the federal agencies would adjust the current Basel I rules for non-Basel II banks so that national competitive disadvantages were eliminated for non-Basel II banks.[172] The NPRs for both projects were projected to overlap in order to give stakeholders the opportunity to compare proposals and comment accordingly (Verdier 2011, 16).

Nevertheless, even thereafter, congressional pressure remained constant since the Senate and the FDIC chairman were still highly concerned about the capital reductions in large banks and the safety and soundness repercussions this could have. While the OCC, after John Dugan had succeeded John Hawke as Comptroller in 2005, was more supportive of Basel II, the FDIC chair Sheila Bair loudly voiced systemic concerns due to reduced capital requirements in Congress (Tarullo 2008, 127–128). The Senate then put pressure on the federal supervisors, particularly the Fed, to renegotiate in the Basel Committee to remedy this problem. Several Senators considered progressing with Basel II to be more problematic than maintaining current US standards. In response, in March 2006 the federal regulators drafted an NPR which took the Senate demands into account, through keeping specific US regulatory safeguard measures (maintenance of the US leverage ratio, as well as the pre-emptive action clauses)[173] and introducing a 10 per cent maximum capital reduction floor on all Basel II banks. It was not long until big American banks countervailed this proposal, when in the Summer of 2006 they asked the agencies to allow for the introduction of the Basel II standardised approach in their institutes. The banks argued that they would suffer substantial competitive disadvantages vis-á-vis EU-based banks and US investment banks, which both could implement the 'international' versions of the Basel II framework without having to meet comparable additional stipulations. The formal NPR in September 2006 did not resolve these issues, but solicited further comments on them.[174]

The tide shifted in January 2007, when a change in the committee chairmanship in the Senate led to support for Basel II implementation, in order to secure the international level playing field of big, internationally active US banks with competitors from other BCBS members. In early 2007, the Treasury, under the stewardship of Secretary Henry Paulson,[175] eventually started to become politically active and pushed towards Basel II implementation. The Treasury put pressure on OCC and OTS to support the removal of the 10 per cent maximum capital reduction floor. In July 2007, chairman Dodd and ranking member Shelby of the Senate's banking committee urged regulators to continue work and reach a consensus soon. Directly responding to this principal's pressure, federal agencies agreed to implement Basel II, not subject to the 10 per cent maximum capital reduction floor, but only to the transitional floors as well as an additional evaluation, and to drop the Basel IA approach in favour of the introduction of the standardised Basel II approach (Verdier 2011, 18–20; Tarullo 2008, 129–130).

Eventually, in November 2007 the US federal supervisors implemented the advanced Basel II rules (A-IRB/AMA) for the most advanced banks, and aimed to adopt the standardised approach of Basel II to all other banks, which demanded capital charges similar to the Basel II banks, in order to sustain domestic competition within the banking sector. After the NPR for the standardised approach in July 2008, however, due to the financial crisis and the shifting agenda of supervisors after the implementation of the advanced options, the standardised approaches were never adopted/implemented and are still under review in the context of the Dodd-Frank Act (Verdier 2011, 18–20). The US, the jurisdiction that initiated the Basel II process against resistance from fellow Basel Committee members, softened the outcome substantially by degrading it to framework status shortly before adoption and failed to adopt considerable parts of the agreement. At the same time, the originally opposed jurisdictions were eager to adopt and implement the framework in their regulatory regimes in order to earn the benefits of the previously undertaken efforts to adapt to the new rules.

Policy outcomes and influential actors

In the final episode, the transnational agreement was softened substantially, while most veto players' key interests were integrated under the roof of a harmonised framework. Specifically, the adjustments integrated the interests of US-based and transnationally oriented banks. Moreover, the problems of global layering continued throughout the adoption and implementation phases. On the one hand, national voice coalitions in the US successfully pursued their competitiveness concerns. Likewise, while in the EU adoption and implementation were swiftly undertaken,[176] the German implementation showed how close regulator-regulatee collaboration within a jurisdiction facilitates competitiveness-boosting, lenient implementation and enforcement after the adoption of global standards.

While the dominant US regulatory agent, the Fed, had set the agenda for the renewal of harmonised banking supervision in the absence of politicians' control, the activation of political oversight by its congressional principals did block this agenda. The regained political control only weakly intervened on behalf of systemic, economy-wide interests, though rather on behalf of those sectoral actors capable of organising voice-based opposition that entered politicians' calculations. Above this threshold, Congress was willing and capable of vetoing the adoption and implementation of the transnational agreement.[177] The success of this US coalition of non-Basel II banks and congressional politicians is reflected in their high integration rates in Figure 4.4 as well as in the high amount of introduced important issues (Table 4.8).

Once locally oriented community banks and further financial institutions, competing with Basel II banks in the US market, overcame the threshold of congressional attention, they achieved a de facto American veto that took effect in two steps: first, on the international level, where instead of an Accord only a framework was adopted; second, through selective US adoption that attempted to ensure a domestic level playing field (even though the latter, due to the onset of the financial crisis in 2007, was not implemented). The veto, however, did not concern the entire framework, but only ensured that (a) certain interests were integrated into the proposal, while (b) domestic implementation was differentiated in favour of influential constituents. The framework approach permitted the Basel Committee to reach an agreement after all, but for the sake of it, further compromise was necessary, adjusting the Basel II content to the benefit of transnationally oriented banks.

On the other hand, the transnational harmonisation coalition's aim of achieving agreement on a global standard resulted in the transnational banking community's late success. This is mirrored in the changes to the capital definition, the resulting reduction in capital levels, and further important issues (as reported in Table 4.8). This was an unintended consequence of the processes triggered by national politicians. The integration of national voice and transnational harmonisation interests at the expense of systemic stability (through reduced capital requirements and increased complexity), is indicative of deficient political control mechanisms.

The combined influence of national voice and transnational harmonisation coalitions resulted in (1) a complex and soft transnational policy outcome, as well as (2) deviant domestic adoption and/or implementation that served special national interests.

The analysis of the fourth period completes the individual episode analysis, and the study moves on to a combined analysis of the entire Basel II process. The following section summarises the empirical insights of the four episodes and outlines how the global, or transgovernmental,

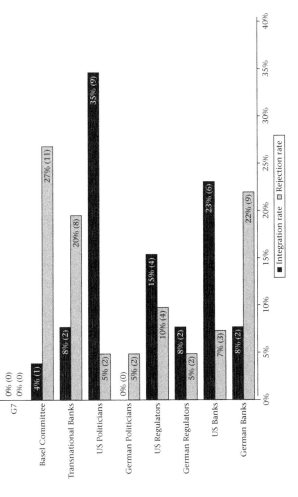

Figure 4.4 Integration and rejection rates in episode 4

Notes: Integration/Rejection rate = percentage of actor i's integrated/rejected positions in relation to all integrated/rejected positions of episode 4 (26 integrated, 41 rejected); values in brackets = number of integrated/rejected proposals.

Source: Own calculations based on correlational content analysis.

Actor type	Crucial integrated positions	Crucial rejected positions	Integration rate		Rejection rate
Global political principal (G7)			—	(—; 0)	— (—; 0)
Transgovernmental network (BCBS)	- Strengthened institutionalisation of BCBS and home-supervisor principle	- Reduced capital levels and capital redefinition (A-)IRB banks - Softened framework (instead Accord)	4%	(8%; 1)	27% (92%; 11)
Transnationally oriented banks	- Reduced capital levels and capital redefinition IRB banks - Securitisation framework based upon US market practices - Strengthened institutionalisation of BCBS and home-supervisor principle	- Credit risk portfolio models - Pro-cyclicality recognition - Capital scaling factor and transition floors with maximum capital reductions	8%	(20%; 2)	20% (80%; 8)
Domestic political principals US Politicians	- Loose framework instead of an Accord - Securitisation framework based upon US market practices - Favourable treatment of credit card commitments - Beneficial treatment of securitised residential mortgages	- Higher capital requirements for A-IRB banks	35%	(82%; 9)	5% (18%; 2)
GE Politicians			0%	(0%; 0)	5% (100%; 2)

(Continued)

Table 4.8 Continued

Actor type	Crucial integrated positions	Crucial rejected positions	Integration rate	Rejection rate
Regulatory agents				
US Regulators	– OCC: Loose framework instead of an Accord – Adoption of Revised framework in 2004	– Fed: Accord with encompassing implementation	15% (50%; 4)	10% (50%; 4)
GE Regulators		– Softened framework (instead of Accord) status	8% (50%; 2)	5% (50%; 2)
Nationally/locally oriented banks				
US Banks	– Securitisation framework based upon US market practices – Loose framework instead of an Accord – Favourable treatment of credit card commitments – Beneficial treatment of securitised residential mortgages	– Capital levels relative to internationally active banks – US Basel IA approach that reduces capital for non-Basel II banks	23% (67%; 6)	7% (33%; 3)
GE Banks		– Parallel partial employment of all credit risk measurement approaches	8% (18%; 2)	22% (82%; 9)

Notes: Integration/Rejection rate = first value depicts percentage of actor i's integrated/rejected positions in relation to all integrated/rejected positions of episode 4; values in brackets: first value describes actor i's integrated/rejected positions in relation to all positions of actor i, second value depicts the absolute count of integrated/rejected positions of actor i; based on coded policy issues, where only those issues are integrated that were coded at least twice; in sum 36 issues.

governance efforts of setting Basel II standards has contributed to regulatory failure underlying the onset of the Great Recession.

4.4　Summary: Basel II, the Great Recession and the global political economy

In sum, then, did the global standard setting of the Basel II initiative contribute to regulatory failure preceding the onset of the Great Recession? The first part of this Basel II conclusion delineates how the exercise diffused standards with substantial regulatory loopholes transnationally, which contributed to regulatory failure. The second part summarises the empirical findings to show how these loopholes were the product of asymmetric influence and how it was conditioned through the transnational governance structure.

Basel II as soft law diffusion mechanism

As outlined before, the Basel Committee's agreements are of a soft law character without immediate legal force. Basel II deepened, but also altered this aspect. On the one hand, it extended the layering of transnational processes and rules through the deepening of the politicisation and institutionalisation of the BCBS as well as the extension of the Basel practices and standards. On the other hand, the rising number of opportunities for national supervisors to undermine global standardisation to the benefit of its regulatees, initiates further competition state strategies of mock compliance, i.e. provides plenty of room for competitiveness-boosting lenient supervision by adopting and/or implementing a specific sub-set or even deviant rules that serve special national interests.

With regard to the transnationalisation of regulatory standard setting, three major aspects underpin the deepening. First, is the augmented transnational role in the development of standards, which is due to the increasing number and importance of the transgovernmental network's working groups. This web of working groups and task forces carried out the bulk of the Committee's work and provided detailed analyses to the BCBS heads. Throughout the Basel II process, their number increased, as did their influence due to the sheer amount of technical decisions that needed to be made. A particularly influential body was the Capital Task Force, which prepared and selected the topics for the Basel Committee meetings. As a consequence, these groups of mid-level hierarchy staffers from domestic supervisory agencies, who communicated extensively with the international banking community, set the agenda regarding several regulatory issues, which were then put on the Basel Committee's agenda merely for agreement.[178]

Second, is the evolutionary character of capital adequacy regulation on the transnational level, which was deepened through the establishment of coordination on implementation and interpretation. The creation of the Accord Implementation Group (AIG) was designed to intensify the information exchange about implementation strategies between supervisors. It raised the Committee's influential role by adding the function of a clearing house for Basel II information.[179]

Third, is the supervisory role of the transgovernmental network, which was strengthened through supervisory coordination mechanisms in supervising internationally active banks. Partly through the development of guiding principles for the supervision of banks (i.e. pillar two), and partly through the further strengthening of the home supervisor in leading the consolidated supervision of globally active banking groups, the regulatory network now intervened slightly more in domestic supervision, and obtained a more pronounced role in the surveillance of international banks. The consolidated supervision of the most advanced measurement techniques of operational and credit risks at the global level of banking groups, and the corresponding regulatory cooperation to minimise the burden of implementation for firms operating in multiple jurisdictions with different Basel II options, was one particular development in this regard.[180]

At the same time, however, Basel II also introduced several options that facilitated cosmetic compliance strategies. The considerable number of such opportunities provide national supervisors with sufficient room to undermine global standardisation to the benefit of its national regulatees.[181] Two major elements were at the basis of this new development. First, the widespread use of optionality and modularity as the governing principle, whereby national jurisdictions can choose which options to implement. As discussed, in many cases even banks obtained the freedom to choose among options for compliance. Accordingly, national agencies can build jurisdictional solutions consisting of particular modules, and individual banks can build their modular solutions within the jurisdiction's limits.

The second factor increasing the potential for cosmetic compliance was the further softening of the agreement's character as a 'framework'. As a result, US compliance was discussed mainly subject to US domestic political concerns, and the range of application there was limited to a set of internationally active banks, while most of the nationally oriented banks were excluded.[182]

The final characteristic defining the actual effectiveness of the Basel II framework relates to its role in the wider policy-web of governing global finance. In other words, how well it works in conjunction with other arrangements among states to enhance the stability of global financial intermediation. While Basel II was designed as club-standard among a selective set of industrialised countries with developed financial systems, at the same time it ensured that the benchmarks of these nations were diffused to emerging and developing nations (Drezner 2007, 119–148). Basel II played an indirect role in this context. The framework's technically advanced best practice standards were, in simultaneous activities, translated into generally applicable and simplified benchmark versions, the so-called Core Principles for Effective Banking Supervision.[183] As discussed before, the result of this, and similar exercises of other transnational regulatory networks, were the 12 key financial codes and standards for the international system. The diffusion of these supervisory principles was enforced through the technical training of emerging market supervisors, as well as through the IMF and World Bank lending to less developed countries and/or assessing of these nations' economic policies – the IFIs officially adopted the 12 codes as part of their assessments in 2002 (Drezner 2007, 135–142). Their scrutiny transformed the voluntary standards into de facto regulatory stipulations, as the positive judgement by these institutions had achieved the status of a 'seal of approval' among investors (see e.g. Gray 2009, 935), making it indispensable for such countries to meet the criteria in order to sustain access to international financial flows. Through these mechanisms, principles developed within the Basel Committee during the creation of Basel II were diffused far beyond the circle of its developers. This strengthened the global authoritative role of the Basel Committee and its standards. As discussed in Chapter 2, while it fostered the IMF's role as global supervisor, it strengthened the BCBS as global regulator – while the Basel Committee is also increasingly involved in supervisory issues due to the supervisory coordination mechanisms established during Basel II and III (see next chapter).

Summing up the framework's effectiveness, i.e. the degree of actual influence of the supervisory decisions, it is helpful to compare it directly with its predecessor, Basel I (a comparatively simple agreement that national supervisors in developed nations adopted stringently): while Basel II deepened and widened the role of the Basel Committee as a transgovernmental network, and even increased its institutionalisation, it did so mainly in a less formal manner. On the contrary, its extensive and invasive character resulted in numerous options and incentives for cosmetic compliance strategies, which softened the character of the Basel II framework. Put succinctly, while the Basel Committee's role evolved more towards a global regulator, the direct impact of its regulatory standard was reduced, or at least subjected to increased national conditioning. In other words, rather than providing a set of gap closing, harmonised standards (either through replacement or complementing of national standards), the Basel II politics extended the layering of transnational processes and rules, while also initiating further competition state strategies of mock compliance.

These results can add to the illumination of Basel II's contribution to the regulatory failure preceding the current crisis, which is still subject to debate. On the one hand, it is argued that Basel II was not readily implemented in banks when the asset bubble was built up and when the turmoil began, and that it would actually have reduced the likelihood of a crisis. On the other hand, it is argued that its recipes increased banks' risk taking and weakened regulators' supervisory capabilities (Tarullo 2008, Goldbach & Kerwer 2012). The causal relationship between the set of harmonised regulatory standards and the worst banking crisis in six decades is one that can only latently and tentatively be established, even in light of an in-depth process tracing analysis. Nevertheless, based on the empirical insights of this as well as Tarullo's (2008) and Buchmüller's (2008) studies of the Basel II process, it can be concluded that it operated as a diffusion mechanism, which led regulators and regulatees to adapt their activities based on the elements of internal risk calculation, internal management and supervisory review processes, and information disclosure of the three-pillar model. Through the Committee and Basel II process, pre-existing practices (in particular those of the US banks and regulators), as well as newly developed standards, were diffused transnationally. A few examples provide a summary of the study's empirical substance for this claim: the three pillars, and the securitisation that both reflected recent developments in the US regulatory regime; the complex internal calculations and credit risk mitigation approaches as provided by the international banking associations; the internal ratings based approaches as promoted by European regulators, in particular the German negotiators.

Some of the harmonised or newly developed standards were rules that *did not prevent, and even created a basis for, regulatory gaps*. They were a basis for regulatory failure, which domestic implementation worsened. As Tarullo (2008, 213) emphasises:

the extent of national discretion and the opaque quality ... breed countless opportunities for the exercise of regulatory discretion in pursuit of national competitive advantage, as well as for sound prudential reasons.

The link between transnational diffusion and financial instability is established through the Basel standards' asymmetric regard of the private, well organised interests of sectoral and national competitiveness vis-á-vis the public good of systemic stability. While this collective action problem also exists in national regulatory regimes, the transnational diffusion of regulatory standards did add further to the dispersion of authority on behalf of stability in the banking systems. The TRR diffusion strengthened global market interaction while merely suggesting that the transnational stability of these interactions is equally ensured. Moreover, the increasing dispersion of authority further weakens the political control mechanism on behalf of the (now partially global) public good, thereby resulting in the asymmetric regard of private interest related regulatory practices. The empirical analysis revealed that the negotiated standards integrated highly complex rules to calculate and manage risks that were in line with private sector (and politicians') interests and, furthermore, a high density of optionality that permitted most actors to pick a standard suitable to their preferences. Moreover, national political interventions on behalf of certain disregarded interests, which led to the shift from transnational regulatory cooperation to rather international negotiations, even weakened the regard of the public good due to the increased focus on comforting all actors capable of blocking the agreement. Several of the regulatory standards that were integrated in this manner and diffused through the Basel II deliberation process are established as being at the root of the recent financial turmoil.

Let us briefly sketch the correlation between causes of the banking crisis and regulatory policies that were diffused during the Basel II process by referring to two central examples, namely securitisation and risk measurement. Excessive risk taking and leveraging, as well as securitisation, were two crucial factors at the root of the banking crisis (for a more encompassing discussion see e.g. Hellwig 2009, Hoshi 2011, Lo 2012, Admati & Hellwig 2013). Excessive risk taking by banks without due capitalisation of those risks, combined with extreme leveraging, was at the heart of the breakdown of most banks (Hellwig 2009). Principles developed under the umbrella of Basel II, however, actually increased the possibilities for excessive risk taking based on complex portfolio and organisational structures in financial conglomerates. While the framework consolidated supervision of these conglomerates, the new standards introduced more complexity and opacity into banking supervision, which facilitated regulatory arbitrage, even though an increasingly sophisticated set of rules came into force. One might say that the new rules made regulatory arbitrage more sophisticated.

Turning to securitisation, these practices were at the heart of imprudent credit intermediation in banks, in particular in the form of securitised sub-prime credits in the United States (Hellwig 2009). The capital requirements on securitised residential mortgages and credit card lines were reduced through the Basel II approach. While the framework did not cause this, it certainly did not prevent it either, but rather legitimised and manifested market practices already in place and evolving in domestic regulatory regimes, in particular in the US. Moreover, both the external ratings on many securitisation tranches and the internal calculations of risks stemming from extending credit and liquidity guarantees to banks' conduits proved – in light of the US Sub-prime Crisis – to be ineffective in assessing risks accurately and identifying imprudent banking behaviour (Tarullo 2008, 158–159).

In retrospect, it is apparent that the project was overburdened with the task of crafting a capital adequacy framework that stabilised global and national banking systems (Tarullo 2008, 260). Nevertheless, its advancement has given rise to substantial changes in the way banking activities are regulated, of which many are unequivocally welcomed. Tarullo (2008, 150, 172–175) emphasises two such broader points, namely the development of a 'common language' on risks in banks as the basis for the regulation of new risk types, and the augmented investments of banks in their internal risk assessment and management systems. Both were goals at the outset of the endeavour, and both are still deemed necessary measures that reduce the likelihood of crises.

In conclusion, while not implemented in the two jurisdictions ex ante the ongoing banking crisis, Basel II operated as a diffusion device of regulatory practices that were at the root of the turmoil. Banks and regulators began early on in the Basel II deliberations to adapt their practices according to the expected new standards: because the new framework with its basic three pillars was consensual and therefore foreshadowing since the first consultative paper in June 1999, which implied substantial adjustment processes, banks began to adapt their internal systems, and regulators their supervisory capacities (Bundestag Finance Committee 2002, Bundesanstalt für

Finanzdienstleistungsaufsicht & Deutsche Bundesbank 2003, Tarullo 2008). Thereby, the risk measurement and management paradigm based on internal banking systems was diffused substantially before the final Basel II agreement and national adoption and implementation. Hence, while not the primary cause of the regulatory failure, the transnational endeavour certainly failed to regulate international banking activity suitably. Moreover, it even contributed to the spread and development of rules prone to regulatory gaps. Excessive risk taking and regulatory arbitrage were not pre-empted and in several cases even facilitated. Thus, while it is difficult to disentangle Basel II effects from other factors of the regulatory regime, the process tracing revealed that the development of new standards was spearheaded and diffused through the Basel II exercise and the Basel Committee's transgovernmental network.

Consequences of asymmetric influence in developing Basel II

In the second part of this Basel II conclusion, I show how the regulatory loopholes were the product of asymmetric influence and how this, in turn, was conditioned through the transnational governance structure. For that purpose, I now evaluate the six explanations of influence on the global political economy of banking regulation – transgovernmental network, transnational capture, global political principal, domestic political principal(s), regulatory agent(s), and nationally/locally oriented banks – based on the entire set of qualitative and quantitative empirical information.

Table 4.9 reflects the episode-specific insights from Tables 4.5, 4.6, 4.7 and 4.8, by adding all empirical information into one succinct overview. The crucial integrated and rejected issues of this summarising table provide an encompassing presentation of all important issues of the Basel II deliberations, whether included or not. All results and conclusions are based on the entire presented empirical material observed during the correlational analysis and process tracing.[184] Figure 4.5 depicts the integration/rejection rates for all actors over the entire Basel II negotiations. The cumulative indicators in the figure and the table are constructed by adding the indicators of the single episodes: for each actor, all integrated/rejected issues are added, the sum of which is then related to the sum of all issues integrated into any of the four consultative papers or the final agreement.

I begin by assessing to which degree the substance of internationally agreed regulatory standards (Basel II for international banking), derived by the transnational network of supervisory agencies (Basel Committee)

Table 4.9 Actors' integrated and rejected interests in Basel II, all episodes combined

Actor type	Crucial integrated positions	Crucial rejected positions	Integration rate	Rejection rate
Global political principal (G7)	– Development of 12 key financial standards – Policy diffusion to emerging markets through IFIs – Consolidated supervision of financial conglomerates	– Increased capital requirements on emerging market banks in case of non-adoption of financial standards	7% (59%; 17)	3% (41%; 12)
Transgovernmental network (BCBS)	– Credit risk calculation via internal rating rather than with internal portfolio model approaches – Strengthened institutionalisation of BCBS and home-supervisor principle (AIG-group) – Market discipline via mandatory pillar three disclosure – Encompassing eligibility criteria for IRB application	– Basel I adaptation instead Basel II agreement – No introduction of external ratings – Banking book interest rate risk capital charge – Reduced capital levels and capital redefinition for IRB banks	18% (40%; 46)	18% (60%; 69)
Transnationally oriented banks	– Reduced capital levels and capital redefinition for IRB banks – Enhanced recognition of internal risk measurement techniques	– Credit risk portfolio models – Pro-cyclicality recognition – No capital scaling factor and transition floors with maximum capital reductions	26% (36%; 67)	31%(64%; 119)

	- Enhanced recognition of credit risk mitigation techniques - Securitisation framework based upon US market practices - Strengthened institutionalisation of BCBS and home-supervisor principle (AIG-group) - Substantial recognition of bank's internal capacities to calculate operational risks under the AMA	- No encompassing eligibility criteria for IRB application - Reduced extent of mandatory disclosures - Lead regulator - Harmonisation of accounting rules - No sub-consolidated supervision	3%(56%; 9)
Domestic political principals US Politicians	- Loose framework instead of an Accord - AMA approach to operational risk - Securitisation framework based upon US market practices - Favourable treatment of credit card commitments - Beneficial treatment of securitised residential mortgages	- Lowered capital requirements for A-IRB banks	2%(44%; 7)

(Continued)

Table 4.9 Continued

Actor type	Crucial integrated positions	Crucial rejected positions	Integration rate	Rejection rate
Domestic principals GE Politicians	(Continued) – Beneficial treatment of SME and retail credits (SME retail portfolio; favourable SME risk weight formula; exception clause allowing to refrain from maturity capital charges on long-term credits) – Exception clauses for banks' commercial shareholding – Introduction of F-IRB approach as less sophisticated IRB alternative – Favourable credit risk weight for commercial collateralised loans (50%)	– Equalisation of requirements for application of standardised and F-IRB approach	5% (41%; 13)	5% (59%; 19)
Regulatory agents US Regulators	– Introduction of the three pillar structure along US practices with internal bank self-regulation, qualitative individual supervision and market surveillance	– Pre-commitment approach – Subordinated debt as additional market surveillance instrument under pillar three – No exception clauses for commercial equity and additional	12% (41%; 32)	12% (59%; 47)

Stakeholder	Column A	Column B	Column C
GE Regulators	– Introduction of external ratings as cornerstone of standardised approach and securitisation – New Basel II agreement – Operational risk capital charge via pillar one – No internal portfolio models, no pre-commitment approach – Constant capital requirement levels – F-IRB introduction and decreased importance of standardised approach – Adoption of Revised framework in 2004	– Basel I adaptation instead Basel II agreement – Basel II Accord instead of a framework – Banking book interest rate risk capital charge 7%(46%; 19)	– maturity capital charges – Banking book interest rate risk capital charge 6%(54%; 22)
Nationally/locally oriented banks **US Banks**	– Widened recognition of credit risk mitigation instruments – Securitisation framework based upon US market practices – Loose framework instead of an Accord	– Equalised capital levels relative to internationally active banks – US Basel IA approach that reduces capital for non-Basel II banks – Less complexity of the framework – Predominantly engaged definition for consolidated supervision 4%(30%; 11)	7%(70%; 26)

(Continued)

Table 4.9 Continued

Actor type	Crucial integrated positions	Crucial rejected positions	Integration rate	Rejection rate
GE Banks	– Beneficial treatment of SME and retail credits (SME retail portfolio; favourable SME risk weight formula; exceptional clause allowing to refrain from maturity capital charges on long-term credits) – Exception clauses for banks' commercial shareholding – F-IRB introduction (reduced focus on external ratings)	– Parallel partial employment of all credit risk measurement approaches – No introduction of external ratings – Sub-consolidated supervision	18% (42%; 47)	17% (58%; 65)

Notes: Integration/Rejection rate = first value depicts percentage of actor i's integrated/rejected positions in relation to all all integrated/rejected positions; of all episodes combined; values in brackets: first value describes actor i's integrated/rejected positions in relation to all positions of actor i, second value depicts the absolute count of integrated/rejected positions of actor i; based on coded policy issues, where only those issues are integrated that were coded at least twice; in sum 369 issues (Episode 1: 86; Episode 2: 109; Episode 3: 138; Episode 4: 36).

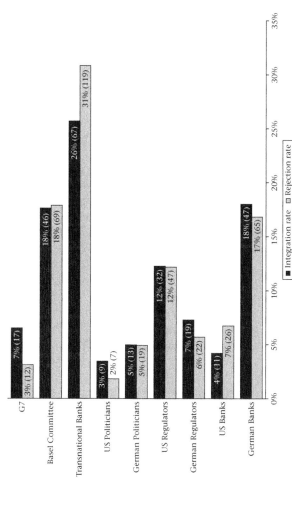

Figure 4.5 Integration and rejection rates in Basel II (sum of all episodes)

Notes: Integration/Rejection rate = percentage of actor i's integrated/rejected positions in relation to all integrated/rejected positions of episodes 1 to 4 (by addition of policies integrated/rejected during the four single episodes; 261 integrated, 386 rejected); values in brackets = number of integrated/rejected proposals.

Source: Own calculations based on correlational content analysis.

was mainly affected by the global political principal of the Basel Committee, namely the G7. They are presented in the first sections of Table 4.9 and Figure 4.5. Compared to the other actors, these – as well as domestic – politicians reveal relatively low integration rates (the black bars), but also lower rejection rates. This, however, is related to their small number of voiced preferences in relation to the further actors, which, in turn, is reflective of the relatively lower involvement in the process. When considering their actor-specific integration/rejection rates (see Table 4.9, each first number in brackets of the specific actor), the principals have relatively higher rates. This implies that politicians raised a relatively lower number of interests, but their interests were integrated to a higher degree.

In sum, political principals only intervened in the policy process to secure (a) the function of banks in overall economic growth, and/or (b) particular interests/constituents. As a result, there was no global political principal, i.e. the G7 did not control the BCBS. At the same time, the national political principals focused almost entirely on the intervention on behalf of those actors capable of exercising the voice option, but failed to duly ensure the public good of financial stability.

There was no conscious delegation strategy (as suggested by Drezner 2007, 64) of G7 governments, but rather silent acceptance by these governments of what their regulatory agents did,[185] presumably, due to politicians' preoccupation with the daily business of keeping the global and domestic financial markets running.[186] Furthermore, only two of the Basel II outcomes can be directly related to openly signalled preferences of the global political principal. First, with recent experiences of crises in emerging countries spilling over to the industrialised world, stabilising these countries' markets was a main interest. This was pursued through the 12 key financial standards, as developed in the transnational regulatory networks, and their enforcement via the IFIs. The second issue was the consolidated supervision of financial conglomerates, which was in substantial part achieved through Basel II. The G7 did not intervene in the BCBS's efforts beyond putting the two issues on the agenda and generally endorsing the Committee's efforts to enhance banking regulation.

The global forum of the G7 summits had an agenda of maintaining global financial market functioning and protecting their national economies from a global cool-down in economic growth. Beyond that, they were interested in pre-empting future spillovers from weakly regulated financial entities and crises in jurisdictions with low regulatory standards, in particular emerging and developing markets.[187]

In order to achieve this goal, the heads of state and government (and in particular their finance ministers) engaged in forum shopping, delegating the development of standards to several fora. The regulation of their own banks, i.e. the standards governing developed countries' banks, were almost entirely disregarded by the global political principal.

With respect to the *domestic political principals*, these politicians, like the G7, also had low Basel II, but relatively high actor-specific, integration rates. They also intervened selectively in the policy process to secure either the function of banks in overall economic growth or particular constituents. The governments and legislatures, if activated at all, focused almost entirely on interventions on behalf of those actors capable of exercising the voice option, but did not enforce systemic stability in banking substantially. Both national principals – the US Congress and the German Bundestag and government – were successful in demanding adjustments to the Basel II rules to better reflect the interests of their main constituencies.

In Germany, these were the small and locally oriented banks, which affected the federal legislative chamber through influential national associations and in some cases locally elected direct representatives. The fifth section from the top down in Table 4.9 reports the relatively high actor-specific integration (but also substantial rejection) rates. The most important achievements were: beneficial treatment of SME and retail credits; exception clauses regarding commercial shareholdings, drafted exclusively for German banks; introduction of the F-IRB, specifically directed at medium-sized German banks. Some issues, however, were blocked throughout the process, for example the parallel partial employment of all credit risk measurement approaches. While the number of rejected issues were lower, the integrated topics were the crucial demands.

In the US, the political principal gained some control over their regulators only after Basel II was already substantially defined. The presidential administration did not affect the outcome at all, but only intervened in national adoption. Both Congress chambers, also at a comparatively late stage, gained control over the regulatory agencies and altered Basel II considerably. This is reflected in the high actor-specific integration rate of Table 4.9. As in Germany, also in the US, small, local banks, specifically the community banks, were quite successful in invoking the voice mechanism. They acted in particular through the House of Representatives, the members of which were highly dependent on these local district constituents. Their crucial achievements were the beneficial treatment of credit card accounts, securitised mortgages and securitisation in general. Interestingly, the US community banks were less successful than their German counterparts.

In sum, national political principals were quite selective in controlling their agents, but in those instances decidedly and insistently in order to ensure that those constituents' interests were reflected in the framework that had a substantial impact on the politicians' utility. Such issues were primarily the beneficial approaches for small and local banks that were conceived of as having a decisive impact on local credit supply and overall national economic growth.

Moving from the public principals to their *regulatory agents*, it is restated that they are conceptualised as independent agents at arm's length of the rather inattentive principal. This, however, is conditional on the principal invoking its control possibilities. In that latter case, the regulators become merely executing agents that bargain on behalf of the domestic political principal's interest in the international negotiation forum of the BCBS.

One important result is that the dominant supervisor of the dominant market power set the agenda and influenced several outcomes substantially: the US Fed, as well as, though to a lesser degree, the US OCC (the two major US supervisors with federal bank supervision authority) integrated a great deal of their interests into the framework: among those were the development of a new Accord, the introduction of the three-pillar approach that added supervisory review and disclosure requirements, the increased reliance on sophisticated bank risk measurement techniques and external rating based risk weights, and the securitisation framework. The third highest integration rate reflects the high influence of US regulators.

The dominant US supervisors drove the German (as well as the other BCBS members') regulators into the development of a new Accord. While in favour of changes to the existing Basel Accord of 1988, they were opposed to the set up of an entirely new one. Therefore, they were clearly less influential than the dominant US regulators. Nevertheless, after this process had been started, the German agencies proved quite successful in integrating, first, their own interests into the first and second consultative papers, as well as, second, their principal's and regulatees' preferences throughout the second and third negotiation rounds.

The *transgovernmental regulatory network* of the BCBS was able to introduce and maintain several of its interests. In particular, the Basel Committee was able to counterbalance the capture by internationally active banks in several regards (credit risk models, operational risk, etc.), but had to give in during the negotiation to several preferences voiced by the transnationally oriented banks (capital levels for A-IRB banks, capital redefinition, securitisation, etc.). The amount of preferences reflected in the framework shifted during the latter episodes from an advantage for the supervisors to one for the banks. Moreover, in the frequent (though by far not universal) instances of a common opinion among the regulators, in particular the BCBS working groups, the Committee can be viewed as one collective supervisory organisation, the interests of which are integrated into global agreements. Accordingly, the transgovernmental explanation receives substantial if only limited support in terms of the number of preferences integrated, as revealed by the high integration and rejection rates in Figure 4.5.

The *transnationally oriented banks*, which in most instances also happen to be the largest and technically most advanced institutions, were widely successful, even though they had to accept many compromises with the transnational regulatory network – the dependence of the supervisors upon these regulatees' cooperation increased during the negotiations. Table 4.9 and Figure 4.5 clearly show the important role of transnational regulatory capture. Complex solutions, which demanded detailed technical knowledge, based on the suggestions of the main international associations, the IIF and ISDA, were introduced that suited the measurement and management methods favoured by those banks (this regards in particular the IRB approaches, operational risk approaches, credit risk mitigation and securitisation models). Nevertheless, in line with the recent findings of Young (2012), we have seen, and Figure 4.5's high rejection rate is indicative of this, that transnational capture is by no means absolute and follows complex causal pathways.

As already outlined with reference to the domestic principals, however, the *locally oriented banks* were also quite successful in utilising the voice strategy to activate domestic politicians to re-invoke their control over the national regulatory agency to negotiate on their interests' behalf in Basel. The surprisingly high integration rates in Figure 4.5 and in particular the high saliency of the integrated issues (as reported in Table 4.9) depict the substantial ratio of integrated positions of these rather small banks into the Basel II framework. Domestic constituents can have a substantial effect in transgovernmental networks and on globally harmonised regulatory standards.

Overall, the issue of the (global) public good of systemic stability was neglected while the sector's, sub-sectors', and several specific national stakeholders' concerns regarding competitiveness found integration into the global standards. Basel II constitutes a prime example of partially globalised policy processes in the global political economy. In the Basel II case, the global governance of regulatory standard setting can be related to regulatory failure, because the governance structure facilitates the simultaneous, unreconciled influence of competition state strategies and global harmonisation efforts, which leads to regulatory loopholes and governance gaps.

Underlying this was an unfavourable, and unintended political dynamic of influence in developing Basel II, which evolved in three stages. First, the transnational regulator-regulatee coalition offered plenty of opportunities for highly influential international banks to capture parts of the political deliberation. Supervisory agencies cooperated with transnationally oriented regulatees to develop standards, thereby balancing heavy pressure from the international banking community on the one hand, and domestic principal interventions on the other. Yet, given that the earlier proposals by the Basel Committee actually revealed the regulators' initial aim to improve systemic stability, both domestic and transnational regulatory capture cannot explain the outcome alone. Rather, these concerns were undermined throughout the further process, in which vetoes made an agreement much more difficult to achieve, to which supervisors then reacted by sacrificing earlier positions to reach an agreement at all.

Second, partially overlapping is the influence of the national voice coalitions between political principals and nationally/locally oriented regulatees. This is a particularly noteworthy finding, since prior studies did not mention this systematic, and crucial impact of competition state strategies as driving the transnational harmonisation project. Particularly interesting in this regard is the collaboration of domestic legislatures with nationally/locally oriented banks to protect the competitiveness of sub-sectors that had a substantial impact on the interests of the political principals. Accordingly, the domestic dimension played a crucial role in determining the outcome of regulatory standards in the TRR. The domestic intervention of the principal, however, while enhancing political accountability of regulators, did weaken the provision of the public good of financial stability. This was because it incentivised the agent to incorporate the principal's specific demands in order to pre-empt further political intervention, which resulted in an implementation that was regardful of the short-term interest of the politicians, but took the overall policy goal of banking system stability less into account (one of the crucial purposes of the authority delegation from politicians to regulators).

As a consequence, the national political principals shifted the inter-jurisdictional actor constellation to a state of increased polarisation on policy issues, which resulted in the changed interaction mode within the Basel Committee. Prior to national intervention that threatened cooperation, supervisors networked in a more like-minded manner to decide which set of standards to agree upon. The working group structure of the Basel Committee provided an excellent forum for crafting these solutions. After intervention of the political principal, the Basel Committee itself (not the working groups) was moved closer towards an international negotiation forum.

Third, this, in turn, led to the seclusion of the transnational network. Domestic supervisors, as well as their transgovernmental network, reacted to the domestic interventions by countervailing these threats to their authority. They counterbalanced and pre-empted further interventions through the seclusion within the transgovernmental regulatory network. Through detailed technical, problem-oriented collaboration in the BCBS working groups and task forces, they ensured coordination and agreement among the informal regulatory regime actors that were necessary to pre-empt political intrusion – i.e. they deepened coalitions among themselves and with the transnationally oriented regulatees.

In abstract terms, the Basel II process as transgovernmental governance effort of setting regulatory standards can be summarised in the following way: the transgovernmental network initiated standard setting, which signalled changes to the domestic market equilibrium; second, national coalitions of private interests became concerned and raised their voice to achieve a selective fire alarm intervention by politicians; transnational coalitions raised their voice with the transgovernmental network (and in addition with domestic regulators and politicians) and achieved integration of their private interests into the global framework; the combined influence weakened the regulators' capacities and incentives to develop standards that protect financial stability.

To summarise, the Basel II framework does reflect the influence of two main coalitions that were dominant in integrating their interests into the framework: first, the transnational network, pro-harmonisation, coalition, i.e. supervisory agencies cooperating with international banks to develop standards – here the pivotal regulators had to balance heavy pressure from the transnational banking community on the one hand, and domestic principal interventions on the other; second, the national voice – or competition state – principal-regulatee coalition(s) to protect the competitiveness of sub-sectors which have a substantial impact on the domestic political principals' utility. Both coalitions focused on the competitiveness of the sector or certain sub-sectors (e.g. small, local banks), but failed to prudently consider negative externalities that threatened systemic stability.

The simultaneous pressure by national voice and transnational harmonisation coalitions – both reinforced through selective political intervention on behalf of concerns of competitiveness – did not only neglect, but in the end even undermined the regard of the public good of financial stability. Due to the unreconciled influence that national and transnational coalitions wielded in the process of setting harmonised standards, regulators were captured and hindered in minimising the risks of negative externalities of imprudent banking on financial stability. Thus, the complex governance constellation of the TRR conditioned the policy process in a manner that was conducive to asymmetric influence of private interest coalitions and the disregard of negative externalities and systemic financial stability.

In sum, in terms of how the governance structure is related to regulatory outcomes, the institutional structure systematically conditions the regard of public versus private interests. Interestingly, regulators at first were quite keen to protect financial stability. It was the intervention by national politicians on behalf of nationally/locally oriented banks that altered and weakened the regulatory framework selectively. While these interventions were numerous, and complemented by selective pressure from transnational banks, advocacy on behalf of the public good of financial stability was disregarded.

Thus, the TRR conditions the policy process of setting globally harmonised standards in a manner that entrenches asymmetric influence of national voice coalitions and transnational harmonisation coalitions, which, in turn, reduces the protection of financial stability. The latter is due to the preferential influence by the private interest coalitions as well as the missing counterbalancing for public good provisioning. In effect, the transnational regulatory regime raises the possibilities for organised special interests to integrate their preferences into policy outcomes, while at the same time decreasing the incentives for, and capacities of, public officials to protect the public good of systemic stability and regulate externalities.

5
Global Banking Regulation after the Great Recession: Basel III, FSB, G20

Has the Great Recession resulted in significant change with regard to the identified deficiencies of global banking regulation? Returning to my initial question, how the transnationalisation in the governance structure of regulating banks conditions the influence of actors in the political process of standard-setting, and, thereby, the content of regulatory standards, as well as the insights on how the TRR conditioned Basel II processes and content, I now review how the post-crisis changes may or may not affect the continued relevance of the prior chapter's findings. Since many reform initiatives are still under way, debated, or in the process of adoption/implementation, the answer provided here can only be preliminary. The ongoing changes of the Financial Stability Board in particular, make any evaluation concerning the altered quality of regulation and regulatory institutions difficult. Therefore, I limit the following analysis to the influence of transgovernmental networks and the transnational regulatory regime dynamics that this study centred on. Accordingly, I identify three main areas of post-crisis reform in the realm of global banking regulation. The main reactions that transcend nation state authority were the development of the Basel III framework to enhance harmonised banking regulation, the strengthening of the G20 as the locus of international coordination for financial regulation, and the reconstitution of the Financial Stability Forum (FSF) as Financial Stability Board (FSB).

This chapter's analysis will reveal that regulatory change in response to the Great Recession was substantial. Yet, with regard to this study's main argument of the conditioning effects that the TRR has on influence and outcomes of regulatory standard setting, the change, to date, is modest. Global governance remains a crucial element of political attempts to embed transnational financial activity. Likewise, does the global layering of national and transnational rules continue to present governance gaps, as the layering of national and transnational processes continues to facilitate the simultaneous, unreconciled influence that creates regulatory loopholes in global standards. In other words, the TRR-structure and transnational networks continue to drive the process, subject to comparable limitations.[1] Looking beyond new detailed rules, likely to be subject to new arbitrage strategies, the potentially lasting change that might alter the TRR dynamics are the recent FSB reforms, which have the potential to transform it from a transgovernmental network into an international organisation. These, however, are potential future changes that have not impacted on the Basel III reforms – the current regulatory regime continues to be governed by the governance structure analysed in the previous chapters. Below, I discuss first the Basel III reforms, and second the changes in the wider global governance structure.

5.1   New policies: Basel III and global systemically important banks

Arguably, the most extensive change has occurred with regard to policy. Disregarding the many other policy changes outside of global bank capital regulation, I focus on the two major initiatives of the Basel III agreement and the additional regulation on systematically important banks.

In December 2010, the Basel Committee adopted one of the crucial cornerstones of the post-crisis governance agenda – the new rules regulating global banking, the Basel III framework (Basel Committee on Banking Supervision 2010b, Basel Committee on Banking Supervision 2010c). Yet, the new package of rules introduced by the Basel Committee often referred to as Basel III rather complements the previous Basel II framework than substituting it – i.e. the rules of Basel II.5 as well as Basel III apply simultaneously.[2] While Basel II.5 and III depict a substantial policy change in terms of new rules and rule restrictiveness, it is only a change within the regime paradigm of capital-adequacy-focused risk regulation, developed and harmonised through the existing TRR (Goldbach & Kerwer 2012, Admati & Hellwig 2013, 167–190). Basel II.5 was the short-term, quick response fighting the fires of the financial crisis, which resulted in quickly applicable, stricter rules.[3] In July 2009 the Committee agreed upon measures to regulate non-hedging securitised assets and other financial instruments of proprietary trading in the trading book. The measures reduce incentives to move assets into the trading book by raising the risk weights and bringing them closer to banking book levels. As a result of these revisions, market risk capital requirements will increase by an estimated average of three to four times for large internationally active banks (Basel Committee on Banking Supervision 2010a). By altering the rules of all three pillars, Basel II.5 raised the (regulatory) costs for trading activities (in contrast to hold-to-maturity investments), and in particular for securitisation, as well as for off-balance sheet assets. By reducing the profitability of the financial instruments that were at the root of the crisis, the regulators made it unattractive for banks to repeat the same mistakes.

Once these urgent revisions had been undertaken, the long-term resilience of the financial system and banks came into focus. Basel III is an extensive and detailed framework, which continues the tradition of complex, risk-based capital calculation in transnational financial regulation. Most of the work concerned pillar I issues, i.e. how much capital banks are required to hold, while less development can be seen regarding Pillar II and III issues, i.e. risk management and its supervision, and market discipline respectively. The new agreement introduced four new elements: increased restrictions concerning capital requirements, new capital buffers, a new leverage ratio, and two new liquidity provisioning requirements.

The minimum capital requirement in relation to risk-weighted assets (RWAs) has been increased to 10.5 per cent, including the new 2.5 per cent capital conservation buffer. In addition, risk-weights of several asset categories have been raised (banking and trading book), particularly concerning securitized assets and derivatives. Moreover, the quality of capital will be improved considerably, as definitions are becoming more restrictive. While capital types of lower quality are either not eligible any more (the previously permitted tier 3 capital) or internationally harmonised (tier 2), the crucial adjustment is the stricter definition of tier 1 capital. Under Basel III, 8.5 per cent have to be common equity, so-called tier 1 capital. From this, 7 percentage points have to be Common Equity Tier 1 (CET1) capital, which is even more restrictively defined capital. An additional 2 per cent can be provided using tier 2, less strictly defined types of, capital. Consequently, the composition of the 10.5 per cent required minimum capital has to be: 7 per cent CET1, 1.5 per cent common equity, 2 per cent tier 2 capital. While the above adjustments affect banks' costs heavily, scepticism is justified concerning the more innovative elements. One new element concerns two capital buffers, one to establish a capital stock that can be drawn from temporarily during bad times, another to be built up during bullish times.

The capital conservation buffer ensures against unexpected losses by building reserves above minimum capital levels. Additional 2.5 per cent of capital requirements are introduced – as discussed above this is part of the 10.5 per cent overall requirement – the distinct feature being that this capital can be drawn down during distressed times (as opposed to minimum capital requirements of 8 per cent). When banks' capital reserves fall into the range between 4.5 and 7 per cent CET1, they are progressively constrained in capital distributions (such as paying dividends, buying back shares, bonus payments, etc.). The logic is that banks want to avoid coming into this range where they are widely restricted in compensating their shareholders and employees, which provides them with the incentives to build higher capital reserves.

The second buffer, the countercyclical capital buffer, provides an incentive to build up buffers during boom times that can be drawn down during bust times – by creating a cyclically stable minimum requirement. In extreme cases it could result in an additional 2.5 per cent of CET1 capital requirements (resulting in the theoretical maximum capital requirement of 13 per cent). Whether, however, banks actually have to provide a countercyclical buffer hinges on a highly complex national process, which leaves room for domestic supervisory discretion. In a complex three-step process a domestic supervisory authority has to (1) identify a boom-episode with system-wide credit risk dissipation, (2) calculate the additional capital requirements (between 0 and 2.5 per cent CET1), for which then banks have 12 months to adjust. Finally (3), the supervisor has to enforce the buffer when banks capital reserves fall below the defined requirement, by progressively constraining capital distributions (stepwise 0-40-60-80-100 per cent of dividends, share buybacks, bonus payments, etc.). The complicated and lengthy process begs the question of whether regulators will be capable of enforcing it in time, i.e. during boom times, when arguments of international competitiveness tend to be dominant.

Furthermore, another innovative element was added to reduce capital arbitrage opportunities. The new leverage ratio defines a minimum level of capital reserves in relation to a bank's portfolio, independent of the risk incurred. It also means equal treatment of balance and off-balance sheet items. The minimum ratio is to act as a backstop to prevent banks from building up excessive leverage that is not prevented via risk-weighted regulatory approaches. It will become a parallel requirement to minimum capital requirements, and will stipulate 3 per cent CET1 capital relative to exposure. Implementation of the requirement as a hard pillar 1 stipulation, however, will not come into force before 1 January 2018, and is explicitly subject to review and potential adjustment. This leaves plenty of room for industry veto.

The most innovative element in transnational banking regulation is the new liquidity provisions that force banks to ensure their portfolios are sustainable within distressed illiquid markets. The standard requires banks to have a higher reserve of short term liquid assets (determined by the liquidity coverage ratio) and longer term liquid assets (determined by the net stable funding ratio). These are not additive to the capital requirements, but overlap. Furthermore, these quantitative requirements are nested within a supervisory framework of liquidity risk management principles (BCBS Principles for sound liquidity risk management and supervision 2008) that give detailed guidance on the risk management for banks and the supervision through the regulatory agencies, as well as the Monitoring Metrics that harmonise the minimum information to be gathered by domestic supervisors.

The Liquidity Coverage Ratio (LCR) stipulates banks to provide sufficient short-term unencumbered high-quality liquid assets to survive a 30-day stress scenario (calculated on the basis of 2007–09 circumstances, albeit not on the worst-case scenario of this period). The aim is for banks to have liquid assets available that can be monetised within a few days to finance 25 per cent of unexpected cash-outflows; banks have to calculate these provisions internally based on stress testing, at least monthly, while ensuring operational capacities for weekly/daily recalculation in stressed situations.

The accompanying Net Stable Funding Ratio (NSFR) aims at limiting over-reliance on short-term wholesale funding during boom times and the underlying revolving market financing of long term credits. It ensures that a bank's maturity structure of assets and liabilities is sustainable over a one-year time horizon. Banks have to undertake internal stress testing of available funds for servicing maturity structures, and report the results at least quarterly.

Basel III was complemented regarding the regulation of globally active banks by the additional capital requirements for Global Systemically Important Banks, the so-called G-SIBs (Basel Committee on Banking Supervision 2013d). The additional regulatory framework sets out the Basel Committee's methodology for identifying G-SIBs and increasing regulatory requirements for these banks. The purpose is to discourage banks from becoming (even more) systemically important. According to this agreement, banks above a certain size – that are deemed to be systematically important banks, and therefore too big to fail – are required to meet additional loss absorbency requirements and to disclose additional information to the public. The rationale is to deal with the cross-border negative externalities created by G-SIBs. The measures are designed to enhance the loss absorbency of G-SIBs and reduce the probability of their failure. The assessment of whether a bank is a G-SIB is based on an indicator-based approach and comprises five broad categories: size, interconnectedness, lack of readily available substitutes or financial institution infrastructure, cross-jurisdictional activity, and complexity. The additional loss absorbency requirements will range from 1 per cent to 3.5 per cent CET1 capital, depending on a bank's systemic importance. The higher loss absorbency requirements will be introduced in parallel with the Basel III capital conservation and countercyclical buffers, i.e. between January 2016 and year end 2018 becoming fully effective on 1 January 2019.

In sum, the three pillar architecture was reinforced by raising quantitative minimum requirements, by increasing qualitative supervisory scrutiny, and by forcing banks to reveal more information to the public. Furthermore, additional lines of defence are erected that are supposed to ensure prudential banking and prevent failures at earlier stages. The existing supervisory architecture has been considerably strengthened. Basel II.5/III, however, clearly did not bring a regime change, as only rules and – in a rather modest manner – decision making procedures were altered (see below), while the guiding principles and norms of the transnational regulatory regime remained untouched. Therefore, all we have seen is change within the existing regime and no change towards another one (Krasner 1982, 187–188). Goldbach & Kerwer (2012, 259–260) summarise their evaluation of the new rules accordingly:

> The Basel Committee continues to adhere to its previous approach to banking risks. Reforms merely amend or add to the three regulatory pillars of Basel II. However, within this framework, standards have changed. The new Basel standards define higher capital requirements, stricter capital definitions, and capital requirements for new types of risk, and apply to a wider range of banks' activities so as to close regulatory loopholes. Internal risk management and public information disclosure have to be enhanced and will be subject to stricter supervision. Moreover, a leverage ratio, capital buffers, and liquidity requirements were introduced. The new capital standards will require banks to shore up their capital reserves. Overall, we thus

find significant, if incremental change. . . . The Committee continues to be guided by the conviction that the uncertain future of financial markets can be transformed into calculable risk.

More than just incremental change in the regulatory regime of banking would include adjustments like the separation of investment and depository banking, size restrictions on banks, etc. Such changes, however, are mostly taking place, if at all, in domestic settings and not within the TRR. Banks may not be able to cause a crisis by using the same profitable, unsustainable financial instruments. Yet, the current imprudent investment in government bonds and other not sufficiently limited instruments provide a breeding ground for comparable business strategies based on different profitable, unsustainable instruments (Admati & Hellwig 2013).

Basel III is a regulatory solution to political challenges – anything else than a regulatory response would be a tremendous surprise. In other words, the decision by political leaders to delegate the responsibility for developing enhanced rules of financial market governance to existing transnationally institutionalised actors resulted in path-dependent negotiation structures that exclude systemic governance revisions (Underhill Forthcoming, 12–18). Basel III won't be able to overcome the risk-regulation regime that necessarily incurs risk and capital arbitrage behaviour and crises. The impressively detailed new framework creates structural incentives of imprudent risk taking similar to those prevailing before the crisis. While the restrictive and newly introduced measures certainly will raise capital requirements and consequently banking production costs substantially, the agreement is likely to become as much subject to capital arbitrage strategies as its predecessors. The arbitrage opportunities will simply move towards other activities – just as regulations move towards additional activities. Highly sophisticated regulatory stipulations always create incentives for identifying profitable loopholes. An industry with highly educated and innovative employees as banking or the financial industry in general will find these loopholes. That this complexity-arbitrage nexus remains under Basel III is a widespread evaluation in policy-making circles, as the remark of Mark Adelson (chief strategy officer at BondFactor Co., a municipal bond-insurance firm, and a former Standard & Poor chief credit officer) on Bloomberg (2013c) plainly suggests: 'Banks will always find loopholes to get around these rules, especially if they are so complicated. With all those formulas, they are like physics books. How can anyone monitor compliance with such complexity?'

Moreover, one should be aware of the obstacles on the path to faithful and effective adoption and implementation. First, the necessary decisions of domestic supervisors to increase capital requirements of banks that do not meet the regulatory standards (as in the case of the countercyclical and the capital conservation buffers) may be politically difficult due to the pressure that banks can put on politicians.[4] Second, the review of the newly introduced measures in combination with lengthy transition periods have already resulted in and are likely to result in further softening of the rules through reinterpretation of the Basel commitments (Howarth & Quaglia 2013b, Young 2013).

Accordingly, one could argue that we are at a point in time at which we witness the clawback of special interests. Cosmetic compliance strategies may weaken the Basel II.5/III results and FSB measures, as much as complexity, optionality and opacity have facilitated regulatory arbitrage during the deliberation, adoption and implementation of Basel II. This means, even if the new rules provided by the regulators are a substantial enhancement in the protection of international financial stability, politicians will react selectively to fire alarms of well-organised interests. At the same time, financial industry groups might gain more influence in the transgovernmental networks again. In other words, if the transnational governance structure continues to have detrimental effects on political processes and policy outcomes, we should witness how well-organized actors are capable of incrementally introducing their competition-related interests throughout the process of policy development, adaptation, and implementation. We could easily derive at that conclusion, if we for a moment compare our current position of the adoption and implementation of Basel III with the comparable situation of the first consultative papers as well as the adoption and implementation of the Basel II framework.

In evaluating Basel III dynamics, it is not yet possible to give an answer as empirically substantiated as the one provided regarding Basel II. Yet, if we aggregate information from press reports and first scientific investigations, we can derive at a first rough vision. Put succinctly, we witness political dynamics of national cosmetic compliance and transnational softening of the Basel III standards (Howarth & Quaglia 2013b, 3, 12). As we know from the last chapter, the first drafts of the Basel II agreement, the consultative papers of 1999 and 2001, outlined rather restrictive approaches to banking regulation, which were softened throughout the negotiation, adoption, and implementation periods. Likewise, following the consultative Basel III paper of December 2009 (the only consultative paper before Basel III adoption), and, furthermore, since the final agreement on the new Basel II.5 and Basel III standards in October 2010 (and the revision in June 2011), attempts to get regulators to substantially soften the adoption and implementation were very successful (see e.g. Howarth & Quaglia 2013b, Underhill Forthcoming, Bloomberg 2014, The Economist 2013, Börsen-Zeitung 2012).

Scholars and journalists have already pointed to the general trend of postponing reform through lengthy transition periods from initially end-2012 to 1 January 2019 (Underhill Forthcoming, Howarth & Quaglia 2013b, Young 2013, Goldbach & Kerwer 2012, The Economist 2013, Börsen-Zeitung 2012), which Young (2013) has coined as a distinct new strategy of the financial industry. Beyond this general phenomenon, political and industry pressure have resulted in major ex post reversals in all three areas of regulatory change.

Moderation in the increase of minimum capital requirements: The long list of reversals began early with the level of minimum requirements at a considerably lower level than initially envisioned – which already is enormously lower than leading experts advise for setting the level (Admati & Hellwig 2013). The finally reached 8 per cent (10.5 per cent including the capital conservation buffer) was the result of a serious veto from the European regulators and politicians – Germany even threatened to veto the agreement (Bloomberg 2013c, Howarth & Quaglia 2013b, 11). Accordingly, the 2010 negotiations led to a watering down of the initial proposal of the 10 per cent initially sought by the United States and Switzerland. As Bloomberg (2013c) reports, 'Germany and France led the opposition, seeking to protect the interests of their biggest lenders, which would have needed to raise more capital than foreign competitors'. Moreover, the definition of capital was – again, as during Basel II negotiations – watered down: American banks were allowed to continue counting some mortgage-linked assets as equity, European banks their minority stakes in other financial firms, and Japanese institutes their deferred tax benefits. As Bloomberg (2013c) reported, 'the last crisis showed that such assets failed to provide a buffer against losses'.

Softening liquidity requirements: The ex post reversals continued with the revisions of the liquidity framework (Basel Committee on Banking Supervision 2014f, Börsen-Zeitung 2012, The Economist 2013, Bloomberg 2013b). Supervisors, arguably reacting to industry influence (Börsen-Zeitung 2012), weakened the Liquidity Coverage Ratio, the new element that forces banks to have liquid assets available according to predefined guidelines, by transforming it from a minimum-requirement reserve into a buffer that can be drawn down during times of market distress. Moreover, supervisors will have discretion to decide whether the reserves lenders keep with central banks will count toward the LCR (Bloomberg 2013b). Second, regulators postponed the deadline of meeting the requirements. Banks now have to meet merely 60 per cent of the LCR obligations by 2015, while the full extent will be phased in annually through 2019, increasing by 10 percentage points each year. Third, the minimum requirements were relaxed, as more assets now count as part of the LCR due to a now extended list of approved assets – including equities and securitized mortgage debt as well as lower-rated sovereign and corporate bonds.[5] Fourth, regulatory authorities agreed to soften the stress test scenario underlying the LCR calculations, assuming a less extreme withdrawal from deposits and a slower income loss (Bloomberg 2013b, The Economist 2013).

As (Bloomberg 2013b) reports, this adaptation was the result of lengthy discussions in the BCBS working groups which endured throughout 2012 without reaching a compromise – that had to be found by a final negotiation between the Governors and Heads of Supervision (GHOS). This dynamic mirrors the Basel II processes of shifting interaction modes within the Basel Committee – transnational networking and international bargaining.

Given that many market participants consider the liquidity provisions as the cornerstone of the new agreements, since the financial crisis and particularly the Lehman collapse was characterised by liquidity shortages, and that these provisions are heavily burdensome for banks, this points to successful industry lobbying to countervail the extensive policy agreement (Börsen-Zeitung 2012).

Postponing and softening minimum leverage ratio: Also the second major new element, the minimum leverage ratio, has become subject to substantial revisions (Howarth & Quaglia 2013b, 12). French and German banks, regulators, and politicians were particularly aggressive in demanding these changes, as their banks' leverage ratios tend to be substantially lower than their US counterparts' (Howarth & Quaglia 2013b, The Economist 2014a, The Economist 2014b). As a result of the European pressure, transition periods were lengthened and the formula for calculating it diluted. Due to the changes, limited netting of repos as well as the integration of certain off-balance sheet exposures in the balance-sheet will be allowed for the calculation of the ratio, which is expected to 'boost' trade finance activities (Financial Times 2014).

This is politically relevant, as 'a rough calculation suggests that [the leverage ratio requirements] have been loosened just enough to allow most big European banks to pass the 3 per cent test. Without the committee's help as many as three-quarters of Europe's big banks might have failed the test' (The Economist 2014a). Moreover, there is still plenty of room for further dilution, as the BCBS '... will carefully monitor the impact of these disclosure requirements. The final calibration of the leverage ratio, and any further adjustments to its definition, will be completed by 2017, with a view to migrating to a Pillar 1 (minimum capital requirement) treatment on 1 January 2018'. (Basel Committee on Banking Supervision 2014a). In other words, arguably German, French, and other interests succeed in keeping the ratio in pillar 2 and in ensuring a potential further softening at a later stage.

This discussion could be extended substantially, since further revisions as in the securitisation framework as well as the trading book are currently in process (Basel Committee on Banking Supervision 2013c, Bloomberg 2013a, The Economist 2012). For example, one of the next steps is the second liquidity-related element, the NSFR, which is still under revision – comments were due in April 2014 (Basel Committee on Banking Supervision 2014b). According to Underhill (Forthcoming, 16) 'controversy with the industry' resulted in the exclusion of the NSFR from the recent liquidity proposal and separate future deliberations. Since government bonds are one of the main types of securities used in repo trades, which would be negatively affected through the current version of the rules, lenders are already warning that an increase in transaction costs caused by the NSFR would affect demand for sovereign debt negatively (Bloomberg 2014). One might imagine how politicians in the eurozone feel about such a threat.

In sum, financial stability was emphasised more strongly in Basel III, through additional and more detailed rules as well as the macroprudential turn (Baker 2013a). Due to the high political salience during the financial crisis, Basel III 'was negotiated in record time' of less than two years Howarth & Quaglia (2013b, 10). Yet, given this study's findings, scepticism whether the agreement in 2010 had, and the subsequent adaptations kept, this strong foundation regarding stability. As (Howarth & Quaglia 2013b, 12) emphasise, the consultative paper of December 2009 was quite 'draconian', yet the intermediary agreement in September 2010 was already much softer concerning several issues; moreover, the December agreement was even further soft-washed. This is in line with a recent study by Young (2013), who finds that financial industry groups have shifted their lobbying efforts towards later stages of the policy cycle, i.e. adaptation and implementation.[6] Thereby, they evaded the spike of public scrutiny after the crisis and strengthened forces during those episodes of technical discourse in the transnational and national networks (i.e. the TRR). Empirical investigation will have to reveal, whether this trend continues in further steps of adoption, adaptation, and implementation (especially during the lengthy transition and implementation periods). Given this study's findings and the vanishing public attention to banking regulation, one can expect further deterioration in the protection of financial stability.

Yet, to evaluate policy- and governance-change, one must look beyond the narrow cage of these agreements: to the transnational regulatory regime, which has a much more continuous impact, than the one-time perspective on agreements suggests. If one takes this perspective, Basel II and III become more alike: first agreement, followed by a lengthy phase of adaptation, transition and more adjustment, national implementation, and – again – transnational re-calibration and re-negotiation. Only this time this latter phase after adoption is even more important, as public scrutiny is vanishing (Young 2013). Certainly, the Basel III aftermath will differ from the Basel II one; however, there is strong evidence in favour of similarities, which should concern us. This is because the remaining prevalence of the TRR – and the layering of transnational and national rules and processes – implies a heightened probability of regulation that fails to protect financial stability.

To conclude the Basel III analysis, policy change has been substantial. The increased attention to system-wide risks andmacroprudential regulatory approaches may even be considered paradigmatic changes (Baker 2013b, Baker 2013a). It seems, however, that 'regulations often respond to the last crisis rather than forestalling the next' (Levinson 2010, 81). With regard to the central question, whether these rules are better suited to ensure prudent bank strategies and financial stability than the predecessor of Basel II, the answer is rather concerning. The continued paradigm of complex risk-calculating and market-driven regulation and supervision remains unsuitable for reducing the systemic stability's high sensitivity to imprudent risk-taking of market actors and banks that are too big to fail (see also Underhill Forthcoming). Given that the rules are becoming even more numerous and complex, two crucial challenges to the supervision of banks remain: (1) the limited resources of supervisory agencies to enforce these rules; (2) the numerous strategies for bank employees to bend or circumvent the rules. This means that the new rules may be more sophisticated rules, but on the basis of flawed assumptions. The risk of negative externalities on financial stability are likely to remain.

Accordingly, we can note within-regime change of continued market-based, risk regulation and the continuing strengthening of special interest clawback. To reduce the likelihood of comparable international spillovers of financial turmoil, this policy-change is insufficient (Admati & Hellwig 2013). It is simply unrealistic to expect a risk-based regulatory system to achieve macroprudential objectives, as the necessary individual supervisory and regulatory decisions remain subject to the well-known collective action problem of free-riding (Olson 1965) that undermines the probability of a public good such as financial stability being provided through a decentral market mechanism.[7]

What is needed is a truly paradigmatic policy-change that relieves regulators from the irreconcilable double responsibilities of ensuring stability and banks' competitiveness simultaneously. In other words, a policy that separates the concerns about the system's stability from those about the competitiveness and credit-creation of banks. As Barth, Caprio & Levine (2012) argue, this is unlikely to happen without institutional change. Therefore, the question of change in the policy process and governance structure as initiator of the strengthening of resilience and stability becomes crucial.

5.2 New layers in the governance structure and the deepening transnational regulatory regime: BCBS, FSB, G20

Of even higher relevance with regard to the validity of this study's findings is the question whether there has been *significant* institutional change – i.e. change that alters how the institutional structure affects the policy process and content/quality. Great Recession induced change is constituted by the three major reconfigurations of the G20, the Basel Committee, and the FSB.

The G20

Since the first leaders' summit in Washington DC in November 2008, the G20 has been considered to have replaced the G7/8. At its 2009 Pittsburgh summit, the member states have declared the G20 as their 'premier forum' (Viola 2014, 117). It could be argued that the G20 was the main locus of regulatory reform, which delegated the development of the details to the transgovernmental network of the Basel Committee and the FSB (Barth et al. 2013). A comparable argument has been put forward by Drezner (2007) regarding the G7/8 delegation of the Basel II development to the Basel Committee – which, however, this study has contested. The ongoing debate rather indicates a less influential role of the G20, comparable to that of the G7/8 during the Basel II negotiations. Several authors consider the forum as a successful crisis committee (Cooper 2010), which, however, has lost momentum after crisis management had been secured during its first three summits (Knaack & Katada 2013). The debate at the moment focuses on the question whether the G20 is merely a crisis committee or whether it has the potential to be a steering committee of global economic governance (Viola 2014, Knaack & Katada 2013).

When it comes to the regulation and politics of their own banks, the G20 continue to rely on the expertise of their regulators. The latter have continued to cooperate within their transgovernmental networks and the broader transnational regulatory regime. In fact, these actors and institutions were the best option for developing new rules available when the crisis hit (Verdier 2013). The global financial architecture continues to be heavily characterised by a transgovernmental structure. The reforms in response to the Great Recession have not altered that, but instead even foster it (Baker 2009). While the extension of the membership in the global financial architecture from G7 to G20 countries has increased inclusion and participation, it fails to create global deliberative equality (Baker 2009, Slaughter 2014). The addition of further bureaucrats into the continuing transgovernmental structure does change the number of states, but not the dominant structural aspects of transgovernmental elitist networks (Baker 2009, 211–212).[8] Andrew Baker (2009, 211) has emphasised this point very clearly:

> Crucially, transgovernmentalism is not just a country-based concept. Indeed, transgovernmentalism's fundamental contribution in its original conceptual form over thirty years ago was to demonstrate that states are structured representations of often splintered and internally conflictual sets of social relations. Simply adding some finance ministries and central banks from selected emerging markets, as in the case of the G-20, is not an adequate application of the principle of representation. This is because of the societal and material interests to which these agencies tend to be closest and, most crucially, the ideas these agencies tend to hold or the ideas they feel they need to espouse in order to be taken seriously by their colleagues from the G7. In this respect, country representation is only part of what is at stake in the global financial architecture. The representation of ideas and sectional interests are just as important.

Certainly, the G20 has concerned itself more with financial regulation than the G7 ever did. Further, it is not possible to give a substantiated answer to the difficult empirical question concerning who drives the agenda – the G20 or the transnational networks – since an in-depth empirical analysis of the many documents has to be undertaken and because the initiation can take place during informal meetings that are difficult to investigate accurately. Nevertheless, I argue that the changes have not yet resulted in altering, and are not likely to do so in the near future, the transnational diffusion dynamics of the transgovernmental governance networks and the transnational regulatory regime. Accordingly, it is important to understand which changes took place within the Basel Committee and which ones concerned the FSB.

The Basel Committee

The continuing dominance of the transgovernmental network logic as a crucial factor characterising global harmonisation of regulatory standards applies similarly to the BCBS. As already outlined, in 2009 following the demand of the G20, the emerging economies were added to the club: Argentina, Australia, Brazil, China, Hong Kong SAR, India, Indonesia, Korea, Mexico, Russia, Saudi Arabia, Singapore, South Africa, and Turkey. Nevertheless, when the Basel Committee adopted the new capital regulation rules, the same informal transgovernmental network of a selective set of developed (and this time emerging market) nations' regulatory agencies remained at the centre of global banking regulation. The BCBS continues to set the rules to protect the global public good of financial stability – even though it had failed to serve this task prior to the crisis. This is because there is no alternative authority – as Verdier (2013) explains, the transgovernmental network remains the core forum for regulatory harmonisation, since no viable alternative is readily available, and because political economy interests are deeply vested within the structures. As a result, it is not surprising that the decision-making mode and political processes after the Great Recession did not differ significantly from the Basel II negotiations (Levinson 2010, Lall 2012, Goldbach & Kerwer 2012, Verdier 2013).

Nevertheless, in evaluating whether the TRR governance structure prevailed after the crisis, a number of incremental internal and external organisational changes need to be considered. Externally, as I already argued above, the G20 did push for regulatory reform, although the content arguably came from the established transgovernmental networks; furthermore, G20 attention is vanishing. Regarding the FSB,

I will argue below that it reinforces the transnational regulatory regime, rather than changing it. In particular, the Board is strongly driven by the same regulatory authorities as is the BCBS, which makes it unlikely that the FSB will interfere with the BCBS work; and, moreover, the Basel Committee is responsible for major elements of the FSB's work (like the systemically important banks framework). Hence, after public scrutiny has vanished, the BCBS remains the central arena in a prevailing TRR, while the FSB deepens, rather than changes, the TRR logic.

The internal organisational changes also are likely to deepen the cooperation through the transgovernmental network and, thus, the TRR logic. As I emphasised in Chapter 2, formalisation and institutionalisation is taking place through an internal reorganisation and a written Charter, where the Committee positions itself as 'primary global standard-setter'. The Charter (Basel Committee on Banking Supervision 2013b) outlines the BCBS organisation, its activities and responsibilities, stipulates member states' responsibilities (ranging from the cooperation to promote financial stability to the faithful implementation and application of the Basel rules), mandates a 'compulsory public consultation process', delineates a periodical review of membership and potential integration of new members as well as the BCBS's relations to other international organisations. In sum, the Charter positions the Basel Committee as a central authority in world politics and how it relates to other elements of this order – another clear indication of formalisation and institutionalisation. Moreover, and this could be the most meaningful and changing reform, the BCBS introduced a detailed monitoring mechanism. Replacing the Accord Implementation Group (AIG), a committee to promote the implementation of Basel standards founded in 2001, Committee members agreed on a strengthened peer review mechanism. Under the Regulatory Consistency Assessment Programme (RCAP) member jurisdictions' implementation of Basel II, II.5, and III will be monitored through a clearly defined mechanism (Basel Committee on Banking Supervision 2013a). The programme consists of two complementary work streams: RCAP 'monitoring' reports on the timely adoption of Basel minimum standards via a self-reporting procedure of domestic regulators; RCAP 'consistency assessments', which involve off- and on-site examinations by an individually assigned RCAP team, and assess the consistency and completeness of the adopted standards. The monitoring exercise is obviously limited due to its basis of self-reporting. The consistency assessments, while not as forceful as they first sound,[9] nevertheless, constitute a transnationally institutionalised regulatory element. There is a complex organisation established under the Committee's Supervision and Implementation Group (SIG), where teams of regulators from non-assessed jurisdictions evaluate documents and data as well as the information from five-day-long visits in the assessed jurisdictions, where interviews are held with market actors, but not regulatory authorities. The following BCBS-internal review and publication process, which leads to a report publicly disseminated via the Committee's website, is also concisely stipulated (Basel Committee on Banking Supervision 2013a) and mirrors further institutionalisation.[10] Certainly, this complex incurs substantial incentives for all involved to not take evaluations as critical when appropriate; moreover, given the Basel standards' complexity, assessment on a 0/1 basis is hardly possible. Yet, taking a wider perspective, this can be seen as an incremental institution-building effort, which, in turn, strengthens the existent transnational norm diffusion processes.

A second, important aspect that was strengthened through further formalisation of principles is the coordinated supervision of internationally active banks by supervisors from multiple jurisdictions. The consolidated supervision of global banking groups are carried out through so-called 'supervisory colleges' (Basel Committee on Banking Supervision 2014c, Basel Committee on Banking Supervision 2010d), which 'refer to multilateral working groups of relevant supervisors that are formed for the collective purpose of enhancing effective consolidated supervision of an international banking group on an ongoing basis' (Basel Committee on Banking Supervision 2010d, 1). While BCBS harmonisation efforts used to be primarily and tend to be interpreted as the transnationalisation of regulatory standard-setting, the principles outlined in this context further the transnationalisation of the supervision of banks. This, again, points towards a deepening of the transnational regulatory regime.

These internal developments are likely to deepen the transnational diffusion of regulatory principles and practices. While both mechanisms (implementation monitoring and supervisory coordination) were already in place before the crisis, the new rules have increased the emphasis on these mechanisms in overcoming regulatory gap challenges. In light of the above discussion on Basel III and its problematic divergence between global layers, i.e. global accord and national implementation, these mechanisms may be(come) crucial. Studies concerned with global banking regulation have yet to investigate systematically the role of supervisory colleges and the implementation of standards. An in-depth analysis of whether these fora help create and diffuse norms, and *how* they actually affect domestic regulatory actions, would add substantially to our understanding of this policy area (and further areas of the international political economy).

In sum, while the inclusion of emerging markets into the BCBS may change the TRR in the long term through increasing policy-diversity, which complicates decision-making and faithful, coherent implementation, the BCBS remains a transgovernmental network of the same community. Moreover, it is still at the very centre of decision-making and constitutes the focal point in the TRR. The internal developments even suggest an incremental increase in the transnationalisation of the governance structure.

The biggest constraint might stem from the FSB, which, however, as we discuss below, does mostly add to the complexity of the TRR structure dynamics, rather than controlling the BCBS.

The FSB

The third main change to the institutional structure, and potentially the most effective adaptation, was the reconfiguration of the Financial Stability Board. Its creation is the most important new element of the international financial governance architecture. Whether it will have a significant impact, namely improved protection of global financial stability, does hinge on how it will perform in two regards. Against the background of this investigation's evidence on the detrimental effects of the TRR structure, the FSB's success will depend on (1) whether it can oppose/overrule banking regulation agreements by the BCBS, if these fail to take stability issues into account, and/or (2) whether it can set standards that have a superior effect vis-á-vis the BCBS rules. In the analysis that follows, I agree with the majority of authors that the prospects for the FSB to wield authority in the above two ways, with the purpose of altering the logic of the transnational regulatory regime, are rather dim. This is because the FSB is not yet a solid fourth pillar of global economic governance – it does not constitute a powerful intergovernmental organisation based on a formal legal contract with according member obligations, but rather another, complementary transgovernmental network that is subject to the same structural characteristics identified in this study.

In April 2009, the former Financial Stability Forum (FSF) was transformed into the FSB by a joint decision of the G20 with the objective to:

coordinate at the international level the work of national financial authorities and international standard setting bodies (SSBs) in order to develop and promote the implementation of effective regulatory, supervisory and other financial sector policies. In collaboration with the international financial institutions, the FSB will address vulnerabilities affecting financial systems in the interest of global financial stability. (Financial Stability Board 2012a, Article 1)[11]

In principle, the new institution has the purpose of safeguarding global financial stability. Hence, it could be the institutional arrangement that reduces the detrimental effects that the TRR structure has with regard to financial stability (i.e. the disproportional regard of well-organised private interests vis-á-vis the public good of financial stability). Considerable scepticism, however, remains, since, to date, the FSB has also preoccupied itself with within-regime changes, although on a truly extensive scale (Donnelly 2012, 274–275). In fact, other authors evaluate the prospects of the FSB as rather dim, since its institutional capacities are not sufficient for the tremendous task of ensuring global financial stability (Baker 2010, Helleiner 2010, Pauly 2010). As the current debate on the future prospects of the FSB mirrors, there are several serious constraints embedded in its institutional design, which may undermine the safeguarding of financial stability (Baker 2010, Griffith-Jones, Helleiner & Woods 2010, Helleiner 2010, Pauly 2010, Donnelly 2012, Moschella 2013, Pagliari 2014, Viola 2014, Wouters & Odermatt 2014). Three of these potential shortcomings are particularly concerning, namely the limited mandate, the organisational design, and its limited resources and highly dependent expertise.

Limited mandate: Arguably, since the amendment of its Charter, the FSB has three sets of mandated tasks: information provisioning, compliance monitoring, and standards development. In accordance with the classic theory on the benefits of international institutions, the FSB's mandatory tasks include mainly information provisioning. Four of the nine explicitly listed tasks (article 2 of the charter) relate to such information collection and provisioning: assessing the global financial system's vulnerability, promoting information exchange among authorities of financial stability, monitoring and advising on market developments and best practices of regulatory standards. Thereby, it provides an important task, yet, its influence does not go much beyond the FSF's information-related role. Several authors have argued that the FSB's information-related responsibilities may not develop much impact during times of boom – much like the FSF and

BIS analyses warning of systemic risks preceding the Great Recession did not have substantial impact (Moschella 2013, Griffith-Jones et al. 2010).

Further, the FSB gains influence through its mandated surveillance of the member states obligations. According to article 6, members of the FSB commit to pursuing the maintenance of financial stability, maintaining the openness and transparency of the financial sector, implementing international financial standards (including the 12 key International Standards and Codes), and agreeing to undergo periodic peer reviews, using among other evidence IMF/World Bank public Financial Sector Assessment Program reports. Arguably, the surveillance of the FSB member states' mandatory implementation of the 12 key financial standards strengthens the FSB's role. This, however, might even augment the role of the transgovernmental networks, where most of these standards originate (Mosley 2009). The Charter amendment strengthened the FSB's role in incentivising member states to implement standards through the explicit mandate to 'promote member jurisdictions' implementation of agreed commitments, standards and policy recommendations through monitoring of implementation, peer review and disclosure' (article 2, paragraph 1(i)). Moreover, it included a new article that gave a stronger mandate to the Standing Committee on Standards implementation (see below). This leads arguably to a strengthened international regime, which is, however, subject to two limitations: first, all Committees function according to consensus rule, which is why the only route to force a member is informal peer-pressure; second, this may result in what Walter (2008) called mock compliance (formally adopting standards, but in reality not enforcing them faithfully).

Prior to the amendment of the FSB Charter, it did not have a strong role in developing standards on its own, leaving this task entirely to the transgovernmental networks of the BCBS, IOSCO, etc. Article 5 (before the amendment article 2), paragraph 2 outlines the relationship between the FSB and the other transgovernmental standard setting bodies. While the latter have to report to the FSB on their regulatory activities, the paragraph clarifies that this 'should not undermine the independence of the standard-setting process'. With regard to banking regulation, this strengthens the Basel Committee by acknowledging its authority. The addition of paragraph 3 to article 5, however, might mirror the incremental change in the FSB's capacity to develop standards itself. This paragraph gives the FSB substantial new formal authority:

The FSB should, as needed to address regulatory gaps that pose risk to financial stability, develop or coordinate development of standards and principles, in collaboration with the SSBs [Standard Setting Bodies] and others, as warranted, in areas which do not fall within the functional domain of another international standard setting body, or on issues that have cross-sectoral implications.

This still limits the influence on the BCBS and regulatory standards for the banking sector. Following the explicit wording, the FSB does not have a lot of room for standards development. Yet, the paragraph provides the FSB with a room for interpretation of which standards do not fall in other SSBs' domains. This new clause could provide a breeding ground for globally harmonised standards to protect financial stability. By going beyond the formal text, the FSB could even intrude in the traditional SSBs' authorities. Given the overlapping membership of these organisations (see below), however, this seems rather unlikely at the moment.

In sum, the FSB's mandatory influence could become a significant change that improves the protection of financial stability by reducing the dangers of international spillovers. Yet, it's institutional and organisational foundation is insufficient for making a strong contribution that overrides the pre-eminence of the transnational standard setters. This is also reflected in the two further problematic elements of the FSB's architecture.

Organisational design: At first sight, the FSB has a much stronger organisational footing compared to its predecessor: first, it's membership was widened to include all G20 jurisdictions. Second, it encompasses many additional actors from the G20's jurisdictions, which includes several (mostly the G7) member states' national political principals, i.e. the finance ministers. The membership consists of political and regulatory representatives from the national authorities, namely finance ministers, central bankers, and financial market regulators. According to Donnelly (2012, 268), 'FSB membership rules ensure that input is dominated by those countries with the greatest combined political and economic clout'. This is ensured by the variation in the number of representatives that a country can send to the FSB. All countries are represented by their central banks, while other countries may also send their finance ministers, and others even their financial market regulator in addition. The distribution of representatives is rooted in the distribution of power. As a result, as Vanoli (2010) demonstrates, the widened membership did not result in a substantial change of the agenda and issues discussed –

much as Baker (2009) argues. This is further fostered by the international organisations which are members of the FSB – the IMF, the World Bank, the BIS, the OECD – and in particular the international standard setting bodies: the BCBS, the BIS's Committee on Payment and Settlements Systems (CPSS), the BIS's Committee on the Global Financial System, the International Accounting Standards Boards (IASB), the International Association of Insurance Supervisors (IAIS), and the IOSCO. Therefore, while the G20 membership is an improvement over the FSF's G7/G10 membership the increase in legitimisation is rather limited, as the core countries of the G7 attempt to maintain their higher power, and include non-G20 countries rather through ad hoc regional committees (Pagliari 2014, 152).

Moreover, the decision-making structure greatly limits the FSB's authority in controlling member states' adherence to their obligations. The FSB plenary is the sole decision-making body in the FSB, which assembles all member state authorities and international authorities (each with an equal vote). It operates on the basis of consensus rule. Hence, while the international forum is in charge of a substantial amount of important decisions – approving the work programme and the budget; adopting standards, reports, principles, and recommendations developed by the FSB – no member state (even no single member state authority) can be forced into any decision against its will. Many authors have agreed that this substantially weakens the FSB – at the moment it is at best a very weak organisation with soft law institutions (Griffith-Jones, Helleiner & Woods 2010, Moschella 2013, Pagliari 2014). The plenary's consensus rule leads to two problems: it could prevent the FSB from opposing imprudent policies during times of economic boom (Griffith-Jones et al., 2010, 8); second, the necessity of consensus limits the leverage that the organisation can have over its member states regarding their obligations to implement certain policies. These problems remain even after the amendment of the Charter, since the FSB continues to be a member-driven, and consensus-based organisation.

Given the constraints of the Plenary, the influence of the FSB as an organisation independent from its member states hinges on the power that the executive agents can exert: the Chair, the Steering Committee, and the Standing Committees. As Pagliari (2014, 150) explains, the Chair does play a central role in steering the organisation. According to article 21, he has to come from a small subset of experts in financial regulation, which is then selected by the plenum. He has (until now only men have served as Chair, first Mario Draghi, and currently Mark Carney) considerable responsibilities in coordinating the FSB's work. He, however, remains on secondment and is paid by as well as principally responsible to the national financial regulatory authority that sends him. One of his key responsibilities can be seen in his proposal of who should serve on the Steering Committee (article 13, paragraph 1), which the Plenary then approves. At the same time, the Chair initiates the selection of Chairs of the Standing Committees and the Secretary General, which are, then, also approved by the Plenary.

The Steering Committee consists of currently (as of 6 January 2014) 41 persons from national financial authorities, and mirrors the FSB membership representation key in the Plenary (with unequal distribution of seats to the different member states). That is, as in the Plenary, the Steering Committee consists of central bankers, financial regulators, and finance ministers. The Steering Committee can function as an important coordinatory body, since it has the assignment to coordinate and conduct policy reviews of the FSB's ongoing projects, coordinate the work with the other transgovernmental networks of standard setting, and might even prepare options for the decision of the Plenary (article 12, paragraph 3). As the current composition of the Steering Committee reveals, it resembles a transgovernmental network structure of national authorities of financial regulation – plus officials from the most important states' ministries of finance.[12] This also characterises the four Standing Committees (on Assessment of Vulnerabilities, SCAV; on Supervisory and Regulatory Cooperation, SCRC; on Standards Implementation, SCSI; on Budget and Resources, SCBR – articles 15–17), which extend the transgovernmental network structure into networked working groups – the transgovernmental network character is extended and deepened even further by the Standing Committees' rights to establish ad hoc working groups with representatives from non-FSB members (whether this includes non-state actors is not obvious); the composition of the Standing Committees lies in the responsibility of each Committee's Chair, who consults with the FSB Chair. The role of the Standing Committees has been put on a strengthened basis in the context of the Charter amendment, since each Committee has now received a particular article, which specifies for each Committee the substantial functions. The just described structural characteristics reveal very clearly the similarity to the transgovernmental network and TRR structures investigated in the present study. The FSB, however, might gain substantial influence, which would imply a change in the organisational logic as compared to the Basel II scenario. This is through its potential capacity to enhance the regard of financial stability in globally harmonised regulatory standards. Arguably, this can take place via two routes, namely the development of particular FSB standards on financial stability and the influence on the standard setting by other bodies like the Basel Committee. As outlined above, according to article 5, paragraph 3, the FSB can develop new standards 'as needed to address regulatory gaps that pose risk to financial stability', which may give the Secretariat and the Standing Committees substantial leverage in pursuing their own regulatory agenda. Moreover, this new paragraph may enable the Board to increase its influence on the standard development in other transgovernmental networks through its increased authority in the coordination of standard development.

Limited resources and dependent expertise: Due to the substantially widened membership as well as its stronger mandate one cannot deny the increased importance of the FSB. Nevertheless, it is crucial to bear in mind that the FSB is not an influential intergovernmental organisation, like the IMF, the World Bank, and the WTO. The major reason lies in its tiny staff of between 15 to 20 employees (Pagliari 2014, Donnelly 2012, 268), which is directed by a Secretary General that is entirely subordinate to the Chair. Also, these employees are either drawn from within the BIS/BCBS or seconded from national regulatory authorities.[13] Further, the Secretariat has no strong formalised rights to put forward a policy agenda – all this remains with the transgovernmental networks and the hubs of the Chair and the Steering Committee.[14]

The FSB Charter's article 23 does explicitly deny the creation of any legal obligation for the member states. Even though the amendments to the Charter and the establishment as association under article 6 of the Swiss Civil Code – by the FSB's articles of association in January 2013 – 'the FSB has a long way to go before it becomes anything like the other pillars [WTO, IMF, World Bank] in terms of legal basis. The FSB articles of association are binding under Swiss law, but at the international level, the Charter remains a non-binding agreement between FSB members' (Wouters & Odermatt 2014, 55). Furthermore, it remains unclear how the FSB can transform into a more permanent organisation (Brummer 2012).[15] As Pagliari (2014, 151) outlines, even after the 2012 amendments the FSB is not 'a treaty-based international organisation [that is] subject to international law and capable of exercising influence independently of its members'. Rather it remains a member driven organisation and its decision making continues to be based on consensus. Against this background, the FSB relies much on transnational diffusion through its membership organisations.

Not only is the FSB insufficiently equipped to be a strong international organisation: even if the FSB can wield significant influence in harmonising regulatory standards for the purpose of safeguarding financial stability, its dependence on Basel Committee expertise makes it highly unlikely to come up with solutions that the BCBS opposes, or even oppose solutions of the Committee. As Donnelly (2012, 270) explains, the FSB is much more a forum that brings together experts from different transgovernmental networks, rather than a hierarchically superior authority. In reality, the FSB is not capable of opposing policies by the transgovernmental networks or even enforcing their policy preferences on the Basel Committee.

In sum, the FSB's reconfiguration changes the global architecture and will alter the future of global banking regulation. Yet, these changes do not alter the existence of the transnational regulatory regime. The FSB's main task continues to be to augment the available information concerning global financial stability and the coordination regarding the topic of financial stability. In the long term, the FSB's creation with its formal structure, official mandate, and organisational body may prove to be a major critical juncture concerning the international cooperation in providing and safeguarding financial stability. Without additional external pressure (such as another crisis), however, this is rather unlikely (Pauly 2010). Pauly draws the parallel to the ineffective League of Nations' Economic and Financial Organization, which was also very limited in its influence due to consensus rules, tiny staff, and a focus on best practice dissemination. Nevertheless, the recent amendment of the FSB's Charter (and the future debate on further development in context of the G20 meeting in Brisbane in 2014) draws our attention to a potential intergovernmental organisation in the (incremental) making. Yet, at the moment global banking regulation continues to be driven by the transnational regulatory regime dynamics revealed by the present study.

If this study's findings remain relevant and the TRR-induced dynamics are accurate theoretical tools for the analysis of the FSB, to strengthen global financial stability this new institution can at best be a complementary element. I discuss the more promising national approaches, which the FSB could complement, in the subsequent chapter. In the short term, however, the FSB is merely another transgovernmental and transnational network with insufficient capacities to come up with its own agenda or counteract selective national fire alarm type special interest clawback. Leading scholars have emphasised in an early volume on the prospects of the reconfigured board that '... the

FSB may suffer the fate of its predecessor, the FSF ... even though it [the FSF] produced often excellent studies warning of systemic risks that were not acted upon' (Griffith-Jones, Helleiner & Woods 2010, 12). In other words, its innovative character as guardian of global financial stability notwithstanding, if the major weaknesses are not overcome, the FSB remains not much more than an additional transgovernmental network that embeds a selective set of domestic actors into an opaque transnational regulatory regime – where incentive structures disadvantage financial stability vis-á-vis special interests. Admittedly, the recent developments related to the amendment of the FSB Charter raise the question as to whether we see the rising of a powerful intergovernmental organisation that could change the dynamics described in this study. Yet, the continued emphasis on member state driven agendas and consensus decision making in the FSB does not lead in this direction. Only time can reveal the meaning of the recent increments.

Considering these institutional changes altogether, I argue that we may witness substantial change as regards long-term international cooperation – the instalment of the FSB as potential fourth pillar of international economic governance and the strengthening of the G20 may in the long term prove to be significant changes. In the short to medium term, however, change is insignificant, because the same transgovernmental/transnational institutions and dynamics continue to dominate political decision making. In other words, this study's theoretical framework of the transnational regulatory regime remains an accurate conceptualisation of how different actors and institutions can affect the content and quality of globally harmonised regulatory standards and how these are then diffused transnationally.

In sum, there can be no doubt that the change that has already occurred or is currently unfolding is tremendous. Therefore, it would be pointless to argue that the current state of the world – characterised by the outlined elements of Basel III, G20, and FSB – can be compared with the Basel II world before the Great Recession in a straightforward manner. Nevertheless, the Basel II findings regarding the (mal-)functioning of global governance in harmonised banking regulation remain valid in the current era following the Great Recession and the subsequent reactions.

Regarding policy, change was substantial – yet, in sum it was rather change within the risk-calculating regime, than a paradigmatic regime change. Moreover, regarding the governance structures, change has not yet addressed the structure and dynamics of the transnational regulatory regime. Hence, transgovernmental networks of national bureaucrats remain in the pivotal position of designing the global governance answers to politically embed global financial activities, while political interventions remain to react selectively to special interests' fire alarms. As a result, global layering of national and transnational rules continues to provide governance gaps, as the layering of national and transnational processes continues to facilitate the simultaneous, unreconciled influence of national and transnational coalitions that creates regulatory loopholes in global standards. In other words, the TRR structure and transnational networks continue to drive the process, subject to comparable limitations.

6
Conclusion: Layers and Gaps in the Global Political Economy

In April and October 2014, the BCBS published its latest progress reports on adoption and implementation of the post Great Recession reforms, finding satisfactory levels of the ongoing efforts (Basel Committee on Banking Supervision 2014d, 2014e). At the same time, the EU and the US pursue adoption adjusted to their specific national circumstances (Howarth & Quaglia 2013a), while industry groups have intensified their transnational and domestic lobbying activities to create loopholes in the new regulations. How effective can such a governance mode be in minimising the risks of repeated global financial turmoil?

I have put forward the argument that such unreconciled simultaneity of national and transnational standard-setting is a major, unresolved problem at the core of global governance, since it constitutes durable disorder and, in consequence, leads to global policy failure. I have emphasised how the unchecked influence of national competition state and transnational harmonisation coalitions have created loopholes in the regulatory architecture that, in conjunction with lenient national rule enforcement, lead to regulatory failure. We saw how the TRR of global banking regulation conditioned influence in a manner that is detrimental to the provisioning of financial stability. Moreover, I revealed that this governance constellation persists after the Great Recession, and that it is the locus of developing the major global regulatory reform efforts – if anything, this structure has been fostered. So, what now?

Randall Germain (2010, 150) has argued that the Great Recession constituted a major historical turning point, as it strengthens the refocusing on national approaches to achieve financial stability. This, however, should not give us a false comforting feeling, since, as I have argued repeatedly in this book, the problematic institutional characteristics that condition the policy process remain in place:

- the crucial importance of big banks to politicians and regulators, combined with the opportunity structures of regulators (and politicians) that incentivise them to regard banks' interests disproportionately;
- the unchecked simultaneous influence of national and transnational coalitions in developing global standards;
- the unreconciled existence of national and transnational standards;
- the missing counterbalance in favour of the public good of financial stability.

Taking these factors into account, while acknowledging the substance of national and global reforms, it is likely that new loopholes will be created and that regulators will remain in a position in which they won't be able to enforce strict rules on banks. Germain points out, as I have done in the previous chapter, that the ultimate responsibility for significant reform lies with politicians, not regulators. Furthermore, Germain explains that hard choices are necessary and will imply losers – actors that profit from the system as it currently functions. I argue that it is because of these losers' capacity to mobilise and the voters' unwillingness to support such tough choices that politicians have few incentives to initiate such reforms. As I have discussed in Chapter 3, the next election is always closer than the next turmoil (at least in the expectations of politicians).

Yet, rather than condemning or praising the entire financial system, 'what we should be worried about ... are the checks and balances which encourage and discourage particular types of behaviour' (Germain 2010, 151). Against the background of an incrementally transnationalising political economy and policy process, it is these political control mechanisms that I turn to in the remainder of this book – first, with a view to the future of global banking regulation, second to global financial governance, and, third, to the global political economy more generally.

6.1 Global banking regulation and financial stability

We began this study against the background of the recent crisis, asking how the transnationalisation in the governance structure of regulating banks and financial stability conditions the influence of actors in the political process of standard-setting, and, thereby, the content of regulatory standards.

This conditioning effect of the governance structure on influence and regulatory outcome is rooted in the evolving transnationalisation or globalisation of politics and political economy. In Chapter 2, I outlined that since the early 1970s we have witnessed an incrementally deepening level of global institutionalisation in the realm of banking regulation. The Basel Committee was introduced as a prime example of the transnationalisation of policy processes and governance structures. The co-evolution of transnational bank activities and banking crises on the one hand and the transgovernmental cooperation on the other hand have established a transnational regulatory regime that augments interdependence through transnational diffusion of regulatory practices. This results in the global layering of institutions and processes and the complex interaction of state-bound and state-transcending mechanisms driving banking regulation.

In light of this partially global political economy, the TRR persists as the governance and opportunity structure of global finance. Thus, I argued that if we aim to understand or explain the recent past and the future of global financial governance, it is necessary to synthesise several explanations of who is influential in global standard setting. Therefore, as outlined in Chapter 3, I propose the TRR-framework that adds to the two-level heuristic by integrating additional intra-level and in particular dynamic inter-level mechanisms. I hope, that the analysis of chapters 4 and 5 convince the reader that transgovernmentally set bank standards are driven by the interaction of state unit-bound mechanisms of a two-level game of international politics – i.e. national intra-level regulatory regime dynamics and interstate G7/20 deliberations – plus transgovernmental and transnational mechanisms as well as dynamic feedback processes between these three arenas. This framework has enabled me to explain, how specific national and transnational coalitions were capable of creating regulatory loopholes in the Basel standards.

It was the aim of my study to reveal how the transnational governance structure is related to regulatory failure since the 1990s. Through measuring the influence of the global political economy's actors and tracing the processes underlying the development of transnational standards it was possible to crystallise how Basel II operated as a diffusion device of regulatory practices that were at the root of the Great Recession. The development of new standards, in particular the risk measurement and management paradigm based on internal banking systems, was spearheaded and diffused through the Basel II exercise and the Basel Committee's transnational network. Hence, while not the primary cause of the regulatory failure, the transnational endeavour certainly failed to regulate international banking activity suitably. Moreover, it even contributed to the spread and development of rules prone to regulatory gaps. Excessive risk taking and regulatory arbitrage were not pre-empted and in several cases even facilitated. Underlying this policy failure was the asymmetric influence of national and transnational coalitions, both of which could introduce their preferred aspects into the Basel II framework.

However, regulatory change in response to the Great Recession was substantial. Nevertheless, my analysis of the reforms of the Basel III and G-SIB agreements as well as the institutional dimensions of the changes of the Basel Committee, the G20, and the FSB revealed that the problematic of rule and process layering remains in light of the persistent transnational governance structure. With regard to this study's main argument of the conditioning effects that the TRR has on influence and outcomes of regulatory standard setting, the change, to date, has been modest – and *not* paradigmatic or significant. The TRR-structure and transnational networks continue to drive the process, subject to comparable limitations. In particular, change has not yet addressed the structure and dynamics of the transnational regulatory regime, since transgovernmental/transnational networks of national bureaucrats remain the pivotal actors. Looking beyond the new detailed rules, likely to become subject to new arbitrage strategies, the potentially lasting change that might alter the TRR dynamics are the recent FSB reforms, which have the potential to transform it from a transgovernmental network into an international organisation. However, the current regulatory regime continues to be governed by the governance structure analysed in the previous chapters.

The theme that guided this book was the relationship between global governance and regulatory failure to provide the public good of financial stability. Underneath this relationship, I identified the overlap of state-bound and state-transcending authority, which leads to the layering of national and transnational (as well as interstate) rules and policy processes, which, in turn, can create considerable loopholes in regulating economic activity, i.e. global governance/regulatory gaps. This is particularly concerning, since these standards can in addition even undermine national authorities' capacity and incentives to enforce strict national rules. Hence, the result could be more, rather than less, gaps.

My main contribution to this research area is the analysis of how these loopholes are created at the stage of developing transgovernmental standards. I have traced how the simultaneous, unreconciled influence that national and transnational coalitions wield in the process of setting harmonised regulatory standards undermines their prudence. In global banking regulation this unreconciled influence is entrenched in the global governance structure. More specifically, I claim that global banking regulation is characterised by a complex governance and opportunity structure, the TRR, that is conducive to policy failure (and the resulting financial instability).

In sum, the core argument is, that the TRR conditions the policy process of setting globally harmonised standards in a manner that entrenches asymmetric influence of national voice coalitions and transnational harmonisation coalitions, which, in turn, reduces the protection of financial stability. The latter is due to the preferential influence by the private interest coalitions as well as the missing counterbalancing for public good provisioning. In effect, the transnational regulatory regime raises the possibilities for organised special interests to integrate their preferences into policy outcomes, while at the same time decreasing the incentives for, and capacities of, public officials to protect the public good of systemic stability and regulate externalities.

As the previous chapter discussed, this governance structure continues to characterise global financial regulation. Instead of asking for an unrealistic choice between national and global solutions, pressing questions relate pragmatically and critically to the balance of a mix of arrangements with differing scopes of societal organisation. The historical record (Helleiner 1994, Pauly 1997, Busch 2009, Germain 2010) suggests that in the short- to medium term (at least) nation state authority will coexist with incrementally deepening transnational governance efforts. In light of partially globalised and incrementally globalising policy processes and political economies, it is worthwhile to think about the implications for power control and political control mechanisms in this state of world politics (Grant & Keohane 2005, Keohane et al. 2009). Thinking about it this way opens the door to considering organisational and institutional adaptations that might provide a better organisation of public authority to balance global private financial activity.

The political economy of the Basel Committee and financial stability

If the reform efforts in the global financial governance structure (BCBS, FSB, G20), as I argue, do not alter the governance structure significantly in terms of opportunity structures for public officials, the incentives for politicians and regulators remain biased in a way that is conducive to repeated regulatory failure in providing financial stability. In the transnational regulatory regime, regulators have de facto obtained a substantial part of legislative authority and political control over the public good of financial stability without being suitably checked and counterbalanced, or being held accountable through effective control mechanisms by the general public or representative public bodies.

This deficiency in political control mechanisms is due to political principals' tendency to weigh the competitiveness of economic actors in their constituency higher than the financial stability of the economy. This occurs for two interrelated reasons, namely short-sighted office-seeking orientation and information/resource deficits to comprehend banking regulation and demand appropriate regulatory standards. On the one hand, politicians of the legislative and government are under pressure from special interests of the industry, which claim that unfavourable standards will result in reduced credit and economic growth and threaten withdrawal of political support. On the other hand, the more complex the policy becomes, the less capable politicians will be of actually scrutinising a regulatory policy in terms of its contribution to financial stability. Politicians, therefore, are likely to enforce control over regulatory agencies to ensure the competitiveness of important constituents, but fail to enforce stability issues accordingly. The described tendency is further aggravated through the persistent policy paradigm of Neoliberalism that guides policymakers.

At the same time, regulatory agents tend to weigh competitiveness higher than stability for two related aspects of the situations of their decision making, namely for reasons of industry capture and selective principal pressure. The everyday close cooperation with the industry results in a bias towards understanding common needs, and in a policy favourable to banks as alternative principals of the supervisors. However, even though regulators still see stability as at least as important, the selective intervention of political principals on behalf of specific interests further weakens their incentives to foster stability, as not giving in to political pressure would likely worsen the agent's utility.

In sum, the informational asymmetries and the dispersed authority between the triangle of political principals, regulatory agents and regulatees, in conjunction with weak political control mechanisms on behalf of financial stability, increase the probability of banking regulation that does not take stability sufficiently into account. Moreover, the opacity of the (T)RR deepens this tendency as it enables specific organised interests' influence through diverse channels, but disables proper regard of the public interest of stability in the everyday decision making of public officials. Consequently, the public good of financial stability is under-provided, since the opportunity structures facing public officials do not provide sufficient incentives to protect financial stability at the expense of banking profitability and growth. In other words, the macro-level task of ensuring systemic stability is not institutionally reinforced during the development of global standards in a way that counterbalances competitiveness-related influence.

Thus, in most regulatory regimes of industrialised nations' banking sectors, there is a tendency to deficient political control mechanisms to provide financial stability. In particular, the study revealed that this tendency is emphasised and deepened through the embedding of domestic regulatory regimes in TRRs, since the additional layer and channels further disperse authority. TRRs increase the possibilities for organised special interests to integrate their preferences into policy outcomes, while at the same time decreasing the incentives for, and capacities of, public actors to ensure systemic stability and the regulation of externalities.

Policy implications

Which policy implications for global banking regulation can be drawn from my findings? In light of this study's insights, it is questionable whether the detailed harmonisation of regulatory standards is really the best solution to reduce the likelihood of financial turmoil and its spreading through transnational spillovers. The problem with detailed harmonisation is that policymakers assume the dangers of regulatory arbitrage to be minimised, while in fact rule and process layering actually increase the number of loopholes and the potential for regulatory arbitrage. Therefore, it might be better to refrain from harmonisation, but continue or intensify supervisory coordination. This, however, is not – at least under the current circumstances – a viable option, due to path-dependent global opportunity structures and entrenched interests (Verdier 2013).

Nevertheless, two realistic changes are possible. First, the policy of banking regulation should be put on a stronger footing, relying less on complex risk-based calculation and more on solid equity. Two leading scholars of the field, Admati & Hellwig (2013), make a strong case for high levels of equity in banks as a major reform element. They argue, since banks and other financial intermediaries continue to have unsustainably high levels of indebtedness (which comes at a very high cost for society), that the best way to regulate them is to increase the level of equity substantially – to levels between 20 to 30 per cent. There is not sufficient room here for a discussion of this reform proposal, instead the reader should consult the work referred to. It is, however, also clear that such significant changes are unlikely given the opportunity structures discussed in the third chapter.

Second, with regard to globally layered institutions and processes, the detrimental dynamics that unfold without intention in the TRR can be reduced, if one examines how domestic politics feed into the transnational regulatory regime. In order to countervail the asymmetric influence of national voice and transnational harmonisation coalitions and reconcile the layering of national and transnational rules, the established national institutional structures provide a baseline on which realistic improvements may be implemented.

In abstract terms, an institutional problematic can be located in the incentives for and capacities of public authorities responsible for providing financial stability. If one attempts to draw a pragmatic policy proposal from this, one might think about altering the existent incentives and capacities of regulators and/or politicians. Accordingly, one could argue for strengthening either the independence of regulatory agencies or propose the opposite, i.e. the strengthening of political control. For several reasons, for which there is not sufficient space to discuss them all here, these proposals are not very promising with regard to reducing the identified problem. For example, increasing regulatory independence might actually result in worsening the situation. Likewise, intensifying political control over regulatory agencies is an unrealistic option. Thinking in another direction, Barth et al. (2012) recently suggested complementing the institutional structure in financial regulation by introducing a sentinel. This would be a publicly institutionalised organisation of independent experts. Their main task would be to assess regulatory standards and provide publicly available information. In particular, the sentinel would have the responsibility to assess whether regulatory standards are suited to serve the public good of financial stability.

In thinking about checks and balances, I suggest a similar, yet different, institutional complement: an institutionalised veto-player. I do not aim to offer a distinct institutional/organisational architecture, but merely highlight potential aspects for improvement, based on the empirical evidence of deficient political control mechanisms. Since cooperation on the international level that is sufficient to provide the global public good of financial stability is highly unrealistic at the moment,[1] realistic institutional approaches have to originate within the nation state (while allowing for continued, incremental transnational institution building in the FSB). The present study's results suggest that two aspects are crucial: first, an institutionally established authority has to be incentivised and provided with sufficient capacities to analyse, whether regulatory standards take systematic repercussions on financial stability sufficiently into account; in other words, such an organisation would need to have the authority, task, interest and resources to control whether financial stability is provided and protected by current and future regulation. Second, this authority needs to be in an institutionally guaranteed position to veto the setting of regulatory standards as well as demanding the alteration of existent rules.

The FDIC in the US, which has the official responsibility to regulate banks in a way that protects customers' deposits, provides an interesting empirical example: as this study showed, the FDIC opposed several Basel II approaches; moreover, the FDIC did not adopt the Basel II standards in the regulation of its banks. The banks under FDIC regulation mastered the turmoil of the financial crisis much better than most other banks in the US (Bair 2013).

Several national innovations in response to the crisis conform to the proposals put forward by Barth et al. (2012) or this study. Examples are the systemic stability councils of the European Union and the United States. Whether, however, these institutions will be capable to vetoing regulatory standards that neglect financial stability, when regulatory failure is not prominent on the media and political agenda, remains to be seen. Moreover, an important remaining question concerns how the new actors and institutions will cope with global rule and process layering.

Since, however, believing in the rational design of institutions with predictable results is clearly wishful thinking, social scientists have to think further. What I mean is that entering the discourse on regulatory and institutional design is important, but raising awareness of unsolvable problems and, thereby, enhancing the level of reflection underlying policy-making is at least equally important. In the context of this study, this implies raising the attention of policy-makers to the unintended consequences of simultaneously pursuing global cooperation and national competitiveness – i.e. how unchecked competition between national and transnational influence in setting rules for global markets results in systematic regulatory failure. If this cannot be counterbalanced through rational institutional design alone, at least political awareness could lead to augmented counterbalancing of asymmetric influence and unintended consequences.

We can look at this problem in another way, from the opportunity structure perspective. If we seriously take into account the decision-making circumstances of all relevant policymakers, it becomes obvious that there is a collective action problematic of providing the partially global public good, since no actor is capable of implementing a solution and no collective action mechanism to overcome this problem is yet in place. National politicians are extremely unlikely to pursue national legislation that *actually* confronts banks with serious limitations. By implication, therefore, regulators are equally unlikely to be successful in pursuing regulation and supervision undermining regulatory arbitrage. On the global level, the G20 has to find a solution that moves within the boundaries of (a) global cooperation (note: logic of appropriateness dictates the withstanding of beggar-thy-neighbour policies and capital controls) as well as (b) does not interfere with national, historically rooted specificities in their political economies. All they can do is to rely on their supervisors to hammer out a technical solution, which is also imprisoned by the necessity to simultaneously achieve (a) and (b). In sum, then, it is first necessary to raise sensitivity to the new 'form of interdependence' (Keohane & Nye 1974, 61) characterising current global governance and its unintended consequences. If policy-makers are increasingly aware of this, it might lead them to take this into account. Recent reforms, however, rather testify to the persistent *unreconciled simultaneity of national and transnational influence* in setting standards and the according governance gap in the hybrid national-transnational reality of regulation and supervision.

Extension of the argument to other areas of global regulation

The findings present relevant insights into other areas of transgovern-mental regulatory standard setting, in particular those of global financial regulation. According to the categorisation of Büthe & Mattli (2011, 18–19), this category is similar to intergovernmental organisations like the International Monetary Fund. While some of my findings, and in particular the core argument, have explanatory value in this area, I expect that since the degree of institutionalisation differs substantially in intergovernmental organisations the findings cannot be simply extended. A category to which our findings present relevant insights are those where the focal institution is a private one – as in the case of the International Accounting Standards Board (IASB) or mixed organisations like the International Organization of Securities Commissions (IOSCO).[2] I now turn to the study's implications for global financial governance more generally.

6.2   Global financial governance and regulatory reform: diligent, but feeble

The Great Recession evoked enormous pressure on public officials, i.e. political principals and regulatory agents, to tighten the freedom of banks. Still, global layering gaps and the opportunity structures of transnational regulatory regimes provide theoretical frames to explain, why post-crisis reforms in financial regulation are 'feeble' (Rixen 2013) and not paradigmatic (Germain 2012, Blyth 2013, Underhill Forthcoming). The reforms are feeble, since their politico-economic substance does not change the crucial threats to financial stability. They are not paradigm shifting, since the prevailing policy paradigm remains Neoliberalism and market-based, arm's length regulation.

As this study has shown that the post-crisis reforms in the area of global banking regulation were not paradigm-shifting or fundamentally problem solving, other studies likewise have revealed comparable shortcomings in other financial policy areas. For example, Underhill (Forthcoming) finds that the responses by IOSCO remained in the confines of the market-based regulatory approach in such important areas as credit rating agencies and hedge funds. Rixen (2013) finds that post-crisis regulation in the area of offshore financial centres and accounting standards is feeble and has largely the character of superficial regulations that satisfy popular demands, while providing the industry with sufficient room for continued regulatory arbitrage (in order to protect the financial sectors' international competitiveness).

For public officials, reforms after the crisis were convenient in that they evaded the really tough decisions that would redistribute away from the financial sector. They were the best compromise for all involved actors to act visibly without really changing the basic system (Helleiner 2014). That is why reforms were substantial but not significant – or diligent, but feeble. This is best demonstrated by the limited innovative character and its convenience to politicians and regulators of the crucial, over-arching – allegedly – new paradigm, the macro-prudential approach. Helleiner (2014, 127–128) demonstrates that this approach is not really that new, but was already part of the pre-crisis (or post – Asian Financial Crisis) agenda, actually a reason why the FSF was established. More importantly, however, it is a perfect reform for public and private actors, as it does not interfere too much with the market-based regulatory approach and the financial power of the industry:

> In this more restricted form, macroprudential ideas in fact provided policymakers with a perfect cover for responding to demands for tighter regulation but in a manner not too radical from the standpoint of the financial sector. The containment of systemic risk became the rallying call for policy-makers and regulators rather than values that might have led to stronger controls on markets, such as distributive concerns relating to wealth and power in the financial sector vis-à-vis public authorities and other societal interests. (Helleiner 2014, 127–128)

I argue, in extending my findings on global banking regulation, that reforms are feeble and not paradigm shifting, since national-transnational layering of the TRR provides opportunity structures of 'paradigm maintenance' (Blyth 2013, 209). What I mean is, that most influential actors in the TRR prior to the crisis have remained the authorities that decide on what were the problems and how can they be fixed (Verdier 2013, Blyth 2013). This occurred since the world's policymakers relied on the transgovernmental networks, as they provided the most convenient, existing organisations available, and since these were driven by the same neoliberal, market-based regulation paradigm. Further-reaching political intervention did not occur, since the fear of a prolonged recession as a result of different policies prevailed among incumbent politicians. In other words, paradigmatic ideational, and therefore policy, change of Hall's third order has not occurred yet, since the locus of authority over the meaning of anomalies has not shifted (Blyth 2013). Thus, in a world in which institutional and ideational factors simultaneously affect policymakers' choices, we fail to see *significant* changes due to the persistence of the authoritative governance structure. A change of Hall's third order typically necessitates a change in the locus of authority over policy (Hall 1993, 280). This, however, has not taken place, since the same transgovernmental communities remain in charge. Leaving the key authority in those transgovernmental networks implies adverse ideational selection (Underhill Forthcoming) – thus feeble and non-paradigmatic change.

Thus, the TRR possesses two aspects of layering that – seen as opportunity structures – reduce the likelihood of paradigmatic change. First, parallel influence of national and transnational coalitions in setting transnational standards like Basel III ensures the due consideration of the different financial sub-sectors' interests, whilst reducing public good concerns. Second, the unreconciled simultaneity of national and transnational rules constitutes a loophole-enabling situation, in which national regulators face increasing pressure to be competitiveness-concerned (and, thus, lenient) in their interpretation and enforcement of global and domestic rules.

This challenge will constitute the status quo for the foreseeable future. The layered, unreconciled national and transnational governing is a convenient reply for most policymakers and private actors. Reconciliation would imply inconvenient collective action efforts, which probably necessitate a more severe shock. The deepened layering, however, may lead to the problematic repercussion that externally enforced supervisory cooperation brings with it, namely unfaithful implementation and enforcement. Accordingly, the schizophrenic (political) pressure to cooperate transgovernmentally and to ensure national competitiveness may lead to the disintegration of the transnational regulatory regime due to countervailing competition state strategies within jurisdictional supervision. Thus, the need to cooperate globally, without an authority that actually makes sure that there is enforcement and reconciliation, while at the same time supervisors are pressured nationally to be competitiveness-concerned in their approach, might result in either (1) the deepening of the layering problem, or (2) the disintegration of transgovernmental standard setting with national supervisors not feeling bound to the global standards. The difference between these options is one of size, not of kind, on a scale of the national faithfulness to transnationally developed rules – whilst arguing that the level of transnational cooperation at least remains constant in the medium-term. (In the long run, however, the non-compliance may lead to the retreat from global cooperation.) In my view the short- to medium term perspective will be closer to the first option. This, however, would imply that the TRR-logic of the policy process and the resulting implications for asymmetric influence and the under-provisioning of the public good of systemic stability continue to characterise the future of global financial governance.

6.3 Layers and gaps in governing the global political economy

Looking beyond the recent financial crisis and the global governance of financial markets, transnational regulatory failure is the result of what Nye & Keohane (1971b, 343), and recently Cohen (2008), have called the 'control gap'.[3] I have outlined that the state aspirations to close this horizontal control gap of economic interdependence result in vertical layering/governance gaps that emerge out of the incomplete compatibility between national and transnational rules and processes.

The resulting relationship between layering and regulatory failure can, in highly simplified terms, be described through four steps: first, transgovernmental cooperation leads to the transnational diffusion of standards, and the layering of institutions and processes creates a breeding ground for loopholes; second, the simultaneous, unreconciled influence of national and transnational coalitions results in the transnational diffusion of rule layers that are prone to asymmetric regard of private over public goods; third, this results in the systematic under-provisioning of the public good; fourth, the existence of transnational standards undermines the domestic capacity/freedom of supervisors to prevent negative externalities (provide the public good) within the jurisdiction. In cases of transnational spillovers and, therefore, partially global public goods, national lenience can have repercussions on other jurisdictions and the entire global political economy.

Furthermore, with regard to similar gaps in other areas of the global political economy, which are characterised by layering and a partial globalisation of the policy process, this book's analysis has revealed three crucial patterns of influence that contribute to such gaps: transnational agenda-setting, selective competition state based national interventions, and, as a result of the first two, deficient political control mechanisms in TRRs. First, leadership is frequently exercised by transnational actors and institutions, rather than international ones, even if the latter signal their lead in directing the global political economy. Referring to the global political principal, the G7/20 achieve their short-term preferences of preserving global banking for the sake of continued economic growth and public debt financing. However, no active intervention in the development of the global regulatory standards for the G7/20's banks is pursued. Political leaders of the most powerful countries do not deliberately delegate the harmonisation of their regulatory standards to the forum of the BCBS. Rather, the G7/20 leaders merely accept the Basel Committee's pre-established agenda. It is regulators who set the agenda and drive the political process. Accordingly, the state-centric view – which considers the most powerful states' leaders to deliberately delegate the realisation of political decisions to transgovernmental networks (Drezner 2007, 119–47) – does not provide sufficient leverage to explain the global harmonisation of banking since the late 1990s, since it underestimates the effect of transnational actors and domestic actors from partially disaggregated states.

In financial regulation, the G summits are not much more than a forum for global crisis management, which is driven by agendas of attention to the currently most pressing debates.[4] Not only do the agents, here the regulatory agencies in their transgovernmental networks, design the policies in the shadow of hierarchy and uninformed principals; they even set the agenda of globally harmonising banking regulation without meaningful control by the global principal. Projecting insights of this onto the future of banking regulation, the G20 is not crucial in explaining global banking regulation. Rather, the transnational networks of regulatory agencies and their regulatees as well as the transnational channels of domestic political economies are at the core of the explanation. The BCBS and the actors capable of gaining influence in this diffusion network are the major global governors – not the concert of the powerful, sovereign nation state leaders. Accordingly, the attempt to close control gaps in the global political economy is heavily driven through transnational forces, be they original transnational organisations or nationally rooted factors.

The second pattern is that a selective set of entrenched national actors can channel their interests (to varying degrees) via domestic institutions into transgovernmental networks. This contradicts those contributions that see transnational banks and/or regulatory communities as the sole drivers of global standard-setting and mourn the demise of the nation state. National political structures remain a central set of variables in global regulatory harmonisation. However, the role of these structures and, as a result, their very nature, change in the face of the transnationalisation of political economies (Cerny 1995). Consequently, the regulatory agencies have become major actors in world politics. The

US regulators, i.e. those of the most powerful jurisdiction, successfully pursued their domestic agenda via transgovernmental agenda-setting. While supervisors representing jurisdictions with less attractive/sizeable markets had to give in to market-based dominance, nevertheless, many of their interests found recognition as a result of mutually preferred transgovernmental cooperation. In the global political economy of banking the US is one of the dominant powers, frequently the most powerful. Yet, it increasingly has to compromise with other BCBS members. In sum, regulatory agencies are crucial actors in the global political economy.

Particularly noteworthy is the substantial influence of domestic politicians and nationally oriented firms. Within the jurisdictions, nationally oriented firms – like German and US community banks – are particularly effective in enforcing their interests through the indirect channel of domestic politicians. For example, the feedback of foreshadowing global rules of US origin resulted in German banks' substantial success in incorporating their interests into Basel II. However, US community banks' capability to oppose Basel II rules demonstrates the significance of domestic–transnational feedback mechanisms in global banking regulation. Moreover, this study has also presented substantial empirical evidence of how national politicians affect transnational agreements. Referring to the political principal explanation, the US Congress and the German Bundestag and government were all successful in demanding an adjustment of the Basel II rules to more appropriately reflect the interests of their main constituents. Yet, they did so via the regulatory channels and indirectly the transgovernmental network – not via traditional fora of international politics. At the root of this is a systematic political mechanism that links national with transnational arenas. Nationally oriented banks alarmed their political representatives, which, once activated by their constituents, forced their regulatory agents to selectively alter the transnational agreement. Through this path, German Sparkassen and US community banks were capable of blocking a global effort to harmonise regulatory standards, and, eventually, substantially adjust the content of Basel II.

In sum, these aspects sketch the changing nature of politics beyond the nation state and the influence that can be wielded in the global political economy. In banking regulation, transnational and domestic forces are more influential than interstate factors: first, transnational coordination drives global harmonisation; second, rather than domestic structures becoming irrelevant, the channels into global politics become transnational, and – as a result – also change the political process and success within nation states. Put succinctly, the political economy is increasingly becoming a global political economy, in which transnational governance patterns as well as international and nation state bound politics interact dynamically.

The third pattern of influence that this study found speaks to an overarching challenge of world politics in the light of governance gaps, namely that accountability is in many instances insufficiently ensured through appropriate mechanisms (Grant & Keohane 2005), which may undermine the legitimacy of rule-setting. Particularly important for ensuring that standards are legitimate with regard to the fair regard of national citizens interests is the concept of political control mechanisms, and specifically ex post control of holding public officials accountable. According to Grant & Keohane (2005, 34, 38–39):

> Effective accountability at the global level will require new, pragmatic approaches: approaches that do not depend on the existence of a clearly defined global public. Attention will need to be paid to delegation problems: exercising control over agents to whom important tasks have been assigned.

> *Transgovernmental networks* do not provide mechanisms for either delegated or participatory accountability. Since these networks are informal, it is often unclear which organizations have delegated powers to them. Furthermore, participatory accountability is minimal: The general public is not involved, and transparency is typically lacking. Abuses of power might in some instances be controlled by the fragmentation of power and conflicts of interest between the participants, but cooperation among the members of such networks could easily become collusion against the interests of outsiders.

Therefore, one might argue that the secluded meetings in Basel, or other transgovernmental arrangements, lead to the circumvention of political control mechanisms, reducing legitimacy of regulatory standards. My findings do not testify in favour of such a claim, at least not in a straightforward version. Interestingly, regulators at first were quite keen to protect financial stability. However, intervention by national politicians on behalf of particular, well organised interests altered and weakened the regulatory framework selectively. While these interventions were numerous, and complemented by selective pressure from transnational banks, advocacy on behalf of the public good of financial stability was neglected. The mounting pressure regarding the competitiveness of local banks in the US, national banks in

Germany, transnational banks, etc. put substantial pressure on the Basel Committee to water down the Basel II framework.

The challenge that global layering and governance gaps pose to political control mechanisms, thus, cannot be solved through simple politicisation of global standard setting, increased transparency, or the involvement of democratically elected politicians. That is because in TRRs, global governance gaps are reinforced through the selective political control of regulators, which are a result of detrimental principal-agent, delegational accountability mechanisms. Therefore, political control instruments need to be suited to counterbalance the unreconciled, simultaneous influence of national and transnational coalitions in standard development. Thus, in policy areas that are governed through TRR-like structures, pragmatic modes of governance accountability have to consider how to counterbalance these deficient control mechanisms that are due to the combination of delegation from political principal to regulatory agent and the embedding of domestic regulatory regimes in TRRs.

The complexities and repercussions of global governance gaps continue to pose many scientifically and politically relevant questions with regard to the future of governing the global political economy. To understand the nature and effects of different layering regimes and governance gaps remains an important field of systematic empirical investigation. One way of approaching these potential gaps is through a problem-oriented conceptualisation and a synthetic analysis of partially globalised world politics that takes all relevant actors, institutions, and ideas into account (Sil & Katzenstein 2010a, 2010b; Lake 2011). While this complicates many aspects, it enables investigators to reveal the dynamic interactions of national, transnational, and interstate mechanisms – and how they shape politics and policies.

Notes

1 The Great Recession, Regulatory Failure and Global Governance

1. A word of clarification is necessary with regard to the use of the terms global, interstate and transnational. International or interstate refer to deliberations/negotiations between sovereign nation states that are represented by their government leaders (or their agents with delegated authority). Transnational refers to interaction across state-borders by private actors and public actors from governmental administrations without formally delegated authority to represent the entire nation state. I use the term *global*, when I refer to a set of different interactions that are directed to affect policymaking that is not constrained by state-borders, where this includes – to varying degrees – transnational and interstate as well as certain national interactions that affect (or are intended to affect) global politics. Accordingly, the terms globalising and transnationalising of politics and the political economy are used distinctively. Globalising refers to the increasing density of political and politico-economic interactions and governance webs beyond national borders, while transnationalising refers to that part of globalisation that is not of an interstate nature.

2. This, however, neglects the fact that regulators may also push for harmonisation, since they face challenges that they cannot solve within their jurisdictional mandate (see Singer 2007 as well as Chapters 2 and 3 of this study).

2 Global Financial Instability and the Evolution of Global Banking Regulation

1. Regulation and supervision are two complementary, yet different tasks: the first refers to the setting of standards, i.e. the development, adaptation and implementation of rules; supervision refers to the active scrutiny and enforcement of regulatees' adherence to the stipulated rules. The words are used interchangeably, unless distinctly emphasised.

2. Due to the focus on regulatory failure to prevent excessive risk taking by banks, I exclude the discussion on consumer protection. For a discussion, see Goodhart et al. (1998).

3. Leveraging means carrying out more lending with less capital, which increases profits but reduces liquidity to serve liabilities in a tightening market.

4. However, the capital adequacy regulation actually has an incentives-based mechanism that makes banks consider actual risks associated with investment in specific assets more strongly. While this is a desirable result, it does not provide sufficient insurance against failure due to illiquidity (since

the capital cannot be used as a buffer during distressed times) or coverage of losses in cases of insolvency (Santos 2001, 52–59).

5. Transgovernmental relations refer to 'sets of direct interactions among sub-units of different governments that are not controlled or closely guided by the policies of the cabinets or chief executive's of those governments' (Keohane & Nye 1974, 43). Transnational defines public and private interaction across borders (that is not interstate) more generally (Nye & Keohane 1971a, 733).

6. As empirical basis for the years 1974–1997 I draw heavily on Goodhart (2011); for the years 1998–2014, I rely substantially on my own empirical analysis of this book's later chapters.

7. Euro-markets are markets in which currencies are deposited/traded outside their home territory, e.g. depositing US dollars in a European country. Banks used these markets to circumvent capital controls and national regulations that restricted private lending.

8. More precisely, the G10 established the 'Standing Committee on Banking Regulations and Supervisory Practices' in December 1974 at one of the monthly G10 central banker meetings. The Basel Committee on Banking Supervision received this current name in 1998 (Goodhart 2011, 7). However, one should be aware that 'the BCBS did not emerge as a pristine organisation; it had behind it in the background the prior experience of the Groupe de Contact.' (Goodhart 2011, 25). This group, which held its first meeting on 29–30 June 1972 in Amsterdam, was a strictly informal group (club) of upper/middle-ranking officials in the banking supervisory authorities of the initial six EEC countries. Their early effort at coordinating supervisory work was a result of the European Community efforts of creating a common market for banking as well as the increasing dangers stemming from unsupervised transnational activity. When the US and other central banks took note of this Group in 1974, but their attempt to get involved was met with some reservation, the G10 Governors took action to establish the BCBS as a group with a reach beyond Europe (Goodhart 2011, 10–24).

9. The Concordat was prepared in 1975, approved by central bank governors in December 1975, made public in 1981, revised in 1983 and again in 1991. The first amendment (second half of the 1970s) of the Concordat recommended consolidated accounting to further strengthen home country control. The home country control-consolidated accounting focus of the Concordat was further strengthened in 1983 in response to the failure of Banco Ambrosiano (1982). The evasion of international regulation by the Bank of Credit and Commerce International in the late 1980s fuelled another amendment. See Goodhart (2011, 96–126) for a detailed description.

10. In addition, the Amendment introduced three further complementary elements to the Basel I Accord: first, the introduction of a trading book; second, the separate treatment of bank and trading book assets (banks' assets are subdivided into two 'books': the banking book contains all assets that are held until maturity, and the trading book encompasses all other activities for trading purposes). This separated the classic banking business from securities trading activities. Third, within the trading book, the Market Risk Amendment introduced the measurement of market risks in addition to the credit risk measures already established in Basel I, by making it mandatory

to also base capital adequacy calculations on general and specific market risks arising from trading activities (that would be held in the trading book) (Goodhart 2011, 224–264). The inclusion of these risks could be undertaken by banks via two routes, namely an internal risk calculation model, or a standard specific risk charge.

11. However, as Goodhart (2011, 413–440) shows, many non-G10 regulators had already turned to the BCBS standards as policy guidelines since the 1980s.

12. The so-called Basel Core Principles provide 25 basic principles that were deemed to be necessary for a supervisory system to be effective.

13. In 1974, the founding member states encompassed the G10 (Belgium, Canada, France, Germany, Italy, Japan, the Netherlands, Sweden, United Kingdom, United States) plus Switzerland (since 1984 also a G10 member) and Luxembourg, and were joined by Spain in February 2001 (Buchmüller 2008, 19–20). In 2009, the G-20 emerging economies were added to the club: Argentina, Australia, Brazil, China, Hong Kong SAR, India, Indonesia, Korea, Mexico, Russia, Saudi Arabia, Singapore, South Africa, and Turkey. In September 2014, the European Central Bank's Single Supervisory Mechanism was granted membership. At the same time representatives from Chile, Malaysia and the United Arab Emirates joined the Committee as observers. Already before that, other observers were the BIS, Basel Consultative Group, European Banking Authority, European Commission, and International Monetary Fund.

14. This arrangement was adopted in March 2003 and introduced in December 2003, mainly as a reaction by G10 central bankers to the Basel II endeavour. Before December 2003 the G10 central bankers were the decision making body which adopted the BCBS proposals. However, as the president of the German federal regulatory agency (BaFin) Jochen Sanio described to German parliamentarians, due to the increasing discontent with Basel II, central bank presidents aimed at distributing responsibility onto more shoulders by including the heads of supervision in the forum that decides on issues of financial regulation (Bundestag Finance Committee 2003a, 56). The first decision the new GHOS approved was the adoption of the Basel II proposal.

15. See the Committee's website at the BIS: www.bis.org/bcbs/about.htm. Last visited on 27 July 2012.

16. I refer to the term 'network' as an organisational mode of recurring, 'reciprocal patterns of communication and exchange' that neither depends upon formal structures nor appears in a social vacuum (Powell 1990, 295).

17. In 1999 there were already more than 20 groups, a number which rose during the Basel II development. Visible groups during the Basel II process were: Capital Task Force, Risk Management Group, Joint Accounting Task Force, Models Task Force, Securitisation Group, Transparency Group, Capital Group. In September 2014, according to the Committee's website (www.bis.org/bcbs/mesc.htm; accessed on 7 September 2014), 23 working groups and task forces were carrying out the BCBS work.

18. Bundesaufsichtsamt für das Kreditwesen & Deutsche Bundesbank (1999), Bundestag Finance Committee (2001d), Basel Committee on Banking Supervision (2001i). The first proposal for a new capital Accord in June 1999 was developed by such a group.

19. See the Committee's website www.bis.org/bcbs/organigram.pdf; accessed on 7 September 2014.
20. The BCBS describes these groups as 'Groups' in its Charter, while calling them 'Main Expert Sub-Committees' on its website (www.bis.org/bcbs/mesc. htm; accessed on 7 September 2014).
21. Soft law comprises legal arrangements that are weakened along one or more of the dimensions of traditional hard law (legally binding obligation, precision, delegation to authority) and that lie on a continuum between hard law and pure political arrangements (Abbott & Snidal 2000).
22. As we will see below, the increasing reliance on qualitative supervision augments these enforcement issues. During the latter half of the 1990s the Committee began to issue principles for qualitative supervision that complemented the quantitative capital requirements, thereby extending its supervisory approach from a purely quantitative to a mixed qualitative-quantitative one. The Basel II framework strengthened the manifestation of the qualitative approach, as it introduced a new (the second) pillar of internal risk management of banks and its qualitative supervision. As Buchmüller (2008, 37) argues, this mirrors a substantial change and results in a fundamentally new harmonisation challenge as principles of individual bank supervision have to be implemented in domestic jurisdictions and harmonised across countries – all in a principle-oriented manner, making the whole process even more diffuse and prone to national deviation.
23. This literature, with the exception of Scott & Iwahara's (1994) analysis of Basel I implementation in the US and Japan, focuses on the adoption and implementation in non-BCBS emerging markets (i.e. non-members before 2009). There is, to my knowledge, no systematic study on implementation in BCBS member states. Hence, there is some level of uncertainty regarding the real empirical – international and comparative national – patterns.
24. Note that this exclusive atmosphere is fostered by the continuity of the same (typically two) persons representing a member state, in most cases over several years (with the exception of Japan, which has a system of rapid exchange). While empirical proof for this practice does only exist for the period 1974–1997 (Goodhart 2011), there are clear signs that this was a guiding principle during Basel II and III too (see Chapters 4 and 5).
25. During that course, the working group structure would facilitate the policy development.
26. For a detailed discussion of interaction modes see Scharpf (1997).

3 Theory: Influence in Global Banking Regulation and the Transnational Regulatory Regime

1. By influence, I refer to the capacity to have an effect on the content of regulatory standards. More specifically, empirically I will operationalise this through the rate of success in integrating interests into transgovernmental agreements.

2. An exception, however, is the work of Duncan Wood (2005), which was among the first to analyse the complex interactive 'politics' characterising the field of global banking regulation.

3. Typological explanations are statements that combine multiple theoretical arguments into a complementary explanation – which is considered a likely outcome due to previous research and theoretical reasoning. The purpose here is to reduce the property space in order to come up with a manageable number of most relevant typologies to be assessed (George & Bennett 2005, 235–248).

4. While I focus on explanations that are a product of the complex interaction between actors and institutions in conditioning processes and outcomes of transnational regulatory standard-setting, however, ideational aspects were and remain important factors explaining interaction and decisions in global banking regulation. We know that two policy paradigms are shaping perception, evaluation and action in the political economy since the late 1970s, namely, first, neoliberal claims of decentral, wealth-creating markets to be supported by the, second, competition state (Cerny 1997, Cerny 2010b). While not at the core of the empirical analysis, my findings confirm the prevailing views in the literature and demonstrates how institutions and ideas combine in their systematic effects on (asymmetric) influence as well as policy outcomes. These dominant ideas are supportive of some actors' preferences, while not of others' (Hall 1993, Underhill Forthcoming). In simple terms, the predominance of the two paradigms advance the influence of actors in favour of global market access and harmonisation on the one hand, and those actors in favour of strengthening domestic industries' international competitiveness (to the benefit of the competition state) on the other hand. In Chapter 6, I will discuss how the non-paradigmatic change in response to the Great Recession is related to the remaining authoritative structure.

5. The latter began their industry cooperation in 1988 (Goodhart (2011), 224–285).

6. I differentiate between the sub-sectors of transnationally and nationally/locally oriented banks, since they differ substantially in production factors (due to different portfolio and customer strategies) and organise within different associations (see Busch (2009) and the discussion in the subsequent chapter).

7. Lütz (2004, 184) refers to this as the convergence towards a 'new hegemonic regulatory model' across industrialised countries. She elaborates that this relates to regulatory agencies as central actors in the two-level game of financial regulation as well as the convergence regarding the instruments used to supervise banks.

8. The datasets are far more comprehensive as they include many developing countries.

9. By extension, this asymmetry becomes even more severe from the perspective of the voting population's attempt to hold political representatives accountable in order to provide financial stability.

10. The chief difference between nationally and locally oriented banks is the political principal to which they are a constituent. This can be neglected here since the main national forum of the transnational harmonisation of

banking regulation is the national political framework, rather than that of the decentral entities.

11. Likewise Pagliari & Young (2014) demonstrate the distinctive interests of different sub-sectoral concerns. While I considered many other actor groups at the outset of the study, however, the empirical material revealed their relatively unimportant roles (as I will discuss in the next chapter).

12. According to Keefer's (2007, 617) empirical data on crisis frequency in developed and developing countries between 1980 and 2000 a crisis occurs in fewer than 1 per cent of the study's country-years.

13. This constellation is facilitated through the policy paradigm of neoliberalism and the concurrent welfare-enhancing growth agenda (Cerny 2010b). It is the conjunction of ideational and institutional factors that facilitates the neglect of financial stability. I return to this discussion in the Chapter 6.

14. The elements of delegated/divided authority and capture in the regulation of banks are crucial theoretical concepts of this study's empirical assessment of banking regulation regimes. Their definition claims a cross-country homogeneity among industrialised countries with developed financial systems, more specifically BCBS members. In light of the apparent differences among national political and economic systems (Gilpin 2001, 148–195), this needs further clarification. What is claimed to be generalisable are the aspects of distant political control mechanisms over regulatory agents with considerable delegated authorities, as well as disadvantaged public good representation in the regulatory regimes.

15. The domestic regulatory regime structure actually presents a plurality of potential coalitions. Four national coalitions are likely to have influence within the politics of the regulatory regime: first, the regulator–regulatee coalition can collaborate in the shadow of hierarchy. Second, regulatees can invoke control by the political principals, the main governmental and/or parliamentary group, if dissatisfied with regulation. In contrast to these private interest coalitions that are rather dedicated to sectoral competitiveness, two drivers in the public interest are possible. Regulators have a mandate to secure financial stability, and might, as a third potential driver, enact and enforce regulatory policies in this sense, which is likely to meet industrial opposition. Fourth, political principals might collaborate with, or force the regulatory agent to augment systemic stability (in the first version it is a coalition, in the second a hierarchical enforcement). Due to capture and delegation, however, the coalitions favouring industry and public interests in competitiveness are likely to prevail over the ones oriented to the public interest.

16. Certainly, one important condition is that there is not a US-centred unipolar power constellation in banking, but rather one with comparably relevant markets and firms – given London's role in finance, this is plausible (Coleman 2003).

17. The interest and capacity to forward one's own preferences is asymmetrically distributed with an increasing advantage for jurisdictional authorities that control access to larger and more attractive markets (Simmons 2001, Drezner 2007, Novembre 2009). In other words, 'the likelihood of a coordination equilibrium at one country's standards is an increasing function of that country's market size' (Drezner 2007, 55–56). In turn, this means that the

adjustment burden to another or new set of standards weighs relatively heavier for large states, and lighter for smaller ones, due to the relative value of increased market access.

18. The argument can be stretched to coalitions of countries – power blocks or *k-groups*: a coalition of a sub-set of countries is powerful enough to enforce an agreement on all BCBS members, if the coalition encompasses sufficient market size that, even with defection by all other countries, the cooperation will benefit the co-operators overall. In such a situation, other countries have an incentive to agree, since they do not want to be excluded from the k-group's markets (Genschel & Plümper 1996, Drezner 2007). An example is the coalition of regulators from the US, UK, and Japan gathering behind a common proposal for the Basel I Accord in 1988, which made it practically impossible for other states to withdraw from this framework due to the feared loss of access to the three then pivotal financial markets (Genschel & Plümper 1996).

19. In this study's context a veto player is understood simply as an actor that can stop harmonised regulatory standards from becoming binding rules within the respective political economy.

20. Transnationally active banks also make use of the possibility of capturing national regulators. The influence on national politicians, however, is more diffuse with regard to the actual contents in global Basel standards and works rather in the form of pushes for general harmonisation and competitiveness (see Chapters 4 and 5).

21. While a banking association will not be able to rally opposition to a regulatory standard, which is irrelevant to most voters, they certainly can use their established political ties to oppose a candidate in an upcoming election or at least reduce previous support (Stigler 1971, 12).

4 Global Banking Regulation Before the Great Recession: The Dynamics of Basel II

1. The G20 did not gain significant political relevance before 2008, when the US administration used the forum as the main channel of communication and coordination during the Great Recession (Keohane & Victor 2011, 11). Accordingly, for the analysis of the Basel II negotiation period, the G7 is the politically relevant forum for international political coordination. This is amplified by the fact that membership in the Basel Committee was not granted to many G20 countries before 2009.

2. Table 4.1 describes the operationalisation of the explanations, i.e. which data sources are used for the measurement of the specific actors. Initially, further actors were considered as potentially relevant (like the IMF, the EU Commission, and rating agencies). These, however, did not play a crucial role and were excluded from the analysis.

3. The bank regulators are: the central bank Federal Reserve (Fed), the Federal Deposit Insurance Corporation (FDIC), the Office of the Comptroller of the Currency (OCC) and the Office of Thrift Supervision (OTS, which was integrated into the OCC after the Sub-prime Crisis).

4. Until 2002 BaKred. See discussion below.

5. Although this changed incrementally prior to, and during, the period of investigation (Höpner & Krempel 2004, 352–353). Nevertheless, banks remain highly important actors in the German political economy (Hardie & Howarth 2009).
6. But see the important discussion of the central role of banks in both varieties of capitalism by Hardie et al. (2013). These authors' findings are consistent with my conceptualisation of banks' influence in both types of political economies.
7. More specifically, in relation to all successful positions. I.e. an integrated issue can deliver two or more successfully integrated positions, in cases where two or more actors pursued the same interest.
8. Again, in relation to all rejected positions, where one rejected issue can result in two or more rejected positions.
9. I.e. all explications of preferred content of regulatory standards were coded as positions of the respective actor. In sum, 74 documents were coded. All presented statistical measures are calculated on the basis of a selective subset of codings operated. Only those issues were integrated in the final analysis that passed the empirical threshold of at least two codings. In sum, 369 issues (from more than 1,000 initially coded issues on the basis of more than 2,400 codings) passed this threshold.
10. An interest is counted as integrated if both the respective actor position and the policy outcome in the Basel II agreement supported a specific issue; this results in an indicator value of '1'. When both values are zero, the indicator consequently also scores '0', which is interpreted as neutral with regard to the issue at hand. When an actor promotes a topic that is not reflected in the framework, he receives a rejection value of '−1'. The same applies if an actor openly rejected a certain policy which was integrated into the agreement nevertheless.
11. For replication, the author's web site (romangoldbach.wordpress.com) provides all documents used for the analysis with the text analysis software TAMS analyzer (developed by Matthew Weinstein; see http://tamsys.sourceforge.net). It comprises all coded text documents, as well as the TAMS analyzer project file of the analysis. It includes a csv-spreadsheet with the exported results of the coding analysis, on the basis of which the integration and rejection rates were built.
12. Readers less interested in the underlying policy details may proceed to Section 4.3. The policy discussion in the next section is (mostly) not necessary to follow the analysis of the aspects of the political economy, which are the subject of the later, major part of the empirical analysis. This detailed discussion, however, is empirically crucial to substantiate the conclusions that I draw, and, furthermore provides an interesting insight into the Basel II policies of global banking regulation.
13. Throughout the chapter, the level of technical detail is kept to a necessary minimum. Some technical debates, however, will be outlined in detail in the context of the process tracing, as these are fundamental for the proposed causal arguments. Readers interested in the deeper analysis of the framework's issues and political discourses should consult the author's website.

14. A simple comparison with the Basel Accord of 1988 shows that this agreement was far less comprehensive and detailed, but faithfully adopted and implemented in all Basel Committee and more than 100 further jurisdictions (Tarullo 2008, 45–87).

15. The analysis of the fourth episode below clearly demonstrates how the emergence of domestic US opposition resulted in the need to incorporate US concerns, and, furthermore, in the Basel Committee's reaction to explicitly design Basel II merely as a framework, the implementation of which being subject to embedding into domestic specifics. For the purpose of concise process tracing, I will refer to the Basel II *Accord* during the first three episodes, and to the *framework* from the fourth episode onwards, when supervisors changed the term. Accordingly, *framework* will also be used when the final results are discussed.

16. In the logic and language of financial intermediation, it is common to differentiate between different risk types, according to which most regulatory actions and investment decisions are structured: credit risk refers to the defaulting probability of a debtor; operational risk refers to banks' operational mistakes in their daily banking and trading activities; interest rate risk refers to the risk from extreme market movements in interest rates; market risk refers to the risk of price changes in an asset due to market volatility; counter-party risk refers to the risk that a counter-party defaults in a derivatives transaction. There are many other risks types such as legal risk, reputational risk, etc. These other categories are not important for the discussions in this study.

17. The Basel II framework refers to internationally active banks, where I speak of transnationally oriented banks. In the following, I use these terms interchangeably.

18. Double or multiple-gearing of capital describes the nominal regulatory reporting of capital at multiple organisational units, which results in a de facto reduction of capital to low, destabilising levels. During the late 1990s and the early 2000s, this was identified as a trend with potentially threatening, system-wide repercussions.

19. Insurance companies, however, are not included.

20. Typically, ratings are solicited by an actor interested in borrowing on financial markets. The external assessment of creditworthiness is supposed to increase transparency for creditors, thereby facilitating borrowing for debtors and reducing interest rates.

21. Credit rating agencies were surprisingly reserved during the Basel II process, even though the regulatory standards increased the demand for their assessments substantially. Their reserved position papers provided to the Basel Committee reflect the fear of public intervention in their business activities (Monro-Davies 1999, Moody's Investors Service 2000, Griep & De Stefano 2001, Moody's Investors Service 2001), which had only been modestly state-regulated up until then (Sinclair 1994, King & Sinclair 2003, Kerwer 2005). They openly rejected stipulations on rating firms under Basel II, which in effect might have resulted in new public regulatory rules for rating agencies in their established business activities. Furthermore, the increased market for ratings might have initiated rising competition. After initial consideration of integrating the rating agencies into the empirical

analysis, they were excluded due to their relatively negligible role in the process compared to other industry actors.

22. See e.g. Institute of International Finance (2001), International Swaps and Derivatives Association (2000).

23. PD describes the expected likelihood of a specific creditor to default. LGD is related to the size of the loss in the case of this default. EAD integrates further factors and defines the exact amount of the bank's exposure in the case of default. Guarantees/credit derivatives are related to the calculation of mitigation effects from such hedging instruments. Maturity-related riskiness internally measures how much the remaining time until amortisation increases risk. For more details, refer to Basel Committee on Banking Supervision (2001b, 2006).

24. Expected losses are those that a bank is expecting from a credit (on average for a pool of similar assets) based on historical loss data. These are usually factored into interest rates charged to the customer. Unexpected losses relate to those losses that are occurring in ways that are not secured directly with a credit transaction, but that occur due to volatility that cannot be planned. Because they cannot be projected, they are managed by general reserves ('provisioning').

25. The 8 per cent level of capital that Basel II demands is divided into 4 per cent core capital (tier one, with rather restrictive definitional limitations) and 4 per cent subordinate capital (tier two, which is much less restrictive and a jurisdictional tool to individually boost the competitiveness of banks' capital levels). So-called tier three capital refers to the specific types of provisions that can be integrated into a maximum amount of 1.25 per cent.

26. For F-IRB banks, this is equal to 95 per cent, 90 per cent and 80 per cent in the first, second and third years, respectively; for A-IRB banks, the same floors apply, except that the first year is one of additional calculation, i.e. A-IRB is introduced one year later.

27. Under the framework of the ICAAP, banks need to measure and manage risks that are not entirely covered under pillar one: credit concentration risk, interest rate risk (which needs to be quantified and stress-tested), liquidity risks, etc.

28. The SREP has to control the adequacy of the capital requirements related to pillar one, as well as the appropriateness of the banks' internal risk management procedures; theoretically, additional capital requirements are possible if banks are insufficiently capitalised in relation to their risks; however, in reality, at least in Europe, additional capital is usually not required, but rather adjustments of management systems are suggested (Buchmüller 2008, 191–192).

29. However unsuccessful this approach has proven to be in the recent financial crisis.

30. Typically, securitised assets are transferred to a legally separate entity. Credit and liquidity facilities are used by the banks to enhance the creditworthi-ness of these conduits – credit enhancements can be understood as credit guarantees for the conduits, liquidity enhancements as cash flow facilities.

31. A haircut is a widely used term in financial economics and refers to a reduction of an interest rate. It is used in many different regards, here it

simply means that the capital requirement is reduced by the size of the hedge.

32. These are reported in issue-specific tables as well as in the case study protocol, both to be found on the author's website: romangoldbach.word press.com.

33. Throughout the chapter, I present process tracing sources in footnotes. To facilitate transparency and the reconstruction of the political process, one can consult the chronological case study protocol of the 300 analysed documents (to be found on the author's website romangoldbach.word press.com).

34. Basel Committee on Banking Supervision (1999).

35. United States Government Accountability Office (1997).

36. The Glass-Stegall Act of 1933 separated depository from investment banking in order to reduce dangers to deposits and prevent systemic instabilities that could emerge from doubts about the safety of deposits. It was officially removed through the Gramm-Leach-Bliley Act in 1999, although the removal of the separation did take place in an incremental manner over several years before this date (Barth et al. 2000, Busch 2009).

37. U.S. House of Representatives (1998a), United States Government Accountability Office (1998, 2000).

38. United States Government Accountability Office (1998, 101–102).

39. Institute of International Finance (1998), International Swaps and Derivatives Association (1998a), International Swaps and Derivatives Association (1998b).

40. Group of Thirty (1997). The Group of Thirty is a private organisation of highly influential scholars and policymakers in the area of international finance. Its main purpose is the exchange of ideas for enhanced supervision and the creation of according reports. The Study Group that created the specific report cited, consisted of 22 experts, of whom 15 were industry managers, five regulators, and two researchers. It was primarily concerned with debating the role of global financial institutions for systemic risks. For an insightful analysis of the group see Tsingou (Forthcoming).

41. De Swaan (1998), in February 1998 executive director of the Dutch central bank and chairman of the Basel Committee, postulated an approach of financial regulation that pursued change in a more continuous and incremental manner. His political positions were clearly cautious in discussing new issues in banking and the resulting pressure for change. In particular, it signalled a hesitant position vis-á-vis the industry and US regulators' (in particular the Fed's) positions of revising Basel I and the supervisory approach in general.

42. McDonough (1998, 11), Wood (2005, 129).

43. Federal Ministry of Finance (1999), Bundesaufsichtsamt für das Kreditwesen & Deutsche Bundesbank (1999).

44. Bundestag Finance Committee (1999, 15).

45. For a detailed description of the credit risk calculation and the IRB approaches see the section in the above policy analysis (pp. 78–81).

46. Bundestag Finance Committee (1999, 15). The banking based credit system of the German financial intermediation system was, and remains, a distinct

feature, less known in market-based financial systems. See the discussion in the preceding chapter.

47. Bundesaufsichtsamt für das Kreditwesen & Deutsche Bundesbank (1999, 15–17).

48. U.S. House of Representatives (1998b), G7 1997a, b, 1998a, b, c, d.

49. The so-called Basel Core Principles provided 25 basic principles that were deemed necessary for a supervisory system to be effective. They were designed as a diffusion instrument to less developed countries and have been regularly updated since then (Basel Committee on Banking Supervision 1997).

50. The BCBS not only holds frequent global or regional conferences, where supervisory practices are diffused to agencies in developing, and in particular emerging, countries, but also provides standard material and courses on prudent supervision through its Financial Stability Institute (FSI), a global learning resource and information centre.

51. The Core Principles became part of the 12 key financial standards, a set of rules for the regulation of financial markets. The remaining 11 standards were developed by similar transnational networks like the Basel Committee. For example, the International Organization of Securities Commissions (IOSCO) crafted the guidelines for securities firms. The G7, IMF and World Bank then adopted these standards, where the latter two integrated them into the evaluations of financial markets of all of their member states. Naturally, for countries depending upon funds from these institutions, the standards are crucial benchmarks to achieve (for a detailed discussion see Mosley 2009).

52. G7 (1999), G8 (1999).

53. Bundestag Finance Committee (2001d, 2003b, 2004), U.S. House of Representatives (2003a, b), U.S. Senate (2003).

54. Lehnhoff (1997), Schröder (1997), Börsen-Zeitung (1999b, c).

55. Yet, it remains unanswered as to whether the main driver was either the US supervisors, with the intention of uploading their regulatory style, or the US-based internationally active banks, with the intent to harmonise regulation according to their interests.

56. The author's website presents for each of the four episodes a detailed table with all relevant topics. Each episode's table reports, for most of the policy issues deliberated during the episode, the successful and defeated actors. This presentation is of relevance to readers interested in issue-specific analyses of the deliberations.

57. Yet, using his statements is still valid, since in his positions McDonough clearly was careful to voice the BCBS interests in general. Furthermore, his rather conservative predecessor as BCBS chairman, Tom De Swaan, also contributed to the BCBS indicator – they also counterbalance the above effect and make the BCBS rates reliable indicators of the transgovernmental network.

58. Basel Committee on Banking Supervision (2001c).

59. Basel Committee on Banking Supervision (2000).

60. Bundestag Finance Committee (2000a, 16), Bundestag Finance Committee (2000a), Federal Ministry of Finance (2000, 13–14).

61. For a detailed description of the credit risk calculation and the IRB approaches see pp. 78–80.
62. Bundesaufsichtsamt für das Kreditwesen & Deutsche Bundesbank (1999, 14–17, 21).
63. Bundestag Finance Committee (2000a, 3), Federal Ministry of Finance (1999).
64. Bundestag Finance Committee (2000d).
65. BaKred (Bundesaufsichtsamt für das Kreditwesen, Federal Banking Supervisory Office) was the predecessor of BaFin. Until April 2002, Germany had three diversified agencies for securities and exchanges, insurance, and banking. The former sole bank regulator BaKred was integrated into the encompassing financial regulatory agency BaFin on 1 May 2002.
66. Bundesaufsichtsamt für das Kreditwesen & Deutsche Bundesbank (1999).
67. Federal Ministry of Finance (1999, 2000).
68. Bundestag Finance Committee (1999, 2000a).
69. Bundestag Finance Committee (1999).
70. Bundestag (2000). Nevertheless, several further preferences were not successfully voiced. E.g. the introduction of an identical master-scale of risk weights for internal and external ratings, or identical minimum requirements for the introduction of both standardised and foundational IRB approaches.
71. Bundestag Finance Committee (1999, 2000a–e), Bundesrat (2000), Bundestag (2000).
72. Bundestag Finance Committee (2000d). Commercial collateralised loans are credits that are secured by physical property, typically real estate. It is a widespread collateral in Germany, typically used as security for bank credits to small- and medium-sized enterprises. The initially proposed 100 per cent risk weight would have increased the existing capital requirements, and thereby disadvantaged German banks' portfolios, and small local banks in particular.
73. The term Mittelstand is a politically decisive concept used in many German debates on economic policy. It refers to small and medium-sized corporations, largely under private ownership and management, which are considered to be a crucial element of the German economy and its growth (Zeitschrift für das gesamte Kreditwesen 1999, Bundestag Finance Committee 2002, Gilpin 2001, 168–171). Building on this common interest, the Mittelstand has stakeholders in the supervisory agencies, federal ministry of finance, parliament, and the umbrella organisation of the German banking industry.
74. Zentraler Kreditausschuss (2000).
75. Federal Ministry of Finance (2000).
76. Although the latter issue was only agreed upon in general, while the specifics were elaborated on during the subsequent third episode.
77. Bundestag Finance Committee (2000d). They particularly refer to the results of the latest Committee meeting on 11/12 July 2000. A particular success was seen in the preferential treatment of collateralised loans, since this reflected a unique German position, opposed by many other Basel Committee members.

78. Institute of International Finance (2000), International Swaps and Derivatives Association (2000).
79. Recognising double default effects means to recognise that certain hedging instruments reduce the risk of losses to solely those cases in which both parties (debtor and guarantor or derivative counter-party) fail. This would have reduced capital requirements.
80. CP-2 encompassed a package of nine documents with a combined 499 pages – the second consultative paper itself (139 pages on its own), two explanatory documents, and six technical documents that provided detailed background information on crucial issues, such as formulas and data upon which the credit risk calculation parameters were based (Basel Committee on Banking Supervision 2001a–h,l).
81. G7 (1999, 2000).
82. The BCBS referred to these emerging-market aspects in CP-1 by explaining how to diffuse regulatory practices through the Core Principles for Effective Banking Supervision.
83. Basel Committee on Banking Supervision (2003c).
84. Bundestag Finance Committee (2001d).
85. Bundestag Finance Committee (2001d, 2002).
86. Bundestag Finance Committee (2001f, 2001h, 2001i).
87. Bundestag Finance Committee (2001i).
88. Federal Ministry of Finance (2001). This success was partly due to the reported shift in several member states' (Japan, France, Spain, Italy) positions towards better treatment of SME businesses (and accordingly the shared interest in reduced capital charges for such firms).
89. Bundestag Finance Committee (2001a–i).
90. Only the thrift association issued an individual position paper, and even this organisation emphasised the unified industry position. One significant difference between locally and transnationally oriented actors emerged with regard to the granularity index and internal portfolio models: the internationally oriented banks of the BdB (as well as the mortgage banks association) favoured the simultaneous recognition of credit risk models – all other associations welcomed the granularity approach as an intermediary step before the later recognition of portfolio models. Both positions were integrated into the common position paper, while the latter was outlined as the main position (Zentraler Kreditausschuss 2001, 79).
91. Bundestag (2001).
92. Bundestag Finance Committee (2002, 14).
93. Frankfurter Allgemeine Zeitung (2002).
94. In the meantime, as explained in Chapter 4, the BaKred was merged into the integrated financial regulatory agency BaFin on 1 May 2002. BaKred President Sanio became president of the BaFin and remained one of the crucial German negotiators (together with the Bundesbank representative).
95. Bundestag Finance Committee (2004).
96. Basel Committee on Banking Supervision (2002a).
97. Bundestag Finance Committee (2002).
98. This relates to the discussion according to which banks using the A-IRB approach would have had to differentiate their credit risk weights in relation to the credit's remaining maturity until amortisation. Here, the

BCBS proposed a rise in the risk weight with longer times until maturity. Since German lending, based on longer time frames via established bank-firm relationships, would have received increased capital requirements, the banking sector and Mittelstand were again expected to be disadvantaged by this stipulation.

99. Zentraler Kreditausschuss (2001).
100. America's Community Bankers (2001), The Bond Market Association (2001), Bank of America (2001), Citigroup (2001), Financial Guardian Group (2001), Financial Services Roundtable (2001), J.P. Morgan Chase (2001), American Bankers Assocciation (2001).
101. Bundestag Finance Committee (2001d).
102. U.S. Banking Supervisors (2001), Office of Thrift Supervision (2001).
103. Bundestag Finance Committee (2001d).
104. Other rejected issues were: overall calibration (too high); securitisation rules slowing the US market development; extending the consolidated supervision too far through the 'predominantly engaged in banking' definition of the BCBS, instead of the US favoured support of a functionally based building block approach (US style); the charge of capital for both unexpected as well as expected losses.
105. In the meantime, US agencies had agreed that the Basel II standards would be applied only to a limited group of 10 to 20 large, internationally active banks. This resulted in the subsequent conflict over an even national level playing field among these and non-Basel II institutes. At the same time, however, other BCBS members planned to apply the new standards to all banks (Bundesanstalt für Finanzdienstleistungsaufsicht & Deutsche Bundesbank 2003, Bundestag Finance Committee 2003b).
106. U.S. Senate (2003).
107. U.S. House of Representatives (2002).
108. U.S. House of Representatives (2003a, b, c), U.S. Senate (2003).
109. U.S. House of Representatives (2002).
110. Maloney (2002).
111. Financial Guardian Group (2001, 2003).
112. U.S. House of Representatives (2003b).
113. U.S. House of Representatives (2003c).
114. The representatives were unaware of which US agencies had a permanent seat, whether the Treasury was involved in the process, how intra-American agency coordination worked, how coordination within the Basel Committee took place, and the non-binding character and possibility of domestically adjusted implementation (U.S. House of Representatives 2003b, c; U.S. Senate 2003).
115. U.S. House of Representatives (2003b).
116. See also Hawke (2003) and Ferguson (2003).
117. This is the approach to supervise consolidated conglomerates that is prevalent in the United States. It allows more differentiated consolidation by, for example, calculating capital of investment firms subject to specific regulatory rules for these enterprises. It would have benefited most US banks.
118. Basel Committee on Banking Supervision (2001m).

119. Previous projections of adoption and implementation dates had been set to the years 2001 and 2003.
120. Basel Committee on Banking Supervision (2001i).
121. The Committee issued several reports in the few months between May and December 2001 (Basel Committee on Banking Supervision 2001m–r).
122. Working group on capital adequacy report (Institute of International Finance 2001, 3).
123. Institute of International Finance (2001), International Swaps and Derivatives Association (2001).
124. Basel Committee on Banking Supervision (2001p)
125. Through several approaches: recognition of loan-specific provisions by allowing them to reduce specific EAD calculations; general loan-loss provisions that go beyond the 1.25 per cent of total capital and 50 per cent tier one/two ratio, by deducting them from EL-related capital charges; future margin income in retail portfolios – A-IRB banks are permitted to calculate their own internal EL-related capital charges.
126. Bundestag Finance Committee (2001d).
127. The QIS exercises are ex ante assessments of proposed regulatory standards. Typically, the BCBS publishes a handout with guidelines to banks, which then exercise simulations with their portfolios in accordance with the Committee's guidelines. Based upon the results, the BCBS evaluates the impact of its suggested rules and, potentially, adjusts them. QIS-1 was exercised in the context of the Basel Accord of 1988.
128. This, however, was already expected since at least May/June of that year, when the banks undertook their own calculations (Bundestag Finance Committee 2001a).
129. Basel Committee on Banking Supervision (2001i, k).
130. Basel Committee on Banking Supervision (2001i).
131. Basel Committee on Banking Supervision (2002b).
132. Basel Committee on Banking Supervision (2002a).
133. Basel Committee on Banking Supervision (2003d), Bundesanstalt für Finanzdienstleistungsaufsicht & Deutsche Bundesbank (2003). Tarullo (2008, 116) comes to the same conclusions.
134. The BCBS was strengthened as a transgovernmental network via three aspects: the establishment of the AIG, which was close to the industry demand for a clearing-house of all information; the strengthening of the two core principles of home country control (and home/host country supervisory coordination), as well as 'mutual recognition' of internationally active banks.
135. G7 (2003).
136. This is analog to what happened to the collaboration between the Committee and the IIF within the context of the Market Risk Amendment of 1996, where substantial public criticism on a first draft led the Committee to work closely with the IIF in redesigning it (Claessens & Underhill 2010).
137. Bundestag Finance Committee (2001a).
138. Mainly driven by locally oriented community banks and further financial institutions competing with potential Basel II banks in the US market

(U.S. House of Representatives 2005a; Bundestag Finance Committee 2003a, 2004).

139. Bundestag Finance Committee (2003a).
140. Bundestag Finance Committee (2004).
141. For (a) see U.S. House of Representatives (2005b); for (b) see U.S. House of Representatives (2005a); for (c) see U.S. Senate (2005, 10–21).
142. U.S. House of Representatives (2003a, b, c).
143. It is noteworthy that a misunderstanding might underlie the discussion regarding the scope of application of the Accord: while in Germany and the EU the Accord was thought to apply to all banks from the beginning, it is not entirely clear what the US position was. It is reasonable to argue that the plan from the very beginning was to exclude local banks (community banks, thrifts, etc.) from the Accord application, or that there was no clear intention in this regard (see also Tarullo 2008, 118–119). Yet, the complex and scattered nature of US supervisory responsibility among four banking supervisory agencies might not have been factored in by all non-US participants, and therefore these expected that the Accord would apply to all banks in the US too. Nonetheless, the cherry-picking of ten to twelve banks constituted a clear-cut deviation from the initial agreement, since it implied excluding certain internationally active, significant banks.
144. Bundesanstalt für Finanzdienstleistungsaufsicht & Deutsche Bundesbank (2003), Bundestag Finance Committee (2003b).
145. Bundesanstalt für Finanzdienstleistungsaufsicht & Deutsche Bundesbank (2003), Bundestag Finance Committee (2003b).
146. U.S. House of Representatives (2003b).
147. Bundestag Finance Committee (2002).
148. Bundestag Finance Committee (2003a).
149. For a detailed description of the credit risk calculation and the UL/EL approaches see the section on policy analysis pp. 78–80.
150. Basel Committee on Banking Supervision (2003a).
151. Basel Committee on Banking Supervision (2003a, b, 2004a, b, c, e, f).
152. Tarullo (2008, 120–121) comes to the same conclusion.
153. At this meeting, the remaining technical issues of the Accord were elaborated in order to provide a final proposal to the BCBS meeting on 11/12 May 2004, where the Accord proposal was to be finalised.
154. Basel Committee on Banking Supervision (2004a, c, e, f).
155. Basel Committee on Banking Supervision (2004a).
156. Basel Committee on Banking Supervision (2003a, b).
157. Basel Committee on Banking Supervision (2003a, b, 2004f).
158. Basel Committee on Banking Supervision (2004b).
159. Bundestag Finance Committee (2004). Further industry demands were resisted: deletion of the use of a test for retail-specific treatments; reductions in data requirements for IRB approaches; disclosure requirements related to risk measurement and risk mitigation techniques.
160. Basel Committee on Banking Supervision (2004d).
161. The EU transmitted Basel II in 2006 into the Banking Directive (2006/48/EC) and the Capital Adequacy Directive (2006/49/EC), both

taking effect on 1 January 2007, with an implementation deadline for banks of 1 January 2008. German supervisors ensured timely implementation through changes of SolvV and MaRisk (BA). According to Buchmüller (2008), Basel II changed German supervision substantially, through the many new stipulations under pillar one, and the general supervisory mode under pillars two and three. The rather principle-oriented regulation, combined with a qualitative supervisory approach that is based on individual bank evaluation, altered the regulatory landscape considerably. The new elements of internal risk management and supervisory review were implemented via the MaRisk regulatory notes that left considerable room for manoeuvre for both supervisors and banks, but at the same time introduced an expansive new range and mode of supervision for BaFin and Bundesbank. In 2008, about 40 German banks were applying for IRB-approaches (15 already registered, 23 still pending), which accounted for about 60 per cent of Germany's banking business.

162. U.S. House of Representatives (2004a).
163. U.S. House of Representatives (2004a, b), U.S. Senate (2004).
164. The US federal regulator of financial markets and securities firms.
165. U.S. House of Representatives (2004b).
166. U.S. Senate (2004).
167. QIS-4 encompasses three impact studies that were individually initiated and undertaken in the United States, Germany and Japan.
168. The NPR is a formally stipulated element of the US process for setting new regulation. Prior to the adoption of new rules, the industry has to be informed about the planned standards and receive sufficient opportunity to comment on the new stipulations, which the supervisory agencies then have to regard within a potential adjustment of the rules.
169. U.S. House of Representatives (2005a).
170. U.S. House of Representatives (2005a, 9).
171. U.S. House of Representatives (2005b), U.S. Senate (2005).
172. Basel IA was a selected set of the less complex Basel II innovations that incorporated several changes favourable to smaller banks, including more sophisticated treatment of residential mortgages and other retail loans that would lessen the competitive disadvantage. Basel IA, however, was adopted instead of the Basel II standardised approach, since the former did not introduce the operational risk capital charge.
173. Pre-emptive action clauses refer to the authority of banking regulators to intervene in banking operations already perceived to be in danger, before actual insolvency or illiquidity has emerged.
174. U.S. Senate (2005), Verdier (2011, 15–18).
175. Until shortly before he took office, Paulson had been chief executive officer of Goldman Sachs, the leading investment bank in the United States (Sorkin 2010).
176. The first directive that translated Basel II into EU law was already adopted in October 2005 (Tarullo 2008, 126–127).
177. Bundestag Finance Committee (2003a, 2004).
178. Bundesaufsichtsamt für das Kreditwesen & Deutsche Bundesbank (1999), Bundestag Finance Committee (2001d), Basel Committee on Banking Supervision (2001i).

179. Basel Committee on Banking Supervision (2001j).
180. Basel Committee on Banking Supervision (2003b, 2004f).
181. Similar to non-tariff barriers as a response to global tariff reductions in the 1980s (Mansfield & Busch 1995).
182. The EU's and Germany's obedient implementation can largely be attributed to the EU's specific adoption process. Nevertheless, national regulators had sufficient room for manoeuvre under the EU directives.
183. Basel Committee on Banking Supervision (1997).
184. Again this depiction is a selection of issues based upon the author's qualitative weighing. The detailed policy issue specific tables on the author's website provide a detailed basis (www.romangoldbach.com).
185. The better rates in Figure 4.5 are mostly due to the G7's successful push of enhanced regulatory standards in emerging markets and the IMF's enforcement of these rules. While this was a very important political success, it also mirrors the low involvement in the regulation of the G7's own banks.
186. The argument here is that regulatory agencies can – in the shadow of crowded G7/20 agendas with topics that affect politicians' current utility most severely – develop their own agenda. Moreover, even conscious delegations are subject to considerable agency losses, as the necessarily imperfect (from the viewpoint of the principal's preferences) forum characteristics result in deviant solutions, as long as the global principal is not re-alarmed through the re-emergence on the G7 agenda.
187. Further important topics during the framework's deliberation are the combating of money laundering (through the OECD), and the enforced raising of regulatory standards in off-shore financial centres (OFCs). Again, these issues did not relate to the regulation of banks in developed countries.

5   Global Banking Regulation after the Great Recession: Basel III, FSB, G20

1. Yet, as Young (2013) reveals, several changes in the policy process have occurred that necessitate careful investigation with regard to whether they mean significant change in governance and its impact on regulatory outcomes.
2. Actually, the Basel Committee provides a collection of 41 documents that constitute what it calls 'Compilation of documents that form the global regulatory framework for capital and liquidity' (available at: http://www.bis.org/bcbs/basel3/compilation.htm (last visited on 29 April 2014).
3. Basel Committee on Banking Supervision (2009a), Basel Committee on Banking Supervision (2009b).
4. The question of lax standard implementation and supervision to increase a nation's banks' competitiveness is a particularly concerning one. Studies concerned with global finance have yet to investigate systematically the domestic implementation efforts of regulatory agencies.
5. For example, the revision extends the range of corporate debt that banks can use, allowing securities with a credit rating of as low as BBB- to be eligible. The 2010 version of the rule stipulated that such debt must have

a rating of at least AA-; banks would also be allowed to use highly rated residential mortgage-backed securities and some equities (Bloomberg 2013b, The Economist 2013).

6. Young (2013) also finds that these groups attempt to affect the agenda in their favour by undertaking pre-emptive self-regulatory efforts.

7. Assuming that a single supervisory or regulatory decision that hampers banks' profitability/competitiveness feedbacks negatively, very directly on the regulator, while decisions contributing marginally to systemic instability are unlikely to be met with negative feedback (rather with a positive one).

8. This does not preclude the fact that the newly included emerging powers, and in particular the BRIC countries, will gain increasing power and thereby change crucial aspects of global economic governance in the long term. In the short to medium term, however, the difference that these additional actors will make with regard to the content and quality of harmonised regulatory standards seems to be rather low, if not even insignificant.

9. While member states agreed to be subject to these assessments, however, this does not force a jurisdiction to adopt all Basel III elements, as is revealed in a footnote to the respective BCBS document: 'In some cases, given the state of financial systems, jurisdictions may choose not to adopt some or all of the advanced approaches of Basel III for the measurement of risks. In the context of the RCAP assessment, these will not be considered as being non-compliant when the relevant provisions of Basel III are assessed. Instead, these provisions may be considered as non-applicable, in line with the approach adopted by the Committee when developing Basel II' (Basel Committee on Banking Supervision 2013a, 2).

10. In the meantime, the Committee has even developed a detailed, 104-page-long questionnaire for national regulators to answer and update regularly (Basel Committee on Banking Supervision 2013e).

11. It is important to note that the FSB charter was subject to considerable amendment. At its Los Cabos summit in June 2012 the G20 decided to establish the FSB on an enduring organisation footing (Financial Stability Board 2012b). As I will discuss below, the addition of six new articles and several new paragraphs incurred substantial adjustments (in addition the FSB was established as an association under article 6 of the Swiss Civil Code in January 2013). In the text, I cite the article reference according to the renewed 2012 version of the charter

12. A crucial question is, whether the inclusion of these mid-level officials from the member countries' ministries can result in change regarding the selective fire alarm mechanisms: higher levels in the ministries could be politically more susceptible to influence from non-special interests. Since, however, the deputies and lower levels of officials are rather technical experts than politicians, this is less likely. This notwithstanding, close empirical investigation should attempt to reveal whether the inclusion of officials from ministries of finance – which is a crucial new element of the FSB, distinguishing it from the transgovernmental networks of regulators – results in an altered level of interest inclusion.

13. From a perspective of incremental institutional development, however, it is highly interesting that the Charter amendment of (now) Article 22, paragraph 5 included a new sentence with regard to the recruitment of

Secretariat staff: 'In appointing the Secretariat staff, the Secretary General shall ... pay due regard to the ... retaining [of] institutional memory by having an adequate proportion of staff on open-ended contracts'. This may open the road to an incrementally growing employment body of an intergovernmental organisation.

14. Yet again the Charter amendment may provide a crucial incremental step towards more power of the FSB as an intergovernmental organisation: article 17 gives the Standing Committee on Budget and Resources considerable agenda setting power in terms of the medium-term budget and resource framework, which provides the transgovernmental network with the possibility to affect the Plenary decision on budget and resources through strategic proposals. The final decision, however, remains with the Plenary, i.e. each member state.

15. At the G 20 meeting in St Petersburg in September 2013, the FSB was requested to review the structure of its representation, on which it will report at the 2014 Brisbane summit.

6 Conclusion: Layers and Gaps in the Global Political Economy

1. Verdier (2013) illustrates the considerable international differences between the different national regulatory regimes, which prevent widespread, substantial international cooperation.

2. Yet, an important difference lies in the public control that politicians can exert over private bodies, since political control mechanisms differ. Politicians have different mechanisms at their disposal to interfere in regulatory agencies' work as compared with private bodies.

3. I am very thankful to Michael Breen for turning my attention to this aspect.

4. One could argue that the actual G7/20-power is exerted during the informal negotiations that take place continuously among the deputy finance ministers (Stone 2011, 6, 58). The agenda developed within these consultations could be transferred via governmental channels into the transnational network. While the quantitative analysis cannot falsify this claim, the process tracing of the consultations within the federal parliaments provides contrasting evidence that rather supports this study's transnational argument.

References

Abbott, Kenneth W. & Duncan Snidal. 2000. "Hard and Soft Law in International Governance." *International Organization* 54(3):421–456.

Admati, Anat & Martin Hellwig. 2013. *The Bankers' New Clothes: What's Wrong with Banking and What to Do about It.* Princeton: Princeton University Press.

American Bankers Assocciation. 2001. "Comments on the Second Consultative Paper of the Basel Committee on Banking Supervision regarding the Basel II Accord." Washington, 25 June 2001. Available at www.bis.org/bcbs/cacomments.htm.

America's Community Bankers. 2001. "Comments on the Second Consultative Paper of the Basel Committee on Banking Supervision regarding the Basel II Accord." Washington, 31 May 2001. Available at www.bis.org/bcbs/cacomments.htm.

Avant, Deborah D., Martha Finnemore & Susan K. Sel, eds. 2010. *Who Governs the Globe?* Cambridge: Cambridge University Press.

Axelrod, Robert. 1984. *The Evolution of Cooperation.* New York: Basic Books.

Bach, David. 2010. "Varieties of Cooperation: The Domestic Institutional Roots of Global Governance." *Review of International Studies* 36(3):561–589.

Bair, Sheila. 2013. *Bull by the Horns: Fighting to Save Main Street from Wall Street and Wall Street from Itself.* New York: Simon and Schuster.

Baker, Andrew. 2009. "Deliberative Equality and the Transgovernmental Politics of the Global Financial Architecture." *Global Governance* 15(2):195–218.

Baker, Andrew. 2010. Mandate, Accountability and Decision Making Issues to be Faced by the FSB. In *The Financial Stability Board: An Effective Fourth Pillar of Global Economic Governance?*, ed. Stephany Griffith-Jones, Eric Helleiner & Ngaire Woods. Waterloo: The Centre for International Governance Innovation pp. 19–22.

Baker, Andrew. 2013a. "The Gradual Transformation? The incremental Dynamics of Macroprudential Regulation." *Regulation & Governance* 7(4):417–434.

Baker, Andrew. 2013b. "The New Political Economy of the Macroprudential Ideational Shift." *New Political Economy* 18(1):112–139.

Bank of America. 2001. "Comments on the Second Consultative Paper of the Basel Committee on Banking Supervision regarding the Basel II Accord." Washington, 31 May 2001. Available at www.bis.org/bcbs/cacomments.htm.

Barr, Michael S. & Geoffrey P. Miller. 2006. "Global Administrative Law: The View from Basel." *European Journal of International Law* 17(1):15–46.

Barth, James R., Chris Brummer, Tong Li & Daniel E. Nolle. 2013. "Systemically Important Banks (SIBs) in the Post-Crisis Era: 'The' Global Response, and Responses Around the Globe for 135 Countries." July 16, 2013). Available at SSRN: http://ssrn.com/abstract=2294641 or http://dx.doi.org/10.2139/ssrn.2294641.

Barth, James R., Gerard Caprio & David S. Levine. 2012. *Guardians of Finance. Making Regulators Work for us.* Cambridge: MIT Press.

Barth, James R., R. Dan Jr. Brumbaugh & James A. Wilcox. 2000. "Policy Watch: The Repeal of Glass-Steagall and the Advent of Broad Banking." *Journal of Economic Perspectives* 14(2):191–204.

Bartley, Tim. 2011. "Transnational Governance as the Layering of Rules: Intersections of Public and Private Standards." *Theoretical Inquiries in Law* 12(2):Article 6.

Basel Committee on Banking Supervision. 1996. "Amendment to the Capital Accord to Incorporate Market Risks." Bank for International Settlements, Basel, January 1996.

Basel Committee on Banking Supervision. 1997. "Core Principles for Effective Banking Supervision." Bank for International Settlements. Basel, September 1997. Available at http://www.bis.org/publ/bcbs30a.htm.

Basel Committee on Banking Supervision. 1999. "A New Capital Adequacy Framework." Consultative Paper 1 of the Basel Committee on Banking Supervision, Bank for International Settlements, Basel, June 1999.

Basel Committee on Banking Supervision. 2000. "Range of Practice in Banks' Internal Ratings Systems." Basel Committee on Banking Supervision, Bank for International Settlements, Basel January 2000. Available at http://www.bis.org/publ/bcbs66.pdf.

Basel Committee on Banking Supervision. 2001a. "Asset Securitisation." Consultative Document (as Supplement to the Second Consultative Paper on the Basel II Accord) of the Basel Committee on Banking Supervision, Bank for International Settlements, Basel, January 2001.

Basel Committee on Banking Supervision. 2001b. "The Internal Ratings-Based Approach." Consultative Document (as Supplement to the Second Consultative Paper on the Basel II Accord) of the Basel Committee on Banking Supervision, Bank for International Settlements, Basel, January 2001.

Basel Committee on Banking Supervision. 2001c. "The New Basel Capital Accord – Second Consultative Paper." Consultative Paper 2 of the Basel Committee on Banking Supervision, Bank for International Settlements, Basel, 16 January 2001.

Basel Committee on Banking Supervision. 2001d. "The New Basel Capital Accord: an explanatory note." Basel Committee on Banking Supervision, Bank for International Settlements, Basel, January 2001.

Basel Committee on Banking Supervision. 2001e. "Operational Risk." Consultative Document (as Supplement to the Second Consultative Paper on the Basel II Accord) of the Basel Committee on Banking Supervision, Bank for International Settlements, Basel, January 2001.

Basel Committee on Banking Supervision. 2001f. "Overview of The New Basel Capital Accord." Consultative Document (as Supplement to the Second Consultative Paper on the Basel II Accord) of the Basel Committee on Banking Supervision, Bank for International Settlements, Basel, January 2001.

Basel Committee on Banking Supervision. 2001g. "Pillar 2 (Supervisory Review Process)." Consultative Document (as Supplement to the Second Consultative Paper on the Basel II Accord) of the Basel Committee on Banking Supervision, Bank for International Settlements, Basel, January 2001.

Basel Committee on Banking Supervision. 2001h. "Pillar 3 (Market Discipline)." Consultative Document (as Supplement to the Second Consultative Paper on the Basel II Accord) of the Basel Committee on Banking Supervision, Bank for International Settlements, Basel, January 2001.

Basel Committee on Banking Supervision. 2001i. "Potential Modifications to the Committee's Proposals." Basel Committee on Banking Supervision, Bank for International Settlements, Basel, 5 November 2001.

Basel Committee on Banking Supervision. 2001j. "Progress Towards Completion of the New Basel Capital Accord." Press Release. Basel Committee on Banking Supervision, Bank for International Settlements, Basel, 13 December 2001.

Basel Committee on Banking Supervision. 2001k. "Results of the Second Quantitative Impact Study." Basel Committee on Banking Supervision, Bank for International Settlements, Basel, 5 November 2001.

Basel Committee on Banking Supervision. 2001l. "The Standardised Approach to Credit Risk." Consultative Document (as Supplement to the Second Consultative Paper on the Basel II Accord) of the Basel Committee on Banking Supervision, Bank for International Settlements, Basel, January 2001.

Basel Committee on Banking Supervision. 2001m. "Update on the New Basel Capital Accord." Basel Committee on Banking Supervision, Bank for International Settlements, Basel, 25 June 2001.

Basel Committee on Banking Supervision. 2001n. "Update on Work on the New Basel Capital Accord." Basel Committee Newsletter No. 2 (Report about the status of work in the Capital Group). Basel Committee on Banking Supervision, Bank for International Settlements, Basel, 21 September 2001. Available at www.bis.org/publ/bcbs_nl2.htm.

Basel Committee on Banking Supervision. 2001o. "Working Paper on Pillar 3 — Market Discipline." BCBS Working Papers No 7. Transparency Group of the Basel Committee on Banking Supervision, Bank for International Settlements, Basel, September 2001.

Basel Committee on Banking Supervision. 2001p. "Working Paper on the IRB Treatment of Expected Losses and Future Margin Income." BCBS Working Papers No 5. Joint Accounting Task Force - Models Task Force Working Group of the Basel Committee on Banking Supervision, Bank for International Settlements, Basel, July 2001.

Basel Committee on Banking Supervision. 2001q. "Working Paper on the Regulatory Treatment of Operational Risk." BCBS Working Papers No 8. Risk Management Group of the Basel Committee on Banking Supervision, Bank for International Settlements, Basel, September 2001.

Basel Committee on Banking Supervision. 2001r. "Working Paper on the Treatment of Asset Securitisations." BCBS Working Papers No 10. Securitisation Group of the Basel Committee on Banking Supervision, Bank for International Settlements, Basel, October 2001.

Basel Committee on Banking Supervision. 2002a. "Basel Committee Reaches Agreement on New Capital Accord issues." Press Release. Basel Committee on Banking Supervision, Bank for International Settlements, Basel, 10 July 2002.

Basel Committee on Banking Supervision. 2002b. "Results of Quantitative Impact Study 2.5." Basel Committee on Banking Supervision, Bank for International Settlements, Basel, 25 June 2002.

Basel Committee on Banking Supervision. 2003a. "Basel II: Significant Progress on Major Issues." Press Release. Basel Committee on Banking Supervision, Bank for International Settlements, Basel, 11 October 2003.

Basel Committee on Banking Supervision. 2003b. "High-level Principles for the Cross-Border Implementation of the New Accord." Basel Committee on Banking Supervision, Bank for International Settlements, Basel, August 2003.

Basel Committee on Banking Supervision. 2003c. "The New Basel Capital Accord – Third Consultative Paper." Consultative Paper 3 of the Basel Committee on Banking Supervision, Bank for International Settlements, Basel, April 2003.

Basel Committee on Banking Supervision. 2003d. "Quantitative Impact Study 3 – Overview of Global Results." Basel Committee on Banking Supervision, Bank for International Settlements, Basel, 5 May 2003.

Basel Committee on Banking Supervision. 2004a. "Changes to the Securitisation Framework." Working Paper. Basel Committee on Banking Supervision, Bank for International Settlements, Basel, 30 January 2004.

Basel Committee on Banking Supervision. 2004b. "Consensus achieved on Basel II proposals." Press Release. Basel Committee on Banking Supervision, Bank for International Settlements, Basel, 11 May 2004.

Basel Committee on Banking Supervision. 2004c. "Continued Progress towards Basel II." Press Release. Basel Committee on Banking Supervision, Bank for International Settlements, Basel, 15 January 2004.

Basel Committee on Banking Supervision. 2004d. "G10 Central Bank Governors and Heads of Supervision Endorse the Publication of the Revised Capital Framework." Press Release. Basel Committee on Banking Supervision, Bank for International Settlements, Basel, 26 June 2004.

Basel Committee on Banking Supervision. 2004e. "Modifications to the Capital Treatment for Expected and Unexpected Credit Losses in the New Basel Accord." Working Paper. Basel Committee on Banking Supervision, Bank for International Settlements, Basel, 30 January 2004.

Basel Committee on Banking Supervision. 2004f. "Principles for the Home-host Recognition of AMA Operational Risk Capital." Working Paper. Basel Committee on Banking Supervision, Bank for International Settlements, Basel, January 2004.

Basel Committee on Banking Supervision. 2006. "International Convergence of Capital Measurement and Capital Standards. A Revised Framework (Comprehensive Version)." Bank for International Settlements, Basel Committee on Banking Supervision.

Basel Committee on Banking Supervision. 2009a. "Enhancements to the Basel II Framework.".

Basel Committee on Banking Supervision. 2009b. "Revisions to the Basel II Market Risk Framework.".

Basel Committee on Banking Supervision. 2010a. "Adjustments to the Basel II market risk framework announced by the Basel Committee." BIS Press Release. Available at: http://www.bis.org/press/p100618.htm. Last visited 25 April 2014.

Basel Committee on Banking Supervision. 2010b. "Basel III: A Global Regulatory Framework for More Resilient Banks and Banking Systems." Bank for International Settlements, Basel, December 2010.

Basel Committee on Banking Supervision. 2010c. "Basel III: International Framework for Liquidity Risk Measurement, Standards and Monitoring." Bank for International Settlements, Basel, December 2010.

Basel Committee on Banking Supervision. 2010d. "Good Practice Principles on Supervisory Colleges." October 2010. Available at http://www.bis.org/publ/bcbs 177.htm. Last visited 21 July 2014.

Basel Committee on Banking Supervision. 2013a. "Basel III Regulatory Consistency Assessment Programme (RCAP)." October 2013. Available at http://www.bis.org/publ/bcbs264.htm. Last visited 23 July 2014.

Basel Committee on Banking Supervision. 2013b. "Charter." January 2013. Available at http://www.bis.org/bcbs/charter.pdf. Last visited 3 September 2014.

Basel Committee on Banking Supervision. 2013c. "Fundamental Review of the Trading Book - Second Consultative Document Issued by the Basel Committee." Press Release, 31 October 2013. http://www.bis.org/press/p131 031. htm. Last visited 21 July 2014.

Basel Committee on Banking Supervision. 2013d. "Global Systemically Important Banks: Updated Assessment Methodology and the Higher loss Absorbency Requirement." July 2013. Available at http://www.bis.org/publ/bcbs255.pdf. Last visited 6 May 2014.

Basel Committee on Banking Supervision. 2013e. "RCAP Questionnaire for Assessing Implementation of Basel III Capital Regulations." October 2013. Available at http://www.bis.org/publ/bcbs264.htm. Last visited 23 July 2014.

Basel Committee on Banking Supervision. 2014a. "Amendments to Basel III's Leverage Ratio issued by the Basel Committee." Press Release, 12 January 2014. Available at http://www.bis.org/press/p140112a.htm. Last visited 21 July 2014.

Basel Committee on Banking Supervision. 2014b. "Consultative Document. Basel III: The Net Stable Funding Ratio (Issued for comment by 11 April 2014)." January 2014. Available at http://www.bis.org/publ/bcbs271.htm. Last visited 21 July 2014.

Basel Committee on Banking Supervision. 2014c. "Principles for Effective Supervisory Colleges." June 2014. Available at http://www.bis.org/publ/bcbs287.pdf. Last visited 21 July 2014.

Basel Committee on Banking Supervision. 2014d. "Progress Report on Implementation of the Basel Regulatory Framework." April 2014. Available at http://www.bis.org/publ/bcbs281.pdf. Last visited 30 September 2014.

Basel Committee on Banking Supervision. 2014e. "Seventh Progress Report on Adoption of the Basel Regulatory Framework." October 2014. Available at http://www.bis.org/publ/bcbs290.htm. Last visited 8 October 2014.

Basel Committee on Banking Supervision. 2014f. "Work on the Liquidity Coverage Ratio finalised by the Basel Committee." Press Release, 12 January 2014. Available at http://www.bis.org/press/p140112c.htm. Last visited 21 July 2014.

Berger, Suzanne. 2000. "Globalization and Politics." *Annual Review of Political Science* 3(1):43–62.

Bloomberg. 2013a. "Banks Face Risk-Model Clampdown in Basel Trading-Book Review." Bloomberg Online. 21 October 2013. Available at http://www.bloomberg.com/news/2013-10-20/banks-face-risk-model-clampdown-in-basel-trading-book-review.html. Last visited on 21 July 2014.

Bloomberg. 2013b. "Banks Win 4-Year Delay as Basel Liquidity Rule Loosened." Bloomberg Online. 7 January 2013. Available at http://www.bloomberg.com/

news/2013-01-06/banks-win-watered-down-liquidity-rule-after-basel-group-deal.html. Last visited on 21 July 2014.

Bloomberg. 2013c. "Basel Becomes Babel as Conflicting Rules Undermine Safety." Bloomberg Online. 2 January 2013. Available at http://www.bloomberg.com/news/2013-01-03/basel-becomes-babel-as-conflicting-rules-undermine-safety.html. Last visited on 21 July 2014.

Bloomberg. 2014. "Deutsche Bank Attacks Basel Plan's Threat to Repo Market." Bloomberg Online. 29 April 2014. Available at http://www.bloomberg.com/news/2014-04-29/deutsche-bank-attacks-basel-plan-s-threat-to-repo-market.html. Last visited on 21 July 2014.

Blyth, Mark. 2013. "Paradigms and Paradox: The Politics of Economic Ideas in Two Moments of Crisis." *Governance* 26(2):197–215.

Börsen-Zeitung. 1999a. ""Sparkassen müssen stärker zusammenarbeiten" – Hoppenstedt: Deutsche Kreditwirtschaft soll ihre Interessen nach außen gemeinsam verfolgen." Börsen-Zeitung, 11. June 1999.

Börsen-Zeitung. 1999b. "Sparkassen wittern Attacke auf das deutsche Bankensystem." Börsen-Zeitung, 3. February 1999.

Börsen-Zeitung. 2012. "Basel lockert Liquiditätskennziffer." Börsen-Zeitung, 10 January 2012.

Brummer, Chris. 2012. "Charter of the Financial Stability Board: Introductory Note." *international legal materials* 51(4):828–829.

Buchmüller, Patrick. 2008. *Basel II. Hinwendung zur prinzipienorientierten Bankenaufsicht.* Baden-Baden: Nomos.

Bundesanstalt für Finanzdienstleistungsaufsicht & Deutsche Bundesbank. 2003. "Testimony at the 38. Finance Committee Meeting (Non-public) in Legislative Period 15." Minutes of the 38. Finance Committee Meeting (Non-public) in Legislative Period 15. Berlin, 22. October 2003.

Bundesaufsichtsamt für das Kreditwesen & Deutsche Bundesbank. 1999. "Testimony at the 46. Finance Committee Meeting (Non-public) in Legislative Period 14." Minutes of the 46. Finance Committee Meeting (Non-public) in Legislative Period 14. Berlin, 15. December 1999.

Bundesrat. 2000. "Entschließung des Bundesrates zum Konsultationspapier des Basler Ausschusses für Bankenaufsicht 'Neuregelung der angemessenen Eigenkapitalausstattung' vom Juni 1999." Minutes of the 58. Finance Committee Meeting (Non-public) in Legislative Period 14. Berlin, 5. April 2000.

Bundestag. 2000. "Antrag der Fraktionen SPD, CDU/CSU, BÜNDNIS 90/DIE GRÜNEN und F.D.P.: Neuregelung der angemessenen Eigenkapitalausstattung von Kreditinstituten und der Eigenmittelvorschriften für Kreditinstitute und Wertpapierfirmen in der EU." Bundestagsdrucksache 14/3523. 7 June 2000.

Bundestag. 2001. "Antrag der Fraktionen SPD, CDU/CSU, BÜNDNIS 90/DIE GRÜNEN, F.D.P. und PDS: Fairer Wettbewerb bei Basel II — Neufassung der Basler Eigenkapitalvereinbarung und Überarbeitung der Eigenkapitalvorschriften für Kreditinstitute und Wertpapierfirmen." Bundestagsdrucksache 14/6196. 31 May 2001.

Bundestag Finance Committee. 1999. "Minutes of the 46. Finance Committee Meeting (Non-public) in Legislative Period 14." Berlin, 15. December 1999.

Bundestag Finance Committee. 2000a. "Minutes of the 58. Finance Committee Meeting (Non-public) in Legislative Period 14." Berlin, 5. April 2000.

Bundestag Finance Committee. 2000b. "Minutes of the 63. Finance Committee Meeting (Non-public) in Legislative Period 14." Berlin, 17. May 2000.

Bundestag Finance Committee. 2000c. "Minutes of the 64. Finance Committee Meeting (Non-public) in Legislative Period 14." Berlin, 6. June 2000.

Bundestag Finance Committee. 2000d. "Minutes of the 69. Finance Committee Meeting (Non-public) in Legislative Period 14." Berlin, 27. September 2000.

Bundestag Finance Committee. 2000e. "Minutes of the 77. Finance Committee Meeting (Non-public) in Legislative Period 14." Berlin, 15. November 2000.

Bundestag Finance Committee. 2001a. "Minutes of the 101. Finance Committee Meeting (Non-public) in Legislative Period 14." Berlin, 27. June 2001.

Bundestag Finance Committee. 2001b. "Minutes of the 102. Finance Committee Meeting (Non-public) in Legislative Period 14." Berlin, 4. July 2001.

Bundestag Finance Committee. 2001c. "Minutes of the 110. Finance Committee Meeting (Non-public) in Legislative Period 14." Berlin, 17. October 2001.

Bundestag Finance Committee. 2001d. "Minutes of the 118. Finance Committee Meeting (Non-public) in Legislative Period 14." Berlin, 11. December 2001.

Bundestag Finance Committee. 2001e. "Minutes of the 119. Finance Committee Meeting (Non-public) in Legislative Period 14." Berlin, 12. December 2001.

Bundestag Finance Committee. 2001f. "Minutes of the 89. Finance Committee Meeting (Non-public) in Legislative Period 14." Berlin, 7. March 2001.

Bundestag Finance Committee. 2001g. "Minutes of the 95. Finance Committee Meeting (Non-public) in Legislative Period 14." Berlin, 9. May 2001.

Bundestag Finance Committee. 2001h. "Minutes of the 96. Finance Committee Meeting (Non-public) in Legislative Period 14." Berlin, 16. May 2001.

Bundestag Finance Committee. 2001i. "Minutes of the 97. Finance Committee Meeting (Non-public) in Legislative Period 14." Berlin, 30. May 2001.

Bundestag Finance Committee. 2002. "Minutes of the 128. Finance Committee Meeting (Public Hearing) in Legislative Period 14." Berlin, 20. March 2002.

Bundestag Finance Committee. 2003a. "Minutes of the 18. Finance Committee Meeting (Non-public) in Legislative Period 15." Berlin, 21. May 2003.

Bundestag Finance Committee. 2003b. "Minutes of the 38. Finance Committee Meeting (Non-public) in Legislative Period 15." Berlin, 22. October 2003.

Bundestag Finance Committee. 2004. "Minutes of the 57. Finance Committee Meeting (Non-public) in Legislative Period 15." Berlin, 5. May 2004.

Busch, Andreas. 2005. "Globalisation and national varieties of capitalism: The contested viability of the 'german model'." *German Politics* 14(2):125–139.

Busch, Andreas. 2009. *Banking Regulation and Globalization*. Oxford: Oxford University Press.

Büthe, Tim & Walter Mattli. 2011. *The New Global Rulers: The Privatization of Regulation in the World Economy*. Princeton: Princeton University Press.

Cerny, Philip G. 1994. "The Dynamics of Financial Globalization: Technology, Market Structure, and Policy Response." *Policy Sciences* 27(4):319–342.

Cerny, Philip G. 1995. "Globalization and the Changing Logic of Collective Action." *International Organization* 49(4):595–625.

Cerny, Philip G. 1997. "Paradoxes of the Competition State: The Dynamics of Political Globalization." *Government and Opposition* 32(2):251–274.

Cerny, Philip G. 2001. "From 'Iron Triangles' to 'Golden Pentangles'? Globalizing the Policy Process." *Global Governance* 7(4):397–410.

Cerny, Philip G. 2010a. "The Competition State Today: From Raison d'Etat to Raison du Monde." *Policy Studies* 31(1):5–21.

Cerny, Philip G. 2010b. *Rethinking World Politics. A Theory of Transnational Neopluralism.* Oxford: Oxford University Press.

Chey, Hyoung-Kyu. 2007. "Do Markets Enhance Convergence on International Standards? The Case of Financial Regulation." *Regulation & Governance* 1(4):295–311.

Chey, Hyoung-kyu. 2013. *International Harmonization of Financial Regulation? The Politics of Global Diffusion of the Basel Capital Accord.* New York: Routledge.

Citigroup. 2001. "Comments on the Second Consultative Paper of the Basel Committee on Banking Supervision Regarding the Basel II Accord." Washington, 31 May 2001. Available at www.bis.org/bcbs/cacomments.htm.

Claessens, Stijn & Geoffrey R. D. Underhill. 2010. The Political Economy of Basel II in the International Financial Architecture. In *Global Financial Integration Thirty Years On*, ed. Geoffrey R. D. Underhill, Jasper Blom & Daniel Mügge. Cambridge: Cambridge University Press pp. 113–133.

Coen, David & Mark Thatcher. 2005. "The New Governance of Markets and Non-Majoritarian Regulators." *Governance* 18(3):329–346.

Cohen, Benjamin J. 1996. "Phoenix Risen: The Resurrection of Global Finance." *World Politics* 48(2):268–296.

Cohen, Benjamin J. 2008. *International Political Economy: An Intellectual History.* Princeton: Princeton University Press.

Coleman, William D. 1994a. "Banking, Interest Intermediation and Political Power." *European Journal of Political Research* 26(1):31–58.

Coleman, William D. 1994b. "Policy Convergence in Banking: A Comparative Study." *Political Studies* 42(2):274–292.

Coleman, William D. 2003. Governing Global Finance: Financial Derivatives, Liberal States and Transformative Capacity. In *States in the Global Economy: Bringing Domestic Institutions Back in*, ed. Linda Weiss. Cambridge: Cambridge University Press pp. 271–292.

Cooper, Andrew F. 2010. "The G20 as an improvised crisis committee and/or a contested 'steering committee' for the world." *International Affairs* 86(3):741–757.

Copelovitch, Mark S. & David Andrew Singer. 2008. "Financial Regulation, Monetary Policy, and Inflation in the Industrialized World." *Journal of Politics* 70(3):663–680.

Crespo-Tenorio, Adriana, Nathan M. Jensen & Guillermo Rosas. 2014. "Political Liabilities: Surviving Banking Crises." *Comparative Political Studies* 47(7):1047–1074.

Davies, Howard & David Green. 2008. *Global Financial Regulation: The Essential Guide.* Cambridge: Polity Press.

De Swaan, Tom. 1998. "Capital Regulation: The Road Ahead." *Federal Reserve Bank of New York Economic Policy Review* 4(3):231–235.

Deeg, Richard & Mary A. O'Sullivan. 2009. "The Political Economy of Global Finance Capital." *World Politics* 61(4):731–763.

Diamond, Douglas W. & Philip H. Dybvig. 1983. "Bank Runs, Deposit Insurance and Liquidity." *Journal of Political Economy* 91(3):401–419.

Donnelly, Shawn. 2012. Institutional Change at the Top: From the Financial Stability Forum to the Financial Stability Board. In *Institutional Change in*

Financial Market Regulation, ed. Renate Mayntz. Frankfurt a.M.: Campus pp. 263–277.

Drezner, Daniel W. 2007. *All Politics is Global: Explaining International Regulatory Regimes.* Princeton: Princeton University Press.

Duffie, Darrell & Henry T. Hu. 2008. "Competing for a Share of Global Derivatives Markets: Trends and Policy Choices for the United States." Rock Center for Corporate Governance at Stanford University Working Paper No. 50. Available at.

Eberlein, Burkard & Edgar Grande. 2005. "Beyond Delegation: Transnational Regulatory Regimes and the EU Regulatory State." *Journal of European Public Policy* 12(1):89–112.

European Systemic Risk Board. 2014. "Is Europe Overbanked?" Report of the Advisory Scientific Committee No. 4/June 2014.

Farrell, Henry & Abraham L. Newman. 2014. "Domestic Institutions Beyond the Nation State: Charting the New Interdependence Approach." *World Politics* 66(2):331–363.

Farrell, Henry & Abraham L. Newman. 2015. "The New Politics of Interdependence. Cross-National Layering in Trans-Atlantic Regulatory Disputes." *Comparative Political Studies* 48(1):497–526

Federal Ministry of Finance. 1999. "Aufzeichnung zu TOP 3 der 46. Sitzung des Finanzausschusses des Deutschen Bundestages am 15. Dezember 1999: Konsultationspapier des Baseler Ausschusses für Bankenaufsicht zur Neuregelung der angemessenen Eigenkapitalausstattung von Kreditinstituten." Minutes of the 46. Finance Committee Meeting (Non-public) in Legislative Period 14. Berlin, 15. December 1999.

Federal Ministry of Finance. 2000. "Aufzeichnung zu TOP 3 der 58. Sitzung des Finanzausschusses des Deutschen Bundestages am 5. April 2000: Konsultationspapier des Baseler Ausschusses für Bankenaufsicht zur Neuregelung der angemessenen Eigenkapitalausstattung von Kreditinstituten." Minutes of the 58. Finance Committee Meeting (Non-public) in Legislative Period 14. Berlin, 5. April 2000.

Federal Ministry of Finance. 2001. "Aufzeichnung zu TOP 4 der 97. Sitzung des Finanzausschusses des Deutschen Bundestages am 30. Mai 2001: Konsultationspapier des Baseler Ausschusses für Bankenaufsicht zur Neuregelung der angemessenen Eigenkapitalausstattung von Kreditinstituten." Minutes of the 97. Finance Committee Meeting (Non-public) in Legislative Period 14. Berlin, 30 May 2001.

Ferguson, Roger W., Jr. 2003. "Testimony at the Hearing 'The New Basel Accord: Sound Regulation or Crushing Complexity?' before the Subcommittee on Domestic and International Monetary Policy, Trade and Technology of the Committee on Financial Services of the U.S. House of Representatives." Washington, 27. February 2003.

Financial Guardian Group. 2001. "Comments of the Financial Guardian Group on the Basel II Accord second Consultative Paper of the Basel Committee on Banking Supervision." Washington, 31. May 2001. Available at www.bis.org/bcbs/cacomments.htm.

Financial Guardian Group. 2003. "Comments of the Financial Guardian Group on the Basel II Accord second Consultative Paper of the Basel

Committee on Banking Supervision." Washington, 31 July 2003. Available at www.bis.org/bcbs/cp3comments.htm.

Financial Services Roundtable. 2001. "Comments on the Second Consultative Paper of the Basel Committee on Banking Supervision regarding the Basel II Accord." Washington, 31 May 2001. Available at www.bis.org/bcbs/cacomments.htm.

Financial Stability Board. 2012a. "Financial Stability Board Charter (Version 2 after 2012 amendments)." Basel.

Financial Stability Board. 2012b. "Report to the G-20 Los Cabos Summit on Strengthening FSB Capacity, Resources and Governance." Basel, 12 June 2012.

Financial Times. 2014. "Banks win Basel concessions on debt rules." Financial Times. 13 January 2014.

Frach, Lotte. 2008. *Finanzaufsicht in Deutschland und Großbritannien. Die BaFin und die FSA im Spannungsfeld der Politik.* Wiesbaden: VS Verlag.

Frankfurter Allgemeine Zeitung. 2002. "Basel II. Durchbruch für den Mittelstand." Frankfurter Allgemeine Zeitung, 3 July 2002.

Frieden, Jeffry A. 1991. "Invested Interests: The Politics of National Economic Policies in a World of Global Finance." *International Organization* 45(4):425–451.

G7. 1997a. "Confronting Global Economic and Financial Challenges." Declaration of the G7 Heads of State/Government for the Denver Summit, 21 June 1997.

G7. 1997b. "Final Report to the G7 Heads of State and Government on Promoting Financial Stability." Finance Ministers Report to the G7 Heads of State and Government at the Denver Summit, 21 June 1997.

G7. 1998a. "Conclusions of G7 Finance Ministers." Finance Ministers' Meetings in Preparation of the G7 Heads of State and Government for the Birmingham Summit on 15 May 1998, 9 May 1998.

G7. 1998b. "Declaration of G7 Finance Ministers and Central Bank Governors." Declaration of the Finance Ministers' Meeting at the G7 Summit in Washington, 30 October 1998.

G7. 1998c. "G7 Leaders Statement on the World Economy." Declaration of the G7 Heads of State/Government at the Washington Summit, 30 October 1998.

G7. 1998d. "Strengthening the Architecture of the Global Financial System." Finance Ministers Report to the G7 Heads of State and Government for the Birmingham Summit, 15 May 1998.

G7. 1999. "Report of G7 Finance Ministers to the G7 Cologne Economic Summit, 18-20 June 1999." Declaration of the Finance Ministers' Meeting at the G7 Summit in Cologne, 18 June 1999.

G7. 2000. "Strengthening the International Financial Architecture." Report from G7 Finance Ministers to the G7 Heads of State and Government, 8 July 2000.

G7. 2003. "Statement of G-7 Finance Ministers and Central Bank Governors." Report of G-7 Finance Ministers and Central Bank Governors. Paris, 22 February 2003.

G8. 1999. "G8 Cologne Summit Communiqué." Declaration of the G8 Heads of State/Government at the Cologne Summit, 20 June 1999.

Genschel, Philipp & Thomas Plümper. 1996. "Wenn Reden Silber und Handeln Gold ist. Kooperation und Kommunikation in der internationalen Bankenregulierung." *Zeitschrift für Internationale Beziehungen* 3(2):225–253.

George, Alexander L. & Andrew Bennett. 2005. *Case Studies and Theory Development in the Social Sciences.* Cambridge: MIT Press.

Germain, Randall. 2010. "Financial Governance and Transnational Deliberative Democracy." *Review of International Studies* 36(2):493–509.

Germain, Randall. 2012. "Governing Global Finance and Banking." *Review of International Political Economy* 19(4):530–535.

Gerring, John. 2007. *Case Study Research. Principles and Practices.* Cambridge: Cambridge University Press.

Gilpin, Robert. 2001. *Global Political Economy: Understanding the International Economic Order.* Princeton: Princeton University Press.

Goldbach, Roman & Dieter Kerwer. 2012. New Capital Rules? Reforming Basel Banking Standards after the Financial Crisis. In *Institutional Change in Financial Market Regulation*, ed. Renate Mayntz. Frankfurt a.M.: Campus pp. 245–260.

Goodhart, Charles A. E. 2011. *The Basel Committee on Banking Supervision. A History of the Early Years, 1974–1997.* Cambridge: Cambridge University Press.

Goodhart, Charles A. E. & Gerhard Illing, eds. 2002. *Financial crises, contagion, and the lender of last resort: a reader.* Oxford: Oxford University Press.

Goodhart, Charles A. E., Philipp Hartmann, David Llewellyn, Liliana Rojas-Suárez & Steven Weisbrod. 1998. *Financial Regulation: Why, how and where now?* London: Routledge.

Goodman, John B. & Louis W. Pauly. 1993. "The Obsolescence of Capital Controls? Economic Management in an Age of Global Markets." *World Politics* 46(1):50–82.

Grant, Ruth W. & Robert O. Keohane. 2005. "Accountability and Abuses of Power in World Politics." *American Political Science Review* 99(1):29–43.

Gray, Julia. 2009. "International Organization as a Seal of Approval: European Union Accession and Investor Risk." *American Journal of Political Science* 53(4):931–949.

Griep, Clifford & Michael De Stefano. 2001. "Standard & Poor's Official Response to the Basel Committee's Proposal." *Journal of Banking & Finance* 25(1):149–169. Standard & Poor's official response to the Basel Committee's proposal (CP1) in December 1999.

Griffith-Jones, Stephany, Eric Helleiner & Ngaire Woods, eds. 2010. *The Financial Stability Board: An Effective Fourth Pillar of Global Economic Governance?* Waterloo: The Centre for International Governance Innovation.

Group of Ten. 2001. Report on Consolidation in the Financial Sector. Technical report Group of Ten.

Group of Thirty. 1997. "Global Institutions, National Supervision and Systemic Risk." Report of the Study Group on the Evolutions of Supervision and Regulation, Washington, July 1997.

Haas, Peter M. 1992. "Introduction: Epistemic Communities and International Policy Coordination." *International Organization* 46(1):1–35.

Hall, Peter A. 1993. "Policy Paradigms, Social Learning, and the State: The Case of Economic Policymaking in Britain." *Comparative Politics* 25(3):275–296.

Hall, Peter A. & David Soskice. 2001. An Introduction to Varieties of Capitalism. In *Varieties of Capitalism: The Institutional Foundations of Comparative Advantage*, ed. Peter A. Hall & David W. Soskice. Oxford: Oxford University Press pp. 1–68.

Hardie, Iain & David Howarth. 2009. "Die Krise but not La Crise? The Financial Crisis and the Transformation of German and French Banking Systems." *Journal of Common Market Studies* 47(5):1017–1039.

Hardie, Iain, David Howarth, Sylvia Maxfield & Amy Verdun. 2013. "Banks and the False Dichotomy in the Comparative Political Economy of Finance." *World Politics* 65:691–728.

Hawke, John D. 2002. "The New Basel Capital Accord: A Status Report." Speech Delivered before the Institute of International Bankers, 4 March 2000, Washington.

Hawke, John D. 2003. "Testimony at the Hearing 'The New Basel Accord: Sound Regulation or Crushing Complexity?' before the Subcommittee on Domestic and International Monetary Policy, Trade and Technology of the Committee on Financial Services of the U.S. House of Representatives." Washington, 27. February 2003.

Helleiner, Eric. 1994. *States and the Reemergence of Global Finance: From Bretton Woods to the 1990s*. Ithaca: Cornell University Press.

Helleiner, Eric. 2010. "What Role for the New Financial Stability Board? The Politics of International Standards after the Crisis." *Global Policy* 1(3):282–290.

Helleiner, Eric. 2014. *The Status Quo Crisis: Global Financial Governance After the 2008 Meltdown*. Oxford: Oxford University Press.

Helleiner, Eric & Stefano Pagliari. 2011. "The End of an Era in International Financial Regulation? A Postcrisis Research Agenda." *International Organization* 65(1):169–200.

Hellwig, Martin. 2009. "Systemic Risk in the Financial Sector: An Analysis of the Subprime-Mortgage Financial Crisis." *De Economist* 157(2):129–207.

Hirschman, Albert O. 1970. *Exit, Voice, and Loyalty. Responses to Decline in Firms, Organizations, and States*. Cambridge: Harvard University Press.

Höpner, Martin. 2003. Der organisierte Kapitalismus in Deutschland und sein Niedergang. In *Politik und Markt. PVS-Sonderheft 34/2003*, ed. Roland Czada & Reinhard Zintl. Wiesbaden: VS Verlag pp. 300–324.

Höpner, Martin & Lothar Krempel. 2004. "The Politics of the German Company Network." *Competition and Change* 8(4):339–356.

Hoshi, Takeo. 2011. "Financial Regulation: Lessons from the Recent Financial Crises." *Journal of Economic Literature* 49(1):120–28.

Howarth, David & Lucia Quaglia. 2013a. "Banking on Stability: The Political Economy of New Capital Requirements in the European Union." *Journal of European Integration* 35(3):333–346.

Howarth, David & Lucia Quaglia. 2013b. "The Comparative Political Economy of Basel III in Europe." Paper presented at the SPERI-Conference at the University of Sheffield in July 2013.

Institute of International Finance. 1998. "Recommendations for Revising the Regulatory Capital Rules for Credit Risk." Report of the Institute of International Finance Working Group on Capital Adequacy, Washington, March 1998.

Institute of International Finance. 2000. "Response to the Basel Committee on Banking Supervision Regulatory Capital Reform Proposals." Report of the Institute of International Finance Working Group on Capital Adequacy, Washington, March 2000.

Institute of International Finance. 2001. "Comments on the Second Consultative Paper of the Basel Committee on Banking Supervision Regarding the Basel II Accord." Washington, 31 May 2001. Available at www.bis.org/bcbs/cacomments.htm.

International Swaps and Derivatives Association. 1998a. "Credit Risk and Regulatory Capital." New York, March 1998.

International Swaps and Derivatives Association. 1998b. "Note of a Consultative Meeting between the German BaKred and ISDA on Credit Risk and Regulatory Capital Proposals." London, 31. July 1998.

International Swaps and Derivatives Association. 2000. "A New Capital Adequacy Framework. Comments on a Consultative Paper Issued by the Basel Committee on Banking Supervision in June 1999." New York, February 2000.

International Swaps and Derivatives Association. 2001. "Comments on the Second Consultative Paper of the Basel Committee on Banking Supervision Regarding the Basel II Accord." Washington, 31 May 2001. Available at www.bis.org/bcbs/cacomments.htm.

Jackson, Particia, Pamela Nickell & William Perraudin. 1999. "Credit Risk Modelling." *Financial Stability Review (Bank of England)* (6):94–121.

Jordana, Jacint, David Levi-Faur & Xavier Fernández i Marín. 2011. "The Global Diffusion of Regulatory Agencies." *Comparative Political Studies* 44(10):1343–1369.

Jordana, Jacint & Guillermo Rosas. 2010. "Financial Governance, Banking Crises, and the Institutional Varieties of Regulation." APSA 2010 Annual Meeting Paper. Available at SSRN: http://ssrn.com/abstract=1641927.

Jordana, Jacint & Guillermo Rosas. 2014. "When do Autonomous Banking Regulators Promote Stability?" *European Journal of Political Research* 53(4):672–691.

J.P. Morgan Chase. 2001. "Comments on the Second Consultative Paper of the Basel Committee on Banking Supervision regarding the Basel II Accord." Washington, 31 May 2001. Available at www.bis.org/bcbs/cacomments.htm.

Kahneman, Daniel. 2012. *Thinking, Fast and Slow*. New York: Penguin.

Kapstein, Ethan Barnaby. 1989. "Resolving the Regulator's Dilemma: International Coordination of Banking Regulations." *International Organization* 43(2):323–347.

Kapstein, Ethan Barnaby. 1992. "Between Power and Purpose: Central Bankers and the Politics of Regulatory Convergence." *International Organization* 46(1):265–287.

Kapstein, Ethan Barnaby. 1994. *Governing the Global Economy: International Finance and the State*. Cambridge: Harvard University Press.

Kaul, Inge, Isabelle Grundberg & Mark A. Stern. 1999. Defining Global Public Goods. In *Global Public Goods. International Cooperation in the 21st Century*, ed. Inge Kaul, Isabelle Grundberg & Mark A. Stern. New York and Oxford: Oxford University Press chapter 1, pp. 2–19.

Keefer, Philip. 2007. "Elections, Special Interests, and Financial Crisis." *International Organization* 61(03):607–641.

Keohane, Robert O. & David G. Victor. 2011. "The Regime Complex for Climate Change." *Perspectives on Politics* 9(1):7–23.

Keohane, Robert O. & Joseph S. Nye. 1974. "Transgovernmental Relations and International Organizations." *World Politics* 27(1):39–62.

Keohane, Robert O. & Joseph S. Nye. 1998. "Power and Interdependence in the Information Age." *Foreign Affairs* 77(5):81–94.

Keohane, Robert O., Stephen Macedo & Andrew Moravcsik. 2009. "Democracy-Enhancing Multilateralism." *International Organization* 63(1):1–31.

Keohane, Robert Owen & Joseph S. Nye. 1977 (1992). *Power and Interdependence. World Politics in Transition.* 3. ed. Longman.

Kerwer, Dieter. 2005. "Holding Global Regulators Accountable. The Case of Credit Rating Agencies." *Governance* 18(3):453–475.

King, Michael R. & Timothy J. Sinclair. 2003. "Private Actors and Public Policy: A Requiem for the New Basel Capital Accord." *International Political Science Review* 24(3):345–362.

Knaack, Peter & Saori N. Katada. 2013. "Fault Lines and Issue Linkages at the G20: New Challenges for Global Economic Governance." *Global Policy* 4(3):236–246.

Krasner, Stephen D. 1982. "Structural Causes and Regime Consequences: Regimes as Intervening Variables." *International Organization* 36(2):185–205.

Lake, David A. 2010. "Rightful Rules: Authority, Order, and the Foundations of Global Governance." *International Studies Quarterly* 54(3):587–613.

Lake, David A. 2011. "Why 'isms' Are Evil: Theory, Epistemology, and Academic Sects as Impediments to Understanding and Progress." *International Studies Quarterly* 55(2):465–480.

Lall, Ranjit. 2012. "From Failure to Failure: The Politics of International Banking Regulation." *Review of International Political Economy* 19(4):609–638.

Lehnhoff, Jochen. 1997. "Letzlich braucht die deutsche Kreditwirtschaft einen sofortigen und absoluten Regulierungsstop auf allen Ebenen." *Zeitschrift für das gesamte Kreditwesen* 50(23):1167–1170.

Levinson, Marc. 2010. "Faulty Basel. Why More Diplomacy Won't Keep the Financial System Safe." *Foreign Affairs* 89(3):76–88.

Llewellyn, David. 1999. The Economic Rationale for Financial Regulation. Fsa occasional paper Financial Services Authority.

Lo, Andrew W. 2012. "Reading about the Financial Crisis: A Twenty-One-Book Review." *Journal of Economic Literature* 50(1):151–78.

Lütz, Susanne. 2004. "Convergence Within National Diversity: The Regulatory State in Finance." *Journal of Public Policy* 24(2):169–197.

MacKenzie, Donald A. 2006. *An Engine, Not a Camera. How Financial Models Shape Markets.* Cambridge, MA: MIT Press.

Majone, Giandomenico. 1997. "From the Positive to the Regulatory State: Causes and Consequences of Changes in the Mode of Governance." *Journal of Public Policy* 17(2):139–167.

Majone, Giandomenico. 2001. "Two Logics of Delegation." *European Union Politics* 2(1):103–122.

Malhotra, Neil & Yotam Margalit. 2010. "Short-Term Communication Effects or Longstanding Dispositions? The Public's Response to the Financial Crisis of 2008." *The Journal of Politics* 72(03):852–867.

Maloney, Carolyn B. 2002. "Letter of the Member of the U.S. House of Representatives Carolyn B. Maloney to the Federal Banking Supervisors concerning issues of Basel II." New York, 14. August 2002 (see Appendix of House of Representatives Hearing on 27 February 2003, Serial No. 108-5).

Mansfield, Edward D. & Marc L. Busch. 1995. "The Political Economy of Nontariff Barriers: A Cross-National Analysis." *International Organization* 49(4):723–749.

March, James G. & Johan P. Olsen. 1998. "The Institutional Dynamics of International Political Orders." *International Organization* 52(4):943–969.

Mattli, Walter & Tim Büthe. 2003. "Setting International Standards: Technological Rationality or Primacy of Power?" *World Politics* 56(1):1–42.

McCubbins, Mathew D. & Thomas Schwartz. 1984. "Congressional Oversight Overlooked: Police Patrols versus Fire Alarms." *American Journal of Political Science* 28(1):165–179.

McDonough, William J. 1997. "The Changing Role of Supervision." Speech Delivered Before the Institute of International Bankers, 10 September 1997, New York.

McDonough, William J. 1998. "Issues for the Basle Accord." Bank for International Settlements Conference on Credit Risk Modeling and Regulatory Implications, 22nd September, Barbican Centre, London, England.

McDonough, William J. 1999. "Credit Risk and the 'Level Playing Field' (Speech Delivered at the Symposium "Challenge Credit Risk" on 24. November 1998)." *Zeitschrift für das gesamte Kreditwesen* 52(3):132–137.

Meyer, Laurence H. 2001. "The New Basel Capital Proposal." Speech Delivered at the Annual Washington Conference of the Institute of International Bankers. Washington, 5 March 2001.

Monro-Davies, Robin. 1999. "Approaches of Rating Agencies (Speech Delivered at the Symposium "Challenge Credit Risk" on 24. November 1998)." *Zeitschrift für das gesamte Kreditwesen* 52(3):126–130.

Moody's Investors Service. 2000. "Moody's Investors Service Response To The Consultative Paper Issued By The Basel Committee On Bank Supervision 'A New Capital Adequacy Framework'." New York and London, March 2000.

Moody's Investors Service. 2001. "Comments on the Second Consultative Paper of the Basel Committee on Banking Supervision regarding the Basel II Accord." Washington, 31 May 2001. Available at www.bis.org/bcbs/cacomments.htm.

Moschella, Manuela. 2013. "Designing the Financial Stability Board: A Theoretical Investigation of Mandate, Discretion, and Membership." *Journal of International Relations and Development* 16(3):380–405.

Mosley, Layna. 2009. Private Governance for the Public Good? Exploring Private Sector Participation in Global Financial Regulation. In *Power, Interdependence and Non-State Actors in World Politics*, ed. Helen V. Milner & Andrew Moravcsik. Princeton University Press chapter 7, pp. 126–146.

Murphy, Dale D. 2005. "Interjurisdictional Competition and Regulatory Advantage." *Journal of International Economic Law* 8(4):891–920.

Niskanen, William A. 1971. *Bureaucracy and Representative Government.* Chicago: Aldine, Atherton.

Niskanen, William A. 1975. "Bureaucrats and Politicians." *Journal of Law and Economics* 18(3):617–643.

Novembre, Valerio. 2009. "The Bargaining Process as a Variable to Explain Implementation Choices of International Soft-law Agreements: The Basel Case Study." *Journal of Banking Regulation* 10(2):128–152.

Nye, Joseph S. & Robert O. Keohane. 1971a. "Transnational Relations and World Politics: A Conclusion." *International Organization* 25(03):721–48.

Nye, Joseph S. & Robert O. Keohane. 1971b. "Transnational Relations and World Politics: An Introduction." *International Organization* 25(3):329–349.

Oatley, Thomas & Robert Nabors. 1998. "Redistributive Cooperation: Market Failure, Wealth Transfers, and the Basle Accord." *International Organization* 52(1):35–54.

Office of Thrift Supervision. 2001. "The New Basel Capital Accord." Memorandum for Chief Executive Officers. Washington, 26 January 2001.

Olson, Mancur. 1965. *The Logic of Collective Action: Public Goods and the Theory of Groups.* Harvard University Press.

Ostrom, Elinor. 2010. "Beyond Markets and States: Polycentric Governance of Complex Economic Systems." *American Economic Review* 100(3):641–72.

Pagliari, Stefano. 2014. Governing Financial Stability. The Financial Stability Board as the Emerging Pillar in Global Economic Governance. In *Handbook of Global Economic Governance*, ed. Manuela Moschella & Catherine Weaver. Abingdon and New York: Routledge pp. 143–155.

Pagliari, Stefano & Kevin L. Young. 2014. "Leveraged Interests: Financial Industry Power and the Role of Private Sector Coalitions." *Review of International Political Economy* 21(3):575–610.

Pauly, Louis W. 1997. *Who Elected the Bankers? Surveillance and Control in the World Economy.* Ithaca: Cornell University Press.

Pauly, Louis W. 2010. The Financial Stability Board in Context. In *The Financial Stability Board: An Effective Fourth Pillar of Global Economic Governance?*, ed. Stephany Griffith-Jones, Eric Helleiner & Ngaire Woods. Waterloo: The Centre for International Governance Innovation pp. 13–18.

Porter, Tony. 2005. *Globalization and Finance.* Cambridge: Polity.

Porter, Tony. 2011. "Public and Private Authority in the Transnational Response to the 2008 Financial Crisis." *Policy and Society* 30:175–184.

Posner, Elliot. 2009. "Making Rules for Global Finance: Transatlantic Regulatory Cooperation at the Turn of the Millennium." *International Organization* 63(4):665–699.

Powell, Walter W. 1990. "Neither Market nor Hierarchy. Network Forms of Organization." *Research in Organizational Behaviour* 12:295–336.

Putnam, Robert. 1988. "Diplomacy and Domestic Politics: The Logic of Two-Level Games." *International Organization* 42(3):427–460.

Rixen, Thomas. 2013. "Why Reregulation after the Crisis is Feeble: Shadow Banking, Offshore Financial Centers, and Jurisdictional Competition." *Regulation & Governance* 7(4):435–459.

Rosenau, James N. 1992. Governance, Order, and Change in World Politics. In *Governance Without Government: Order and Change in World Politics*, ed. James N. Rosenau & Ernst-Otto Czempiel. Cambridge: Cambridge University Press pp. 1–29.

Rosenau, James N. 1995. "Governance in the Twenty-first Century." *Global Governance* 1(2):13–43.

Rosenbluth, Frances & Ross Schaap. 2003. "The Domestic Politics of Banking Regulation." *International Organization* 57(2):307–336.

Ruggie, John Gerard. 1982. "International Regimes, Transactions, and Change: Embedded Liberalism in the Postwar Economic Order." *International Organization* 36(2):379–415.

Santos, Joao A. C. 2001. "Bank Capital Regulation in Contemporary Banking Theory: A Review of the Literature." *Financial Markets, Institutions & Instruments* 10(2):41–84.

Scharpf, Fritz W. 1997. *Games Real Actors Play. Actor-Centered Insititutionalism in Policy Research.* Oxford: Westview Press.

Scholte, Jan Aart. 2013. "Civil Society and Financial Markets: What is Not Happening and Why?" *Journal of Civil Society* 9(2):129–147.

Schröder, Gustav Adolf. 1997. "Wir wollen kein 'KWG-light', aber wir benötigen für kleine und mittlere Institute verstärkt sinnvolle Bagatell- und Ausnahmeregelungen." *Zeitschrift für das gesamte Kreditwesen* 50(23):1172–1176.

Scott, Hal & Shinsaku Iwahara. 1994. *In search of a level playing field: the implementation of the Basle Capital Accord in Japan and the United States.* Group of Thirty.

Sil, Rudra & Peter J. Katzenstein. 2010a. "Analytic Eclecticism in the Study of World Politics: Reconfiguring Problems and Mechanisms across Research Traditions." *Perspectives on Politics* 8(2):411–431.

Sil, Rudra & Peter J. Katzenstein. 2010b. *Beyond Paradigms: Analytic Eclecticism in the Study of World Politics.* Basingstoke: Palgrave Macmilian.

Simmons, Beth A. 2001. "The International Politics of Harmonization: The Case of Capital Market Regulation." *International Organization* 55(3):589–620.

Sinclair, Timothy J. 1994. "Between State and Market: Hegemony and Institutions of Collective Action under Conditions of International Capital Mobility." *Policy Sciences* 27(4):447–466.

Singer, David Andrew. 2007. *Regulating Capital. Setting Standards for the International Financial System.* Ithaca and London: Cornell University Press.

Slaughter, Anne-Marie. 2004. *A New World Order.* Princeton: Princeton University Press.

Slaughter, Steven. 2014. "The Transnational Policy Networks of the G20." Paper presented at the ECPR Joint Sessions 2014 in Salamanca, Workshop Mapping the emerging hybrid world order. How Global Governance networks and regimes interact with shifting inter-state hierarchies in shaping global policies.

Sorkin, Andrew R. 2010. *Too Big to Fail. Inside the Battle to Save Wall Street.* New York: Penguin.

Stigler, George J. 1971. "The Theory of Economic Regulation." *Bell Journal of Economics and Management Science* 2(1):3–21.

Stone, Randall W. 2011. *Controlling Institutions. International Organizations and the Global Economy.* Cambridge: Cambridge University Press.

Strange, Susan. 1994. *States and Markets.* 2. ed. London: Continuum.

Strange, Susan. 1996. *The Retreat of the State. The Diffusion of Power in the World Economy.* Cambridge: Cambridge University Press.

Tarullo, Daniel K. 2008. *Banking on Basel: The Future of International Financial Regulation.* Washington, D.C.: Peterson Institute for International Economics.

Thatcher, Mark. 2005. "The Third Force? Independent Regulatory Agencies and Elected Politicians in Europe." *Governance* 18(3):347–373.

The Bond Market Association. 2001. "Letter to the Basel Committee commenting on the second consultative proposal on Basel II." New York, 2 May 2001.

The Economist. 2012. "Half-cocked Basel. Stop-gap Rules on Banks' Trading Books may Add Perilous Complexity." The Economist. 7 January 2012.

The Economist. 2013. "Go with the Flow. Global Regulators Soften their Stance on Liquidity." The Economist. 13 January 2013.

The Economist. 2014a. "Leavened. Regulators go easy on Europe's Overstretched Banks." The Economist. 18 January 2014.

The Economist. 2014b. "A Worrying Wobble. Bank Regulators should not have Weakened Rules that Limit Leverage." The Economist. 18 January 2014.

Thiemann, Matthias. 2014. "In the Shadow of Basel: How Competitive Politics Bred the Crisis." *Review of International Political Economy* 21(6):1203–1239.

Toniolo, Gianni. 2005. *Central Bank Cooperation at the Bank for International Settlements, 1930–1973*. Cambridge: Cambridge University Press.

Tsingou, Eleni. 2010. Regulatory Reactions to the Credit Crisis. Analyzing a Policy Community under Stress. In *Global Finance in Crisis: The Politics of International Regulatory Change*, ed. Eric Helleiner, Stefano Pagliari & Hubert Zimmermann. New York: Routledge pp. 21–36.

Tsingou, Eleni. Forthcoming. "Club Governance and the Making of Global Financial Rules." *Review of International Political Economy* Published online before print(doi:10.1080/09692290.2014.890952):1–32.

Underhill, Geoffrey R. D. 1995. "Keeping Governments out of Politics: Transnational Securities Markets, Regulatory Cooperation, and Political Legitimacy." *Review of International Studies* 21(3):251–278.

Underhill, Geoffrey R. D. Forthcoming. "The Emerging Post-Crisis Financial Architecture: The Path-Dependency of Ideational Adverse Selection." *The British Journal of Politics & International Relations* Published online before print(doi: 10.1111/1467-856X.12056):1–33.

Underhill, Geoffrey R. D. & Xiaoke Zhang. 2008. "Setting the Rules: Private Power, Political Underpinnings, and Legitimacy in Global Monetary and Financial Governance." *International Affairs* 84(3):535–554.

United States Government Accountability Office. 1997. "Foreign Banks. Internal Control and Audit Weaknesses in U.S. Branches." Report to the Subcommittee on Financial Institutions and Consumer Credit of the Committee on Banking and Financial Services of the U.S. House of Representatives (GAO/GGD-97-181).

United States Government Accountability Office. 1998. "Multilateral Development Banks: Public Consultation on Environmental Assessments." Report to the Congress (GAO-NSIAD-98-192), 8 September 1998.

United States Government Accountability Office. 2000. "Risk-Focused Bank Examinations. Regulators of Large Bank Organizations Face Challenges." Report to Congressional Requests (GAO/GGD-00-48).

U.S. Banking Supervisors. 2001. "Letter of the U.S. Banking Supervision Agencies to Regulated Entities Soliciting Comments from the US Banking Industry on the Second Consultative Paper Concerning the Basel II Accord." Joined Letter by the Federal Reserve, Federal Deposit Insurance Corporation and Office of the Comptroller of the Currency. Washington, 16 January 2001.

U.S. House of Representatives. 1998a. "Bank Mergers." Hearing before the Committee on Banking and Financial Services of the U.S. House of Representatives. Washington, 29. April 1998.

U.S. House of Representatives. 1998b. "East Asian Economic Conditions." Hearing before the Committee on Banking and Financial Services of the U.S. House of Representatives. Washington, 30. January 1998.

U.S. House of Representatives. 2002. "The European Union's Financial Services Action Plan and its Financial Services Industry." Hearing before the Committee on Financial Services of the U.S. House of Representatives. Washington, 22 May 2002.

U.S. House of Representatives. 2003a. "Legislative Proposal H. R. 2043: To establish a mechanism for developing uniform United States positions on issues before the Basel Committee on Banking Supervision at the Bank for International Settlements, to require a review on the most recent recommendation of the Basel Committee for an accord on capital standards, and for other purposes." Representatives in the Subcommittee on Financial Institutions and Consumer Credit of the Committee on Financial Services of the U.S. House of Representatives. Washington, 9 May 2003.

U.S. House of Representatives. 2003b. "The New Basel Accord: In Search of a Unified U.S. Position." Hearing before the Subcommittee on Financial Institutions and Consumer Credit of the Committee on Financial Services of the U.S. House of Representatives. Washington, 19. June 2003.

U.S. House of Representatives. 2003c. "The New Basel Accord: Sound Regulation or Crushing Complexity?" Hearing before the Subcommittee on Domestic and International Monetary Policy, Trade and Technology of the Committee on Financial Services of the U.S. House of Representatives. Washington, 27. February 2003.

U.S. House of Representatives. 2003d. "United States Monetary and Economic Policy." Hearing before the Committee on Financial Services of the U.S. House of Representatives. Serial No. 108–24. Washington, 30 April 2003.

U.S. House of Representatives. 2003e. "US Regulator Urges Basel II Dialogue with Congress." Global Risk Regulator Email news service November 2003.

U.S. House of Representatives. 2004a. "The New Basel Accord: Private Sector Perspectives." Hearing before the Subcommittee on Financial Institutions and Consumer Credit of the Committee on Financial Services of the U.S. House of Representatives. Serial No. 108–96. Washington, 22 June 2004.

U.S. House of Representatives. 2004b. "Oversight of the Office of the Comptroller of the Currency: Examination of Policies, Procedures and Resources." Hearing before the Committee on Financial Services of the U.S. House of Representatives. Serial No. 108–78. Washington, 1 April 2004.

U.S. House of Representatives. 2005a. "Basel II: Capital Changes in the U.S. Banking System and the Results of the Impact Study." Joint Hearing before the Subcommittee on Financial Institutions and Consumer Credit and the Subcommittee on Domestic and International Monetary Policy, Trade and Technology of the Committee on Financial Services of the U.S. House of Representatives. Serial No. 109–27. Washington, 11 May 2005.

U.S. House of Representatives. 2005b. "Private Sector Priorities for Basel Reform." Hearing before the Subcommittee on Financial Institutions and Consumer Credit of the Committee on Financial Services of the U.S. House of Representatives. Serial No. 109—57. Washington, 28 September 2005.

U.S. Senate. 2003. "Review of the New Basel Capital Accord." Hearing before the Committee on Banking, Housing, and Urban Affairs of the U.S. Senate. Washington, 18. June 2003.

U.S. Senate. 2004. "Examination of the Current Condition of Banking and Credit Union Industries." Hearing before the Committee on Banking, Housing, and Urban Affairs. Washington, 20 April 2004.

U.S. Senate. 2005. "The Development of New Basel Capital Accords." Hearing before the Committee on Banking, Housing, and Urban Affairs of the U.S. Senate. Washington, 10 November 2005.

Vanoli, Alejandro. 2010. FSB: Current Structure and Proposals for a More Balanced Representation. In *The Financial Stability Board: An Effective Fourth Pillar of Global Economic Governance?*, ed. Stephany Griffith-Jones, Eric Helleiner & Ngaire Woods. Waterloo: The Centre for International Governance Innovation pp. 23–28.

Verdier, Pierre-Hugues. 2011. "U.S. Implementation of Basel II: Lessons for Informal International Law-Making." SSRN Working Papers. Available at: http://ssrn.com/paper=1879391.

Verdier, Pierre-Hugues. 2013. "The Political Economy of International Financial Regulation." *Indiana Law Journal* 88(4):1405–1474.

Viola, Lora Anne. 2014. The G-20 and global financial regulation. In *Handbook of Global Economic Governance*, ed. Manuela Moschella & Catherine Weaver. Abingdon and New York: Routledge pp. 115–128.

Vogel, Steven K. 1996. *Freer Markets, More Rules: Regulatory Reform in Advanced Industrial Countries*. Ithaca: Cornell University Press.

Walter, Andrew. 2008. *Governing Finance: East Asia's Adoption of International Standards*. Ithaca: Cornell University Press.

Way, Christopher R. 2005. "Political Insecurity and the Diffusion of Financial Market Regulation." *Annals of the American Academy of Political and Social Science* 598(1):125–144.

Weingast, Barry R. & Mark J. Moran. 1983. "Bureaucratic Discretion or Congressional Control? Regulatory Policymaking by the Federal Trade Commission." *Journal of Political Economy* 91(5):765–800.

Wood, Duncan R. 2005. *Governing Global Banking: The Basel Committee and the Politics of Financial Globalisation*. Aldershot: Ashgate Publishing.

Wouters, Jan & Jed Odermatt. 2014. "Comparing the 'Four Pillars' of Global Economic Governance: A Critical Analysis of the Institutional Design of the FSB, IMF, World Bank, and WTO." *Journal of International Economic Law* 17(1):49–76.

Wyplosz, Charles. 1999. International Financial Instability. In *Global Public Goods. International Cooperation in the 21st Century*, ed. Inge Kaul, Isabelle Grundberg & Mark A. Stern. New York and Oxford: Oxford University Press pp. 152–189.

Young, Kevin. 2012. "Transnational Regulatory Capture? An Empirical Examination of the Transnational Lobbying of the Basel Committee on Banking Supervision." *Review of International Political Economy* 19(4):663–688.

Young, Kevin. 2013. "Financial Industry Groups' Adaptation to the Post-Crisis Regulatory Environment: Changing Approaches to the Policy Cycle." *Regulation & Governance* 7(4):460–480.

Zeitschrift für das gesamte Kreditwesen. 1999. "Nicht gleich richtig aufgepaßt?" *Zeitschrift für das gesamte Kreditwesen* 52(20):5–6.

Zentraler Kreditausschuss. 2000. "Comment on the Consultative Paper 'A New Capital Adequacy Framework' of the Basel Committee on Banking Supervision." Letter to the Bundesaufsichtsamt für das Kreditwesen (10. March 2000). Supplement to the Minutes of the 58. Finance Committee Meeting (Non-public) in Legislative Period 14. Berlin, 5. April 2000.

Zentraler Kreditausschuss. 2001. "Comments of the Zentraler Kreditausschuss on the Basel Committee's Consultative Document of 16 January 2001 on a New Capital Adequacy Framework for Banks." Berlin, 28 May 2001.

Index

CPSIA information can be obtained at www.ICGtesting.com
Printed in the USA
LVOW04*2120250915

455759LV00009B/196/P